spaghetti

cooking up a STORM

AN ALL-PURPOSE COOKBOOK

FAVORITE RECIPES® OF OKLAHOMA
FUTURE HOMEMAKERS OF AMERICA

© Favorite Recipes Press/Nashville EMS MCMLXXXII
P. O. Box 77, Nashville, Tennessee 37202

Library of Congress Cataloging in Publication Data
Main entry under title:

Cooking up a storm.

Compiled and sponsored by the Oklahoma Future
Homemakers of America.
Includes index.
1. Cookery, American--Oklahoma. I. Oklahoma
Future Homemakers of America. II. Favorite Recipes
Press.
TX715.C7844   1982   641.5   82-20982
ISBN 0-87197-147-X

Page 1, recipes on pages 130 and 131.

Page 2, recipe on page 56.

The Oklahoma Future Homemakers of America has the honor of recognizing the first lady of Oklahoma, Mrs. Donna Nigh, Honorary State Chairman of the Oklahoma Building Campaign Fund for the National Leadership Headquarters in Reston, Virginia.

We salute Mrs. Nigh for her personal contribution and support of this special project!

EXPRESSION OF APPRECIATION

The Oklahoma Future Homemakers of America, the compilers and sponsors of this cookbook, do here publicly thank and express our appreciation to all those who furnished recipes, who assisted in the compiling of sales of books, or in any other way contributed to the publication of this book.

A thank you goes to Pat Kellner, FHA Adviser, from Okeene, Kim Heinze, West District State Vice-President, Okeene, and Kathy Kimbrell, North District State Vice-President who worked so diligently with this project.

Without their many hours of typing recipes and coordinating the project, the Oklahoma Future Homemakers of America would not have achieved this outstanding cookbook.

Edna Crow

Edna Crow, State Adviser
Oklahoma Association, FHA/HERO

Task Force Nutrition Team at the Oklahoma State Fair. Left to right, Pat Kellner, Local Chapter Adviser; Edna Crow, State Adviser; Dede Speed, State President; Kathy Kimbrell, North District Vice-President; Kim Heinze, West District Vice-President.

Contents

Appetizers and Salads 8

Main Dishes 26

Vegetables 58

Breads 74

Desserts and Beverages 94

Cakes 114

Candies and Cookies 128

Fun-Raiser Ideas 142

Calorie Chart 157

Candy Testing Chart 160

Metric Conversion Chart 160

Equivalent Chart 161

Substitutions Chart 162

Index 163

Appetizers
and Salads

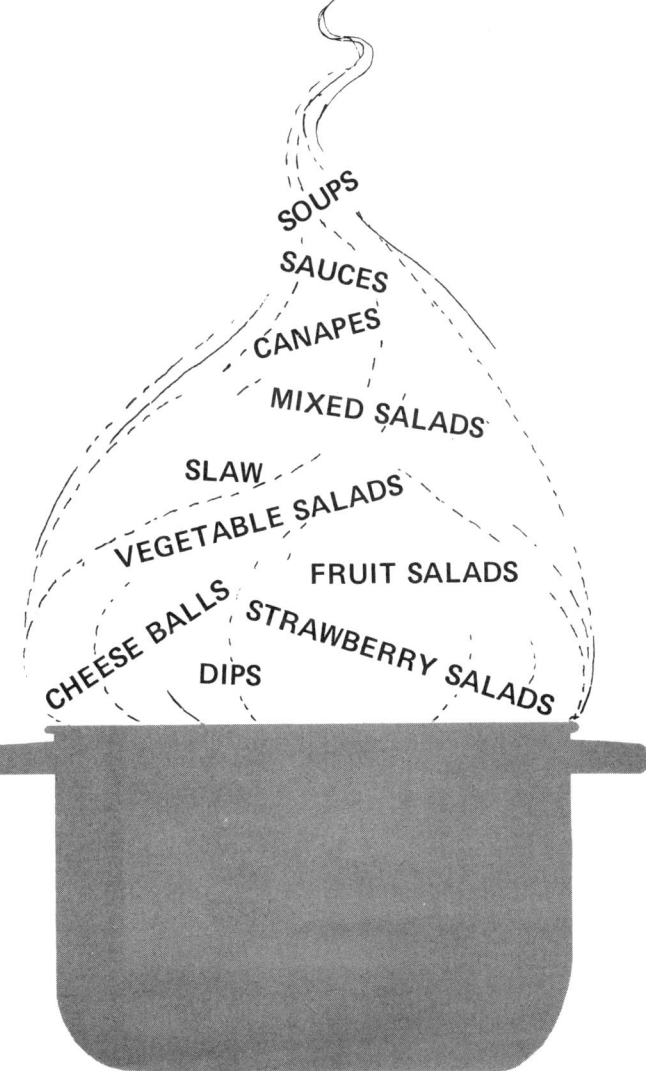

SOUPS

SAUCES

CANAPES

MIXED SALADS

SLAW

VEGETABLE SALADS

FRUIT SALADS

CHEESE BALLS

STRAWBERRY SALADS

DIPS

ANTS ON A LOG

Celery
Peanut Butter
Raisins

Cut . . . . celery into 3 to 4-inch pieces.
Fill . . . . with peanut butter.
Top . . . . with raisins.

Beth Felder Weber
Okeene Public School, Okeene, Oklahoma

ARTICHOKE BALLS

1 14-oz. can artichokes, drained,
  mashed
1 tbsp. lemon juice
2 cloves of garlic, minced
2 tbsp. Parmesan cheese
2 eggs
1 c. seasoned bread crumbs

Combine . . . . all ingredients in bowl, mixing
            well.
Shape . . . . . . into quarter-sized balls.
Roll . . . . in additional Parmesan cheese.
Place . . . . on baking sheet.
Bake . . . . at 350 degrees for 10 minutes.

Relda I. Coley
Binger H. S., Binger, Oklahoma

BITE-SIZED PIZZA

1 recipe biscuit dough
Tomato sauce
Oregano to taste
Garlic powder to taste
1/2 lb. sausage, cooked, drained
1 c. grated mozzarella cheese
Parmesan cheese

Roll . . . . biscuit dough on floured surface
            into 4-inch circles.
Place . . . . on baking sheet.
Spoon . . . . . . tomato sauce onto dough.
Sprinkle . . . . with oregano and garlic powder.
Spread . . . . . sausage over sauce.
Sprinkle . . . . cheeses over top.
Bake . . . . at 425 degrees for 10 to 12
            minutes.
Yields . . . . . . 10 servings.

Charla Wood
Cyril H. S., Cyril, Oklahoma

CHILI NACHOS

1 15-oz. can chili without beans
1 8-oz. jar Cheez Whiz with jalapeno
  peppers
1/4 c. chopped green peppers
1 8-oz. package tortilla chips
2 c. shredded lettuce
1 c. chopped tomatoes
1/2 c. sour cream
1/4 c. chopped black olives

Combine . . . . first 3 ingredients in saucepan.
Cook . . . . until heated through.
Alternate . . . layers of half the tortilla chips
            and chili mixture on serving
            plate.
Top . . . . with remaining ingredients in
            order listed.

Bobbie D. Cook
Waynoka H. S., Waynoka, Oklahoma

FRIED CHEESE BALLS

4 tsp. flour
1 c. grated American cheese
1/4 tsp. salt
Dash of pepper
2 egg whites, stiffly beaten
Dried bread crumbs
Oil for deep frying

Combine . . . . first 4 ingredients in bowl, mix-
            ing well.
Fold . . . . in egg whites.
Shape . . . . . . by teaspoonfuls into balls.
Roll . . . . in bread crumbs.
Fry . . . . in 390-degree deep fat until
            golden brown.
Yields . . . . . . 18 balls.

Brenda L. Brainard
Oklahoma Dairy Princess
Stillwater, Oklahoma

HAM AND CHEESE PINWHEELS

Dry onion soup mix to taste
1 8-oz. package cream cheese, softened
Chopped green onions to taste
2 pkg. long-sliced boiled ham
1 pkg. long-sliced Swiss cheese

Combine . . . . first 3 ingredients in bowl, mix-
            ing well.

Spread ..... over ham slices.
Top .... with Swiss cheese slices.
Roll .... as for jelly roll.
Chill .... in refrigerator.
Slice .... into 1/2 inch thick slices.
Arrange ..... on serving plate.
Yields ...... 24 slices.

Lawanna Basks
State HERO Officer
NEO Vo-Tech School, Pryor, Oklahoma

PEPPERONI BALLS

1 pkg. hot roll mix
1/4 lb. mozzarella cheese, cubed
1/4 to 1/2 lb. pepperoni, thinly sliced
Oil for deep frying

Prepare ..... roll mix according to package directions omitting egg and using 1 cup water.
Place .... 1 cheese cube on 1 pepperoni slice.
Wrap .... each with a small piece of dough, shaping into ball.
Fry .... in hot deep oil for 5 minutes or until brown.

Carolyn Sanders
Sweetwater School, Sweetwater, Oklahoma

PICKLE-FRUIT KABOBS WITH HAM ROLLS

1/2 c. sweet mixed pickles
12 melon balls
12 pineapple chunks
12 tangerine or orange sections
1/4 c. pineapple juice
2 tbsp. sweet pickle liquid
1 lb. creamed cottage cheese
8 slices boiled ham

Alternate ... pickles, melon balls, pineapple and tangerine sections on 4 skewers.
Place .... in shallow dish.
Pour .... pineapple and pickle juices over top.
Chill .... covered, turning once.
Mix .... 2 tablespoons marinade with cottage cheese.
Spoon ...... onto long side of each ham slice.
Roll .... as for jelly roll.

Arrange ..... on platter with kabobs.
Spoon ...... remaining marinade over ham rolls.
Yields ...... 4 servings.

Photograph for this recipe on this page.

POCO PEPPER SNACKS

1 3-oz. package cream cheese, softened
1/2 c. shredded Cheddar cheese
2 tbsp. chopped green chiles
2 tbsp. chopped olives
1 tsp. instant minced onion
5 drops of Tabasco sauce
1 can quick crescent rolls

Combine .... first 6 ingredients in bowl, mixing well.
Separate .... dough into 4 rectangles.
Press .... perforations together to seal.
Spread ..... 1/4 of the cheese mixture over each rectangle.
Roll .... as for jelly roll.
Slice .... each roll into 10 slices.
Place .... cut side down on greased baking sheet.
Bake .... at 400 degrees for 12 to 15 minutes or until browned.
Yields ...... 40 appetizers.

Ronda R. Harris
Okeene H. S., Okeene, Oklahoma

SPICY CHEESE DROPS

2 c. flour
1 tsp. red pepper
1/2 tsp. salt
1 c. finely chopped pecans
2 tsp. caraway seed
1 c. butter, softened
2 c. shredded sharp Cheddar cheese

Combine .... first 5 ingredients in bowl, mixing well.
Cream ...... butter and cheese in bowl.
Add .... to dry ingredients, mixing well.
Shape ...... by teaspoonfuls into balls.
Place .... on cookie sheets.
Bake .... at 350 degrees for 15 to 18 minutes or until golden brown.
Yields ...... 10 dozen.

Bobbie Rogers
Duncan H. S., Duncan, Oklahoma

PARTY SNACK

2 c. hearty granola cereal
1 c. pretzel sticks
1/2 c. peanuts
1/2 tsp. seasoned salt

Combine .... cereal, pretzels and nuts in 9-inch pan.
Sprinkle .... with seasoned salt, stirring to season evenly.
Bake .... at 300 degrees for 8 to 10 minutes.
Yields ...... 3 1/2 cups.

Photograph for this recipe on this page.

CHEESE FOOTBALL

1 env. Lipton Onion Soup Mix
2 c. sour cream
1/4 c. Port
1 8-oz. package cream cheese, softened, cubed
2 c. shredded Cheddar cheese
1/2 c. finely ground soda crackers
1/3 c. chopped cashews
Pimento strips

Blend .... soup mix and sour cream in bowl.
Place .... with Port in blender container.
Add .... cheeses gradually, processing until smooth after each addition.
Stir .... in cracker crumbs and cashews.
Pack .... into 4-cup bowl.
Chill .... until firm.
Unmold .... onto plate.
Shape ...... ends to resemble football.
Decorate .... with pimento strips for laces.
Yields ...... 3 1/2 cups spread.

Photograph for this recipe on page 35.

DEDRIA'S CHEESE ROLL

1 8-oz. package cream cheese, softened
1 sm. jar pimentos
8 green onions
1 stick butter
2 c. chopped pecans

Place .... first 4 ingredients in blender container.
Process ..... until smooth.
Shape ...... into 2 large rolls.
Roll .... in pecans.

Dedria Anderson
Ringwood H. S., Ringwood, Oklahoma

DEVILED PECAN BALL

2 8-oz. packages cream cheese, softened
2 c. shredded sharp cheese
1 can deviled ham
2 tbsp. chopped pimento
2 tsp. Worcestershire sauce
2 tsp. grated onion
1 tsp. dried parsley flakes
1 tsp. lemon juice
1 tsp. dry mustard

3/4 tsp. each seasoned salt, paprika
2 to 4 drops of hot sauce
2 c. chopped pecans

Combine .... first 3 ingredients in bowl, mixing well.
Add .... remaining ingredients except pecans.
Shape ...... into 2 balls.
Roll .... in pecans.

Linda M. Lamle
Okeene H. S., Okeene, Oklahoma

ERWANA'S CHEESE BALL

2 8-oz. packages cream cheese, softened
1 8-oz. can crushed pineapple, drained
2 tbsp. chopped onions
1/4 c. chopped green pepper
1 tbsp. seasoned salt
2 c. chopped pecans

Combine .... first 5 ingredients with 1 cup pecans in bowl, mixing well.
Shape ...... into ball.
Chill .... until firm.
Roll .... in remaining 1 cup pecans.

Erwana Ferrell, Advisor
McLoud H. S., McLoud, Oklahoma

PARTY CHEESE ROLL

1 12-oz. package American cheese
1 8-oz. package cream cheese, softened
2/3 tsp. garlic powder
1/2 c. chopped nuts
Chili powder

Mix .... first 4 ingredients together in bowl.
Shape ...... into 2 long rolls.
Roll .... in chili powder.
Chill .... until serving time.
Serve .... sliced with crackers.

Sandra Whitman, Advisor
Porum School, Porum, Oklahoma

DAZZLE DIP

1 6-oz. package pimento cream cheese, softened
1/2 c. sour cream

1/2 tsp. paprika
1/4 tsp. Tabasco sauce
1/2 tsp. Worcestershire sauce
1/2 tsp. salt
4 tbsp. catsup

Combine .... first 6 ingredients and 2 tablespoons catsup in bowl, mixing well.
Swirl .... remaining 2 tablespoons catsup on top.
Serve .... with shrimp, meatballs and chips.
Yields ...... 6-8 servings.

Linda Skrdla, President
Medford H. S., Medford, Oklahoma

DIP AND CRUNCH

1 3-oz. package cream cheese, softened
1/2 c. mayonnaise
3 tbsp. catsup
Carrots, cut in diagonal slices
Lettuce, cut in chunks
Cauliflowerets
Cherry tomatoes
Celery pieces

Combine .... first 3 ingredients in small bowl, mixing well.
Serve .... with vegetables for dipping.
Yields ...... 1 cup.

Photograph for this recipe on page 69.

GUACOMOLE DIP

2 ripe avocados, mashed
2 med. tomatoes, chopped
Juice of 1/2 lemon
1/4 tsp. garlic powder
1/2 tsp. salt
1 tbsp. finely chopped onion

Place .... avocados in blender container.
Process ..... until creamy.
Add .... remaining ingredients, mixing well.
Serve .... with tortilla chips.
Yields ...... 1 1/2 cups.

Debra Thompson
Mountain View H. S., Mountain View, Oklahoma

HOT CHILI-CHEESE DIP

1 8-oz. package cream cheese
1 can tomato soup
1 tbsp. instant minced onion
1 1/2 tsp. chili powder
1/2 tsp. Tabasco sauce
1 2-lb. package frozen French-fried
   potatoes, cooked

Cut .... cream cheese into 8 pieces.
Heat .... with soup and onion in saucepan
               until melted.
Stir .... in seasonings.
Serve .... with French-fried potatoes for
               dipping.

Photograph for this recipe on page 8.

EASY MEXICAN DIP

2 cans tomatoes, mashed
2 sm. cans chopped green chiles
2 tbsp. dried minced onion
1 tbsp. chili powder
1 tsp. ground cuminseed
Liquid red pepper seasoning to taste

Combine .... all ingredients in bowl, mixing
               well.
Adjust ...... seasonings to taste.
Chill .... until serving time.
Yields ...... 4 cups.

Van Ansley
Mooreland H. S., Mooreland, Oklahoma

MICROWAVE HOT BEEF DIP

1 2 1/2-oz. jar dried beef, chopped
1/2 c. Parmesan cheese
1/2 c. sour cream
1/4 c. chopped green onion
1/4 c. salad dressing
1 8-oz. package cream cheese, softened
1 tbsp. dried parsley flakes

Combine .... dried beef and 1 cup water in
               4-cup glass measuring cup.
Microwave .. on High for 3 minutes.
Drain ...... well.
Stir .... in remaining ingredients, mixing
               well.
Microwave .. on Roast to 120 degrees on food
               sensor.

Stir .... before serving.
Yields ...... 3 cups.

Carolyn Ames
Mooreland H. S., Mooreland, Oklahoma

MACHO NACHO CHEESE DIP

1 12-oz. can Cheddar cheese soup
1 tbsp. picante sauce
1/4 c. stewed tomatoes
Nachos

Combine .... first 3 ingredients in saucepan.
Cook .... over medium heat until blended.
Serve .... hot with nachos.

Sheri Huff
Moore West School, Oklahoma City, Oklahoma

OLIVE DIP

2 tomatoes, chopped
2 cans chopped ripe olives
1 can green chiles, chopped
3 green onions, chopped
2 tbsp. oil
Salt and pepper to taste

Combine .... all ingredients in bowl, mixing
               well.
Chill .... in refrigerator overnight.
Serve .... with chips or vegetables.

Mary Jo Drummond
State Dept. of Vo-Tech Ed.
Stillwater, Oklahoma

SKINNY DIP

1 bunch green onions with tops,
   chopped
2 firm tomatoes, chopped
1 4-oz. can chopped green chiles
1 4-oz. can chopped ripe olives
3 tbsp. olive oil
3 tbsp. taragon vinegar
Pinch of garlic salt
1 tsp. (or more) salt
Pepper to taste

Combine .... first 4 ingredients in bowl.
Mix .... oil, vinegar and seasonings
               together.

Pour . . . . over vegetable mixture.
Marinate . . . . for 2 hours or longer.
Yields . . . . . . about 2 cups.

Anna Lou Harris
Watonga H. S., Watonga, Oklahoma

TACO PIZZA DIP

2 cans refried beans
1 pkg. taco seasoning
2 cans frozen guacamole dip, thawed
2 sm. cans chopped chiles
Chopped tomatoes
Chopped green onions
1 sm. can chopped black olives
1 pt. sour cream
Grated cheese
Doritos

Blend . . . . . . first 2 ingredients in bowl, mixing well.
Mix . . . . guacamole and chiles in bowl.
Combine . . . . tomatoes, onions and olives in bowl.
Layer . . . . . . bean mixture, guacamole, sour cream, vegetable mixture and cheese on serving plate in order listed.
Serve . . . . . . with Doritos.
Yields . . . . . . 8-10 servings.

Jennifer Ann Walsh
Union City H. S., Union City, Oklahoma

TWO-MEAT DIP

1 lb. ground beef, cooked, drained
1 lb. sausage, cooked, drained
2 cans Ro-Tel
1 lb. Velveeta cheese, cubed

Combine . . . . ground beef, sausage, 1 can drained Ro-Tel, 1 can undrained Ro-Tel, and cheese in saucepan.
Heat . . . . until cheese melts, stirring constantly.
Serve . . . . . . warm.

Lana Byrd
Moore West Mid-H. S., Oklahoma City, Oklahoma

TANGY FRESH VEGETABLE DIP

2 c. mayonnaise
1 c. cottage cheese

3/4 c. chopped onion
1 1/2 tbsp. horseradish
1 1/2 tbsp. Worcestershire sauce
1 1/2 tsp. caraway seed
1 tsp. garlic salt
Dash of Tabasco sauce
1/2 tsp. seasoned salt

Combine . . . . all ingredients in bowl, mixing well.
Serve . . . . with fresh vegetables or chips.

Trina Morse
Wilson H. S., Wilson, Oklahoma

VEGETABLE CONFETTI

1   8-oz. package cream cheese, softened
1/2 c. sour cream
1 tbsp. dry mustard
1 tsp. salt
1/2 tsp. pepper
1 green pepper, chopped
1 tomato, chopped
1 bunch green onions, chopped

Cream . . . . . . first 2 ingredients in bowl.
Blend . . . . . . in mustard, salt and pepper.
Stir . . . . in vegetables.
Serve . . . . with corn chips.

Cari Starkey, President
McLoud School, McLeod, Oklahoma

CABBAGE PATCH SOUP

1 lb. ground beef
1 sm. onion, chopped
3 cans chicken broth
3 cans ranch-style beans
1 can tomatoes
1 sm. head cabbage, shredded
1 c. chopped celery
1/2 tsp. cuminseed
1/2 tsp. chili powder

Saute . . . . . . ground beef and onion in skillet until beef is crumbly.
Combine . . . . with remaining ingredients in 4-quart saucepan.
Simmer . . . . . until vegetables are tender.

Deanna Reeves
Granite H. S., Granite, Oklahoma

CLAM CHOWDER

3/4 lb. minced clams
1 c. finely chopped onions
1 c. finely diced celery
2 c. diced potatoes
3/4 c. butter, melted
3/4 c. flour
1 qt. half and half
1 1/2 tsp. salt
Pepper to taste
1/2 tsp. sugar

Drain . . . . . . juice from clams and set clams aside.
Combine . . . . clam juice with vegetables and water to cover in medium saucepan.
Cook . . . . for 20 minutes or until potatoes are tender.
Blend . . . . . . butter and flour in saucepan.
Cook . . . . for 1 or 2 minutes.
Stir . . . . in cream.
Cook . . . . until smooth and thick, stirring constantly with whisk.
Add . . . . undrained vegetables and clams.
Cook . . . . until heated through.
Season . . . . . with salt, pepper and sugar.

Margaret J. Kelly
State Dept. of Vo-Tech Ed., Stillwater, Oklahoma

CHICKEN GUMBO

1 lg. fryer, cut up
2 tsp. salt
1/2 tsp. pepper
Oil
1/2 c. flour
1 lg. onion, chopped
1/2 c. chopped celery
1/3 c. chopped green pepper
1/2 tsp. file (opt.)

Season . . . . . chicken with salt and pepper.
Saute . . . . . . in oil in skillet until brown on both sides; drain and set aside.
Combine . . . . 1/2 cup oil and flour in heavy skillet to make roux.
Cook . . . . until golden brown, stirring constantly.
Add . . . . onion, celery and green pepper.
Cook . . . . until vegetables are tender.

Heat . . . . 2 quarts water to boiling point in large soup pot.
Add . . . . roux mixture and chicken to water.
Simmer . . . . . until chicken is tender.
Stir . . . . in file.
Serve . . . . in bowls over rice.

Shelley Williams
McLoud School, McLeod, Oklahoma

SHRIMP AND OKRA GUMBO

2 c. fresh diced okra
2 tbsp. oil
1 stick margarine, melted
4 tbsp. flour
1 onion, chopped
1 green pepper, chopped
2 stalks celery, chopped
2 cloves of garlic, minced
1 tbsp. Worcestershire sauce
2 lb. fresh peeled shrimp
Creole seasoning to taste

Saute . . . . . . okra in oil in heavy saucepan for 10 minutes, stirring constantly.
Remove . . . . okra and set aside.
Blend . . . . . . in margarine and flour, stirring to make roux.
Cook . . . . until golden brown, stirring constantly.
Add . . . . next 4 vegetables and okra.
Cook . . . . for 5 minutes.
Stir . . . . in 3 quarts water and Worcestershire sauce.
Simmer . . . . . for 1 to 2 hours.
Add . . . . shrimp.
Simmer . . . . . for 1/2 hour or until tender.
Season . . . . . to taste with creole seasoning.
Serve . . . . over rice garnished with chopped scallions and file.
Yields . . . . . . 8 servings.

Kasey Faye
Cyril H. S., Cyril, Oklahoma

LORETTA'S HOT SAUCE

2 cans tomatoes
1 mild onion, chopped
1 tsp. pepper
3 tsp. pepper juice

4 peppers, finely chopped
1 tsp. salt

Combine . . . . all ingredients in saucepan.
Simmer . . . . . until flavors are well blended.

Loretta Lane
Rush Springs H. S., Rush Springs, Oklahoma

HORTON'S HOT SAUCE RELISH

8 to 10 jalapeno peppers
3 med. tomatoes
1 med. onion
1 sm. carrot

Force . . . . . . all ingredients through food grinder.
Place . . . . in bowl.
Let . . . . stand until serving time.
Yields . . . . . . 2-3 cups. Enough to get you hot and keep you that way.

Andrea Horton
Mustang H. S., Mustang, Oklahoma

GLADYS' BARBECUE SAUCE

1 lb. margarine
1 c. packed brown sugar
4 bay leaves
1 bottle of catsup
1 bottle of mustard
1 bottle of Worcestershire sauce
4 cloves of garlic, minced
Salt and pepper to taste

Combine . . . . all ingredients in saucepan.
Boil . . . . for 3 minutes.
Chill . . . . in refrigerator.
Brush . . . . . . over cooked meat or chicken.
Cook . . . . until heated through.

Gladys Cassell
Eisenhower Jr. H. S., Lawton, Oklahoma

NEVER-FAIL BARBECUE SAUCE

1/4 c. barbecue spice
1/4 c. packed brown sugar
1/4 c. Worcestershire sauce
1/4 c. liquid smoke
2 tbsp. vinegar
1 32-oz. bottle of catsup

Combine . . . . all ingredients in 2-quart saucepan.
Simmer . . . . . covered, for 15 minutes.
Use . . . . for basting meats, adding to beans or serving with leftover roast.
Yields . . . . . . 1 quart sauce.

Geneva Perry
Alex School, Alex, Oklahoma

SUE'S BARBECUE SAUCE

1 med. onion, chopped
2 tbsp. drippings
1 32-oz. bottle of catsup
1 1/2 tbsp. Worcestershire sauce
2 tbsp. liquid smoke
Dash of Tabasco sauce
1/4 to 1/2 c. sugar
Cooked meat

Saute . . . . . . onion in drippings in skillet until light brown.
Add . . . . next 5 ingredients and 2 cups water.
Simmer . . . . . until blended.
Add . . . . meat.
Simmer . . . . . for 15 minutes.

Sue Wolfe
Rush Springs H. S., Rush Springs, Oklahoma

APRICOT FRUIT SALAD

1 6-oz. package apricot gelatin
1 8-oz. package cream cheese, softened
1 15-oz. can pineapple
2 jars apricot baby food
1 8-oz. carton Cool Whip

Dissolve . . . . gelatin in 2/3 cup hot water in large bowl.
Add . . . . cream cheese, beating until smooth.
Stir . . . . in pineapple and apricots.
Chill . . . . until partially congealed.
Fold . . . . in Cool Whip.
Pour . . . . into 8 x 12-inch dish.
Refrigerate . . covered, until firm.
Yields . . . . . . 10-12 servings.

Brenda Kopf
Waynoka Public School, Waynoka, Oklahoma

CHERRY FLUFF SALAD

1 can sweetened condensed milk
1 lg. carton Cool Whip
1 can cherry pie filling
1/2 c. nuts
1 c. crushed pineapple, drained
Juice of 1 lemon

Blend ...... condensed milk and Cool Whip in large bowl.
Fold .... in remaining ingredients.
Chill .... until serving time.

Jeri Starcher
Sentinel H. S., Sentinel, Oklahoma

CHERRIES AND CREAM SALAD

1 lg. can crushed pineapple, drained
1 can sweetened condensed milk
1 can cherry pie filling
1 lg. carton Cool Whip

Combine .... all ingredients in bowl, mixing well.
Chill .... until serving time.
Yields ...... 6-8 servings.

Marinelle McPherson
Bartlesville Mid-H. S., Bartlesville, Oklahoma

KAREN'S CRANBERRY SALAD

1 orange, grated with rind
1 apple, grated with peel
1 lb. cranberries, ground
2 c. sugar
1 8-oz. can crushed pineapple, drained
1 3-oz. package lime gelatin
1 3-oz. package orange gelatin

Combine .... first 5 ingredients in bowl, mixing well.
Let .... stand for 1 hour.
Dissolve .... gelatins in 2 cups boiling water.
Add .... 1 cup cold water.
Mix .... with fruit.
Chill .... until firm.

Karen Long
Francis Tuttle Vo-Tech Center
Oklahoma City, Oklahoma

LEMON SALAD

1 8-oz. package cream cheese, softened
1 can sweetened condensed milk
1 15-oz. can crushed pineapple, drained
1 can lemon pie filling mix
1 9-oz. carton Cool Whip
1 c. grated longhorn cheese (opt.)

Blend ...... cream cheese and condensed milk in bowl until smooth.
Add .... pineapple, pie filling and Cool Whip, mixing well.
Stir .... in cheese.
Garnish .... with additional grated cheese or chopped nuts.
Refrigerate .. for several hours before serving.
Yields ...... 12 servings.

Tamara L. Fischer
Okeene Public H. S., Okeene, Oklahoma

ORANGE-TUNA TUBS

2 7-oz. cans tuna
1 1/2 c. Florida orange sections, cut into bite-sized pieces
1/2 c. chopped celery
1 lg. tomato, chopped
1/3 c. mayonnaise
1 tbsp. Florida orange juice
4 round rolls
2 Florida orange slices, cut in half

Combine .... first 4 ingredients in bowl.
Blend ...... mayonnaise and orange juice in small bowl.
Add .... to tuna mixture, mixing well.
Cut .... thin slice off top of rolls.
Scoop ...... out centers.
Fill .... with tuna mixture.
Thread ..... orange slices on 4 long food picks.
Top .... with paper pennant, cherry tomato or olive for sails.
Place .... picks in side of each roll.

Photograph for this recipe on page 36.

MANDARIN ORANGE MOLD

2 11-oz. cans mandarin oranges
2 3-oz. packages orange gelatin

1 13 1/2-oz. can crushed pineapple
1 pt. orange sherbet

Drain . . . . . . oranges, reserving syrup.
Add . . . . enough water to syrup to mea-
sure 1 1/2 cups liquid.
Bring . . . . to a boil in saucepan.
Remove . . . . from heat.
Add . . . . gelatin, stirring until dissolved.
Stir . . . . in remaining ingredients.
Pour . . . . into mold.
Chill . . . . . . until firm.
Unmold . . . . on serving plate.
Garnish . . . . . with watercress, orange segments
and strawberries.

Callie Heinze
Pawhuska H. S., Pawhuska, Oklahoma

ACINI DEPEPE SALAD

1 c. macaroni DePePe
1 tsp. salt
1 16-oz. can pineapple tidbits
2 cans mandarin oranges
1 c. sugar
3 tbsp. flour
3 eggs, beaten
1 c. miniature marshmallows
1 lg. carton Cool Whip

Cook . . . . macaroni in boiling salted water
in saucepan until tender; drain.
Drain . . . . . . pineapple and oranges, reserving
juices.
Combine . . . . juices, sugar, flour and eggs in
saucepan.
Cook . . . . over low heat until thickened,
stirring constantly. Cool.
Mix . . . . with cooled macaroni and fruit
in large bowl.
Refrigerate . . overnight.
Fold . . . . marshmallows and Cool Whip.
Note . . . . R. F. Acini DePePe is found in
pasta or gourmet section of
store.

Tamara Culberson
Canute H. S., Canute, Oklahoma

DARN GOOD SALAD

1 3-oz. package lime gelatin
1 8-oz. package cream cheese, softened
36 miniature marshmallows

1 pkg. Dream Whip
1 sm. can crushed pineapple
1 c. grated carrots
1 c. coconut
1 c. chopped nuts

Dissolve . . . . gelatin in 1 cup boiling water in
bowl.
Beat . . . . in cream cheese and marsh-
mallows.
Chill . . . . . . until partially set.
Prepare . . . . . Dream Whip using package
instructions.
Add . . . . with remaining ingredients to
gelatin mixture.
Pour . . . . into mold.
Chill . . . . . . until set.

Staci Shaw
Mustang H. S., Mustang, Oklahoma

DELICIOUS FRUIT SALAD

1 lg. carton Cool Whip
1 can sweetened condensed milk
1 14-oz. can crushed pineapple, drained
1 can cherry pie filling
1/2 c. pecans
1 c. flaked coconut
1 c. miniature marshmallows

Blend . . . . . . Cool Whip and condensed milk
in large bowl, mixing well.
Refrigerate . . for 1 hour.
Stir . . . . in remaining ingredients.
Refrigerate . . overnight.

Mrs. Norman A. Lamb
Enid, Oklahoma

DEBI'S FRUIT SALAD

1 can mandarin oranges
1 can pineapple chunks
1 sm. jar maraschino cherries,
cut in half
1 sm. box vanilla instant pudding mix
3 bananas, sliced

Combine . . . . all ingredients in bowl, mixing
well.
Chill . . . . . . until serving time.
Yields . . . . . . 10 servings.

Debi Hunko
Moore West H. S., Oklahoma City, Oklahoma

FRUIT SALAD A LA MODE

Crisp greens
1/2 cantaloupe, peeled
6 to 8 Bing cherries
1/2 peach
1/2 pear
1 slice watermelon, cut in wedges
1/2 c. raspberries
1 yellow plum
1 sm. bunch grapes
1/4 c. blueberries
3 med. scoops vanilla ice cream

Arrange . . . . . greens on serving plate.
Place . . . . cantaloupe in center with all fruits except blueberries arranged around edges.
Fill . . . . cantaloupe with ice cream.
Top . . . . with blueberries.
Yields . . . . . . 1 serving.

Photograph for this recipe above.

ICED MELON CUPS

2 c. sugar
Lemon juice to taste
1/2 tsp. rum flavoring or 1 tsp.
orange marmalade
3 cantaloupes, halved
1 pt. fresh strawberries, stemmed
2 bananas, sliced
1/4 lb. green grapes, stemmed
1   16-oz. can pineapple chunks, drained

Boil . . . . sugar and 4 cups water in large saucepan for 5 minutes; cool.
Add . . . . lemon juice and flavoring or marmalade.
Pour . . . . into ice cream freezer container.
Freeze . . . . . . following manufacturer's instructions.
Place . . . . cantaloupe halves on individual salad plates.

Combine .... strawberries, bananas, grapes and pineapple in bowl, mixing well.
Spoon ...... into cantaloupe halves.
Top .... with scoops of lemon ice.
Garnish ..... with stemmed maraschino cherries.
Yields ...... 6 servings.

Margaret Scott, Advisor
Cyril H. S., Cyril, Oklahoma

PRETZEL SALAD TORTE

2 2/3 c. crushed pretzels
2 sticks margarine, melted
Sugar
1 8-oz. package cream cheese, softened
1 lg. container Cool Whip
1 lg. package gelatin
1 10-oz. package frozen fruit, thawed

Mix .... first 2 ingredients with 3 table-spoons sugar in bowl.
Pat .... into 9 x 13-inch baking pan.
Bake .... at 350 degrees for 10 minutes.
Blend ...... cream cheese and 1 cup sugar in bowl.
Spread ..... over cooled crust.
Cover ...... with Cool Whip; chill.
Dissolve .... gelatin in 2 cups boiling water.
Stir .... in fruit and 3/4 cup cold water.
Chill .... until partially set.
Spread ..... over Cool Whip.
Chill .... until serving time.

Angela Moddie
Snyder H. S., Snyder, Oklahoma

CHAMPAGNE SALAD

1 8-oz. package cream cheese, softened
3/4 c. sugar
1 12-oz. carton frozen strawberries, thawed, drained
1 lg. can pineapple tidbits, drained
2 bananas, diced
1 c. chopped pecans
1 10-oz. carton Cool Whip

Combine .... cream cheese and sugar in bowl, mixing well.
Stir .... in fruit and nuts.
Fold .... in Cool Whip.
Spoon ...... into paper-lined muffin cups.

Freeze ...... until firm.
Yields ...... 18 servings.

Traci Oglesby
Eakly School, Eakly, Oklahoma

STRAWBERRY-SOUR CREAM SALAD

1 sm. package strawberry gelatin
1 pkg. unflavored gelatin
1 pkg. frozen strawberries
1 sm. can crushed pineapple
1 pkg. cherry gelatin
1 can cranberry sauce
3 or 4 bananas, sliced
1 8-oz. carton sour cream

Combine .... strawberry gelatin, 1/2 package unflavored gelatin and 1 cup boiling water in bowl, stirring until dissolved.
Stir .... in strawberries and pineapple.
Pour .... into rectangular serving dish.
Chill .... until firm.
Dissolve .... cherry gelatin and remaining unflavored gelatin in 1 cup boiling water in bowl.
Stir .... in cranberry sauce until smooth.
Chill .... until partially set.
Fold .... in bananas.
Spoon ...... sour cream over strawberry mixture.
Pour .... cranberry mixture over sour cream.
Chill .... until firm.

Shirley Novosad
Union City H. S., Union City, Oklahoma

SWEET AND SPICY AVOCADO KABOBS

1/2 avocado, peeled
12 pineapple chunks
12 mandarin orange segments
1/4 c. French dressing

Cut .... avocado into 12 chunks.
Thread ..... alternately with pineapple and oranges on 6 wooden skewers.
Serve .... with dressing.

JoAnn Massingill
Wilson H. S., Wilson, Oklahoma

BEAN SALAD

1/3 c. sugar
1/4 c. oil
1/4 c. red wine vinegar
3/4 tsp. salt
1   16-oz. can French-style green
       beans, drained
1/2 c. chopped onion
1 can English peas, drained
1 green pepper, chopped
4 stalks celery, chopped
1 c. chopped pimentos

Combine .... first 4 ingredients in saucepan.
Heat .... to boiling point.
Mix .... remaining ingredients in serving
                bowl.
Pour .... hot dressing over vegetables.
Refrigerate .. for 24 hours or longer.

Pam Lind
Hydro H. S., Hydro, Oklahoma

BANNER SALAD

2 c. cauliflowerets, cooked, drained
1 c. chopped tomatoes
1/2 c. sliced celery
1/2 c. red onion rings
1/4 c. chopped green pepper
Italian dressing
1 qt. shredded lettuce

Combine .... first 6 ingredients in bowl, mix-
                ing well.
Refrigerate .. covered, for several hours.
Drain ...... reserving marinade.
Combine .... lettuce, vegetables and reserved
                marinade, tossing lightly.

Emma Ellen Bunyard
Jenks H. S., Jenks, Oklahoma

BROCCOLI-CAULIFLOWER SALAD

2 carrots, chopped
1 head broccoli, chopped
2 cucumbers, chopped
1 head cauliflower, separated into
     flowerets
1 onion, chopped
1   10-oz. package mushrooms, sliced
1 bottle of Italian dressing
1 tsp. garlic powder

Combine .... all ingredients in serving bowl,
                mixing well.
Refrigerate .. for 1 hour.
Yields ...... 10-12 servings.

Renee Romero
Vanoss School, Ada, Oklahoma

BROCCOLI IN TOMATO MAYONNAISE

1 bunch broccoli, trimmed, cut into
     flowerets
1 med. onion, chopped
1 clove of garlic, minced
2 tbsp. butter
1 tbsp. oil
2 lg. fresh tomatoes, chopped
Pinch of sugar
Pinch of dried basil
1/2 tsp. fresh oregano
2/3 c. mayonnaise
Salt and freshly ground pepper to taste

Cook .... broccoli in boiling salted water
                for 3 minutes or until tender-
                crisp; drain.
Saute ...... onion and garlic in butter and oil
                in saucepan for 5 minutes.
Add .... chopped tomatoes, sugar, basil
                and oregano.
Cook .... for 15 mintues or until soft, stir-
                ring occasionally; cool.
Place .... in food processor container.
Process ..... until smooth.
Combine .... with mayonnaise in bowl, mix-
                ing well.
Add .... broccoli, tossing well.
Season ..... with salt and pepper to taste.
Chill .... until serving time.
Garnish ..... with tomato slices.
Yields ...... 4-6 servings.

Peter A. Butorovich
Setauket, New York

CARROT SALAD

1 med. onion, diced
1 green pepper, diced
1 can tomato soup
1 c. sugar
1/2 c. oil
1/2 c. vinegar

1 tsp. dry mustard
1 tsp. salt
Pepper to taste
2 lb. carrots, sliced, cooked, cooled

Combine .... all ingredients except carrots in saucepan.
Bring .... to a boil.
Add .... carrots, mixing well.
Refrigerate .. covered, overnight.
Yields ...... 10 servings.

Mary P. Boechman
Okeene, Oklahoma

FROZEN VEGETABLE SALAD

1 10-oz. package frozen carrots, thawed
1 10-oz. package frozen cauliflower, thawed
1 10-oz. package frozen broccoli, thawed
1 7 3/4-oz. can pitted ripe olives
1 4 1/2-oz. can whole mushrooms
1 8-oz. can sliced water chestnuts
2/3 c. Italian salad dressing

Combine .... first 6 ingredients in large bowl.
Add .... salad dressing, tossing to mix.
Refrigerate .. covered, for 3 hours, stirring occasionally.
Yields ...... 8 cups.

Donna Nigh, Oklahoma Governor's Wife
Honorary Fund Raising Chairman for FHA/HERO
Oklahoma City, Oklahoma

SAUERKRAUT SALAD

1 20-oz. can sauerkraut, drained
1 c. sugar
1 c. chopped onions
1 c. chopped celery
1 med. green pepper, chopped
1/2 c. oil
1/3 c. vinegar

Combine .... first 5 ingredients in bowl, mixing well.
Heat .... oil and vinegar in saucepan.
Pour .... over vegetables.

Patty Harper
Okeene Public School, Okeene, Oklahoma

POM-POM SALAD

3 c. shredded cabbage
3 c. shredded red cabbage
2 c. shredded carrots
1/2 c. peanuts
1/2 c. raisins
1 c. Wish-Bone Sweet 'n Spicy French
    or Russian Dressing
1/4 tsp. ground ginger (opt.)

Combine .... first 5 ingredients in medium bowl.
Blend ...... dressing and ginger.
Pour .... over vegetables, tossing to mix well.
Chill .... overnight.
Yields ...... 8 servings.

Photograph for this recipe on page 35.

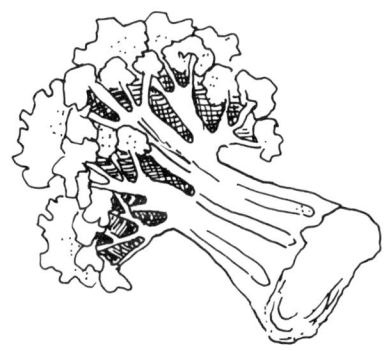

FRESH MUSHROOM SALAD

1 c. sliced fresh mushrooms
1 sm. potato, thinly sliced
1 c. bean sprouts
2 c. alfalfa sprouts
1/2 c. fresh peas

Mix .... all ingredients in large serving bowl.
Chill .... until serving time.
Serve .... with oil-based dressing.
Yields ...... 4 servings.

Christinia Mack
Drummond H. S., Drummond, Oklahoma

PEANUT BUTTER-POTATO SALAD

1/4 c. vinegar
1/4 c. peanut oil
1 tsp. salt
1/4 tsp. pepper
3 c. diced hot cooked potatoes
1 c. diced celery
1/4 c. chopped green onions
1 c. diced ham
1/2 c. mayonnaise
1/2 c. peanut butter

Combine .... first 4 ingredients in bowl, mixing well.
Stir .... in potatoes, mixing lightly.
Chill .... in refrigerator.
Add .... celery, onions and ham.
Mix .... mayonnaise and peanut butter in bowl.
Spoon ...... over potato mixture, tossing to mix.
Yields ...... 6 cups.

Photograph for this recipe on page 67.

SALAD FLORENTINE

1   12-oz. can Spam, cut into 1/2-inch cubes
3 tbsp. oil
1/4 c. vinegar
1 tbsp. sugar
1/4 tsp. pepper
1/4 tsp. onion salt
9 c. fresh spinach leaves

Brown ...... Spam in oil in skillet.
Add .... 2 tablespoons water and remaining ingredients except spinach.
Simmer ..... for 2 minutes, stirring constantly.
Pour .... over spinach, tossing lightly.
Garnish ..... with tomato slices and sliced hard-boiled eggs.

Debbie Perkins
Okeene Public School, Okeene, Oklahoma

HERMAN'S SLAW

1 head cabbage, shredded
6 carrots, shredded
3 onions, thinly sliced
Juice of 2 lemons
1 tbsp. vinegar
1/4 c. sugar
1 1/2 tsp. salt
1/4 c. oil
1/4 tsp. garlic powder

Combine .... first 3 ingredients in bowl, mixing well.
Mix .... remaining ingredients together in small bowl.
Pour .... over vegetables.
Refrigerate .. for 24 hours or longer.
Note .... will keep for weeks in refrigerator in plastic container.
Yields ...... 8-10 servings.

Relda I. Coley
Binger H. S., Binger, Oklahoma

JUDY'S COLESLAW

4 c. finely shredded cabbage
1/4 c. chopped onion
1/2 c. sour cream
1/4 c. mayonnaise
1/2 tsp. dry mustard
Dash of pepper

Combine .... cabbage and onion in large bowl.
Blend ...... remaining ingredients in small bowl.
Pour .... over cabbage mixture; toss.
Garnish ..... with paprika.
Yields ...... 6-8 servings.

Judy Smith
Springer H. S., Springer, Oklahoma

CONFETTI COLESLAW

4 c. shredded cabbage
1/2 c. shredded carrot
1 tsp. salt
1 tsp. sugar
1/2 c. mayonnaise
1 tbsp. vinegar

1 tbsp. milk
1 sm. red apple, chopped

Combine .... cabbage and carrot in bowl.
Sprinkle .... with salt and sugar.
Mix .... mayonnaise, vinegar and milk in small bowl.
Add .... to cabbage mixture, mixing well.
Chill .... in refrigerator.
Stir .... in apple just before serving.
Yields ...... 8 servings.

Photograph for this recipe on page 69.

SEVEN-LAYER SALAD

1 head lettuce, chopped
1 c. celery, chopped
1 lg. green pepper, chopped
1 purple onion, diced
1 pkg. shredded Cheddar cheese
Tomato wedges (opt.)
1 c. mayonnaise
2 tbsp. sugar
1 pkg. frozen peas, thawed

Combine .... first 6 ingredients in serving bowl, tossing lightly.
Mix .... mayonnaise and sugar together in bowl.
Spread ..... over vegetables.
Refrigerate .. for 4 to 8 hours.
Add .... peas just before serving, tossing all ingredients.

Brenda Moss
Ryan Public School, Ryan, Oklahoma

SWEET-SOUR SALAD

3/4 c. sugar
1/2 c. oil
1 c. vinegar
1 can whole kernel corn, drained
1 can English peas, drained
1 can French-style green beans, drained
1 can carrots, drained
Celery, pimento, salt, pepper to taste

Combine .... first 3 ingredients in small bowl, mixing well.

Mix .... remaining ingredients in large bowl.
Pour .... dressing over vegetables.
Refrigerate .. for 4 hours or longer.
Yields ...... 12-15 servings.

Mrs. Leo Laubach
Okeene, Oklahoma

SWEDISH VEGETABLE SALAD

1 can white Shoe Peg corn, drained
1 can French-style green beans, drained
1 can English peas, drained
1 jar pimento, chopped
1 c. chopped celery
1 green pepper, chopped
1 c. sugar
1/2 c. oil
1/2 c. vinegar
Salt and pepper to taste

Combine .... all vegetables in large serving bowl, mixing well.
Mix .... remaining ingredients together in bowl.
Pour .... over vegetables.
Refrigerate .. overnight.
Note .... will keep for 1 week in refrigerator.

Mrs. Art Scheffler
Hitchcock, Oklahoma

TREASURE ISLAND SEASHELL SALAD

1/2 c. mayonnaise
3 tbsp. Florida orange juice
1 tbsp. sugar
8 oz. shell macaroni, cooked, drained
1 1/2 c. Florida orange sections, cut into bite-sized pieces
1/2 c. chopped green pepper
1/3 c. shredded carrot

Blend ...... mayonnaise, orange juice and sugar together in bowl.
Add .... remaining ingredients; toss to mix well.
Yields ...... 4-6 servings.

Photograph for this recipe on page 36.

Main Dishes

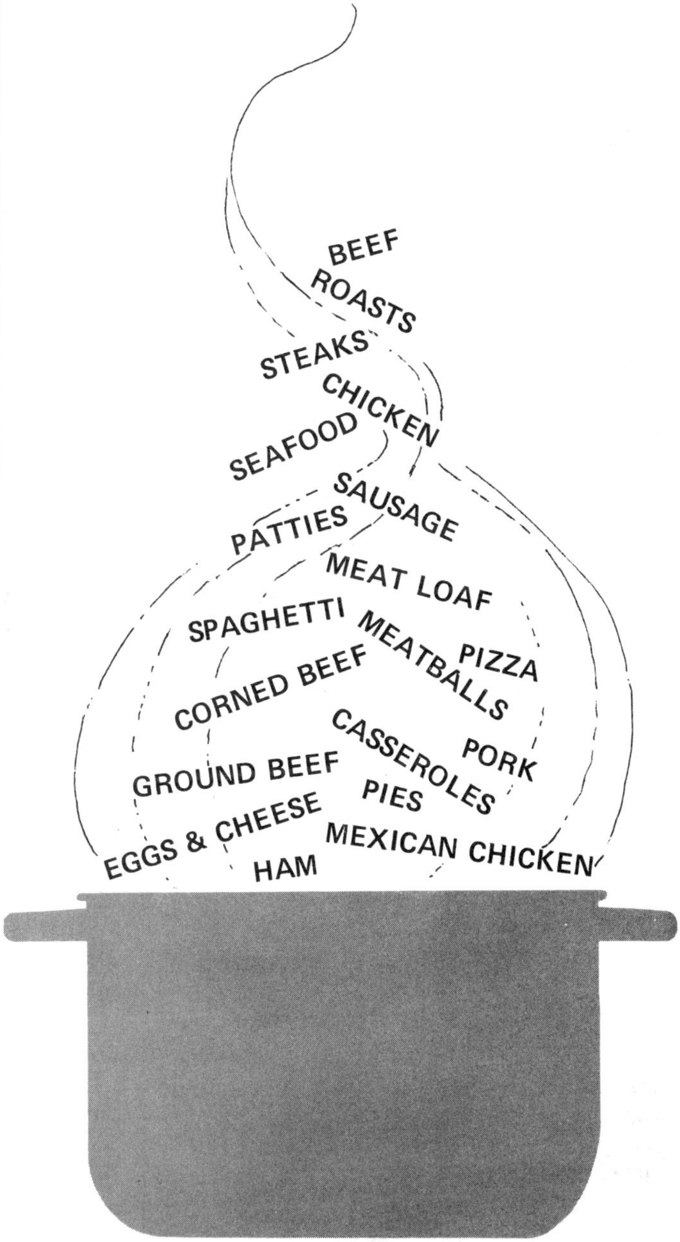

BEEF
ROASTS
STEAKS
CHICKEN
SEAFOOD
SAUSAGE
PATTIES
MEAT LOAF
SPAGHETTI MEATBALLS PIZZA
CORNED BEEF
CASSEROLES PORK
GROUND BEEF
PIES
EGGS & CHEESE MEXICAN CHICKEN
HAM

BARBECUED BEEF IN BUNS

1   3 to 4-lb. chuck roast
1 can tomato sauce
1/2 bottle of catsup
3 tbsp. mustard
3 tbsp. Worcestershire sauce
1/2 tsp. salt
1/4 tsp. pepper
1/2 tsp. garlic powder
2 tbsp. chili powder
1/4 tsp. celery salt
2 or 3 drops of liquid smoke
1 green pepper, chopped
1 onion, chopped
Buns

Place . . . . roast in pan with water to cover.
Cook . . . . covered, over low heat for 8 hours or until meat falls from bones.
Drain . . . . . . and shred; set aside.
Combine . . . . remaining ingredients except buns with 1 sauce can water in large saucepan, mixing well.
Simmer . . . . . for 1 hour or longer.
Add . . . . meat, mixing well.
Cook . . . . until heated through.
Serve . . . . on buns.

Shelia Mapp
Wilson H. S., Wilson, Oklahoma

BEEF SKILLET MEAL

1 1/2 lb. round steak, cut in serving pieces
1/2 c. flour
2 tsp. salt
1/2 tsp. pepper
4 tbsp. shortening
1 can cream of mushroom soup
1 tbsp. Worcestershire sauce
1 lg. onion, sliced
6 med. potatoes, diced
6 lg. carrots, diced

Coat . . . . steak with mixture of flour, salt and pepper.
Brown . . . . . . in shortening in skillet.
Add . . . . remaining ingredients.
Simmer . . . . . covered, for 1 1/4 hours.
Yields . . . . . . 4-6 servings.

Karla Eischen
Okarche Public School, Okarche, Oklahoma

BAKED CHILI

1 lb. chopped beef
1 lg. onion, chopped
1 lg. green pepper, chopped
3 1/2 c. tomatoes
1 can Ro-Tel
1 1/2 tsp. salt
1/8 tsp. paprika
1/8 tsp. cayenne pepper
3 whole cloves
1 bay leaf
1 to 2 tbsp. chili powder
1/2 tsp. cumin
2 sm. red peppers
1/2 tsp. oregano

Brown . . . . . . beef, onion and green pepper in Dutch oven.
Stir . . . . in remaining ingredients.
Bake . . . . covered, at 300 degrees for 2 hours or until beef is tender.

Susan Brown
Empire H. S., Duncan, Oklahoma

DEVILISH BEEF STEW

1 1/2 lb. beef stew meat, cut into 1-inch cubes
1/3 c. flour
2 tbsp. oil
1 tbsp. dry mustard
1 1/2 tsp. salt
1 clove of garlic, minced
1 tsp. chili powder
1 tsp. Worcestershire sauce
1/4 tsp. pepper
4 med. potatoes, peeled, quartered
6 sm. onions, quartered
4 carrots, quartered
2 stalks celery, cut into 1-inch pieces

Coat . . . . beef cubes with flour.
Brown . . . . . . 1/3 at a time in oil in large saucepan; remove from heat.
Combine . . . . meat, seasonings and 2 cups water in saucepan.
Simmer . . . . . covered, for 1 to 1 1/2 hours or until meat is almost tender.
Add . . . . 1 1/2 cups water and vegetables.
Simmer . . . . . covered, for 30 minutes longer or until vegetables are tender.

Remove	meat and vegetables from saucepan; skim fat.
Blend	1/4 cup cold water into remaining flour until smooth.
Stir	into hot liquid gradually.
Cook	until thick, stirring constantly.
Return	meat and vegetables to saucepan; heat.
Yields	8 servings.

Sonya Tilmon
Nowata H. S., Nowata, Oklahoma

GOULASH ON NOODLES

2 lb. beef, cubed
2 tbsp. shortening
1 c. chopped onions
1 8-oz. can tomato sauce
1 tbsp. each sugar, paprika
1 tsp. salt
2 tbsp. vinegar
2 tsp. Worcestershire sauce
Pinch each of garlic powder, pepper
2 bay leaves
2 tbsp. flour

Brown	beef in hot shortening in skillet.
Add	remaining ingredients, except flour, with 1 cup water, mixing well.
Simmer	covered, for 1 1/2 to 2 hours or until tender.
Remove	bay leaves and excess fat.
Blend	flour with 1/4 cup cold water.
Stir	into goulash.
Cook	until thick, stirring constantly.
Serve	over noodles.

Kay Howard
Wilson H. S., Wilson, Oklahoma

MEXICAN FRICASSEE

1/2 c. chopped green pepper
1/2 c. chopped onion
2 tbsp. butter
1 can chili beef soup
1 can tomato soup
2 c. cubed cooked beef

| Saute | green pepper and onion in butter in skillet until tender. |
| Stir | in remaining ingredients with 1/2 cup water. |

| Simmer | until heated through. |
| Serve | over rice and garnish with shredded Cheddar cheese. |

Tinaliesa Forrest
Locust Grove H. S., Locust Grove, Oklahoma

SOUTHERN-STYLE SPAGHETTI

1 c. diced cooked beef
1 med. green pepper, sliced
1 med. onion, sliced
1/4 to 1/2 tsp. chili powder
1 clove of garlic, minced
1 can tomato soup
2 slices crisp-cooked bacon, crumbled
6 oz. spaghetti, cooked

Saute	first 5 ingredients in a small amount of bacon drippings in skillet until tender.
Add	soup, bacon and 1/2 soup can water, mixing well.
Simmer	covered, for 30 minutes, stirring frequently.
Serve	over spaghetti.

Molly Abner
Hydro H. S., Hydro, Oklahoma

AUNT CATHERINE'S BEEF STROGANOFF

1 onion, finely chopped
1 green pepper, finely chopped
2 sticks butter
2 lb. beef, cut in finger-sized strips
1 lg. can mushrooms
Worcestershire sauce to taste
Garlic salt and ground pepper to taste
1 lg. carton sour cream
1 c. whipping cream
1 pkg. Rice-A-Roni, prepared

Saute	onion and green pepper in butter in large skillet until tender.
Add	beef.
Cook	until light brown.
Add	remaining ingredients except Rice-A-Roni; mixing well.
Heat	through. Do not boil.
Serve	over Rice-A-Roni.

Marlene Baker
Coyle H. S., Coyle, Oklahoma

SUKIYAKI

1 lb. boneless beef tenderloin,
     very thinly sliced cross-grain
2 tbsp. oil
2 tbsp. sugar
1/2 c. beef stock
1/3 c. soy sauce
2 c. diagonally sliced green onions
2 c. diagonally sliced celery
1 c. small spinach leaves
1 1-lb. can bean sprouts, drained
1 c. thinly sliced fresh mushrooms
1 5-oz. can sliced water chestnuts,
     drained

Stir-fry ..... beef in oil in wok for 1 to 2 minutes or until brown.
Sprinkle .... with sugar.
Pour .... combined stock and soy sauce over beef, moving beef to side.
Stir-fry ..... onions and celery for 1 minute and move to side.
Stir-fry ..... remaining ingredients 1 at a time for 1 minute each, moving ingredients to side as each is cooked.
Serve .... with rice.

Vicki Kidd
Ryan H. S., Ryan, Oklahoma

COUNTRY-STYLE POT ROAST

1 3 to 4-lb. beef pot roast
Flour
1/4 c. butter
1 tsp. salt
1/8 tsp. pepper
1 beef bouillon cube
6 to 8 med. onions, peeled
1 lb. carrots, peeled, quartered
3 to 4 lg. potatoes, peeled, quartered
1 1/3 c. drippings
1 c. sour cream

Coat .... roast with flour.
Brown ...... in butter in Dutch oven.
Season ..... with salt, pepper and bouillon cube dissolved in 1/2 cup hot water.
Bake .... covered, at 350 degrees for 1 1/4 to 1 1/2 hours.
Add .... onions and carrots.
Bake .... for 15 minutes longer.

Add .... potatoes and additional salt to taste.
Bake .... for 30 to 40 minutes or until vegetables are tender.
Remove .... roast to warm platter.
Pour .... drippings into saucepan.
Add .... 3 tablespoons flour mixed with 1/4 cup cold water.
Cook .... until thick, stirring constantly.
Cook .... for 2 minutes longer.
Place .... sour cream in bowl.
Stir .... gravy into sour cream.
Pour .... into saucepan.
Cook .... over low heat until heated through.

Photograph for this recipe on opposite page.

DRIP BEEF

2 tsp. each salt, pepper, oregano,
     rosemary, seasoning salt, garlic powder
1 5-lb. beef roast

Stir .... seasonings into 1/2-inch water in heavy pan.
Place .... roast in pan.
Bake .... at 250 degrees for 8 hours or until roast falls apart.

Teanna L. Grisham
Broken Arrow H. S., Broken Arrow, Oklahoma

NEW ENGLAND POT ROAST

1 4-lb. beef chuck roast
1/4 c. flour
1 1/4 tsp. pepper
5 1/2 tsp. salt
2 tbsp. shortening
1 jar horseradish (opt.)
8 sm. potatoes, pared, quartered
8 med. carrots, quartered

Rub .... roast with mixture of flour, pepper and 5 teaspoons salt.
Brown ...... roast in shortening in Dutch oven.
Spread ..... horseradish on both sides of roast and add 1 cup water.
Bake .... at 325 degrees for 3 hours.
Add .... vegetables and 1/2 teaspoon salt.
Bake .... for 1 hour longer.

Georgia Penner
Ringwood H. S., Ringwood, Oklahoma

SUPER BEEF ROAST

2 pkg. dried onion soup mix
1 4-lb. beef roast
2 cans mushroom soup
12 med. potatoes
12 carrots

Spread ..... soup mix in Dutch oven.
Add .... roast, mushroom soup and 2 soup cans water.
Bake .... covered, at 325 degrees for 2 hours.
Add .... potatoes and carrots.
Bake .... for 45 mintues longer.
Yields ...... 10 servings.

Emma Jane Welch
Helena, Oklahoma

CHICKEN-FRIED ROUND STEAK

1 1/2 to 2 lb. round steak
2 eggs, beaten
2 tbsp. milk
1 c. fine cracker crumbs
1 c. shortening
Salt and pepper to taste

Cut .... steak into serving-sized pieces, pounding with meat mallet to tenderize.
Combine .... eggs with milk, mixing well.
Dip .... steak in egg mixture.
Coat .... with crumbs.
Brown ...... slowly on both sides in hot shortening in skillet.
Season ..... with salt and pepper.
Cook .... tightly covered, over very low heat for 45 to 60 minutes or until tender.

Michelle Musueami
Moore West H. S., Oklahoma City, Oklahoma

PEPPER STEAK

1 round steak, cut in strips
2 cloves of garlic, minced
3 beef bouillon cubes
1 c. sliced onion
2 green peppers, chopped
2 tbsp. cornstarch
1/4 c. soy sauce
2 fresh tomatoes, chopped

Brown ...... steak in skillet.
Add .... garlic and bouillon cubes dissolved in 1 1/2 cups hot water.
Simmer ..... covered, for 30 minutes.
Stir .... in onion and peppers.
Cook .... for 5 minutes longer.
Add .... cornstarch and soy sauce blended with 1/4 cup water.
Cook .... until thickend, stirring constantly.
Stir .... in tomatoes.
Cook .... for 2 minutes longer.
Serve .... over rice.

Loretta Grove
Union City H. S., Union City, Oklahoma

SPANISH STEAK

1/2 c. each chopped onion, green pepper
1/2 tbsp. oil
2 1/2 lb. chuck steak cut 1 in. thick
1 tsp. salt
1/4 tsp. pepper
1 bay leaf
2 8-oz. cans tomato sauce

Saute ...... onion and green pepper in oil in skillet.
Brown ...... steak on both sides in skillet; pour off excess drippings.
Add .... remaining ingredients with 1/4 cup water.
Simmer ..... covered, for 2 hours.

Katrina Tennyson
Moore West Mid-H. S., Oklahoma City, Oklahoma

CROCK•POT SWISS STEAK

1 round steak, cut in serving pieces
1 c. flour
1 tsp. salt
1/4 tsp. pepper
1 tsp. paprika
3 tbsp. oil
2 tomatoes, quartered
2 green peppers, quartered
1 onion, chopped
1 can tomato sauce

Coat .... steak with seasoned flour.
Brown ...... in oil in skillet.
Place .... in Crock•Pot with remaining ingredients.
Cook .... on High for 1 hour.
Cook .... on Low for 30 minutes.
Yields ...... 4-6 servings.

Durene French
Cameron H. S., Cameron, Oklahoma

SWISS STEAK

2 lb. round steak, cut in pieces
Flour
1 sm. onion, sliced
1 can whole stewed tomatoes
1 can cream of mushroom soup
1 can onion soup
1 1/2 tsp. Worcestershire sauce

Coat .... steak with flour.
Brown ...... on both sides in a small amount of oil in skillet.
Arrange ..... onion over steak.
Cover ...... with tomatoes.
Blend ...... remaining ingredients with 1 soup can water in bowl.
Pour .... over all.
Simmer ..... covered, for 2 hours or until tender.
Serve .... over rice or noodles.

Pat Wright
Okeene Public Schools, Okeene, Oklahoma

CORNED BEEF BUN CAMPER

1 can corned beef, flaked
1 sm. onion, finely chopped
2 tbsp. sweet relish
1/2 stick longhorn cheese, diced
1/2 c. salad dressing
1 pkg. hamburger buns

Combine .... first 5 ingredients in bowl, mixing well.
Spread ..... on buns.
Wrap .... in foil.
Bake .... at 425 degrees until heated through.

Charlotte McCombs
Penny McCombs
Okeene Public School, Okeene, Oklahoma

NEW ENGLAND CORNED BEEF DINNER

1 sm. clove of garlic
1 bay leaf
1 2 1/2-lb. corned beef brisket
6 sm. potatoes, peeled, halved
6 med. carrots, peeled, halved
1 sm. head cabbage, quartered
1 sm. rutabaga, coarsely chopped
4 peppercorns

Combine .... garlic and bay leaf with 1 cup water in 6-quart pressure cooker.
Place .... brisket on rack in cooker; close cover securely.
Cook .... at 15-pounds pressure for 45 minutes.
Let .... stand until pressure drops.
Add .... remaining ingredients, closing cover securely.
Cook .... at 15-pounds pressure for 6 to 7 minutes.
Place .... under cold running water to reduce pressure quickly.
Yields ...... 6 servings.

Freda Sue Smith
Ryan Public School, Ryan, Oklahoma

PEACH-GLAZED CORNED BEEF

1 3-lb. corned beef brisket
4 sm. apples, halved, cored
1/3 c. peach preserves
1/4 tsp. ground ginger

Rinse ...... brisket in cold water.
Place .... fat side up on rack in shallow roasting pan containing 2 cups water.

Roast ...... covered, at 325 degrees for 2 hours.

Drain ...... discarding liquid.

Arrange ..... apples skin side up around brisket with 1/2 cup water.

Roast ...... uncovered for 30 minutes longer.

Blend ...... preserves and ginger.

Turn .... apples skin side down.

Spoon ...... preserves over brisket and apples.

Roast ...... until glaze is heated through.

Kim Marie Wales
Sentinel H. S., Sentinel, Oklahoma

SUPER HERO

1 loaf French or Italian bread
Wish-Bone Creamy Bell Pepper Dressing
4 slices cooked turkey
4 slices cooked corned beef
4 slices American cheese, halved
4 tomato slices, halved

Slice .... bread into 15 slices, cutting to but not through bottom.

Spread ..... alternate slices generously with dressing.

Place .... 1 slice turkey or corned beef, 1/2 slice cheese and 1/2 tomato slice on each prepared slice.

Chill .... wrapped in foil.

Bake .... at 350 degrees for 30 minutes or until heated through.

Yields ...... 8 sandwiches.

Photograph for this recipe on page 35.

BEEF BOLOGNA

2 lb. lean ground meat
2 tbsp. meat tenderizer
1/4 tsp. onion powder
1/8 tsp. garlic powder
1 1/2 tsp. liquid smoke

Mix .... all ingredients with 1 cup cold water in bowl.

Shape ...... into 2 or 3 long rolls.

Wrap .... in plastic wrap.

Chill .... for 24 hours.

Remove .... plastic wrap.

Place .... on baking sheets.

Bake .... at 300 degrees for 45 minutes.

Slice .... when cool.

Serve .... hot or cold.

Joyce Stockton
Ninnekah H. S., Ninnekah, Oklahoma

GLAZED MEAT LOAF

2 eggs. beaten
2/3 c. milk
2 tsp. salt
1/4 tsp. pepper
3 slices bread, cubed
2/3 c. finely chopped onion
2/3 c. shredded raw carrots
1 1/2 c. shredded Cheddar cheese
2 lb. ground beef
1/4 c. packed brown sugar
1/4 c. catsup
1 tbsp. prepared mustard

Mix .... first 9 ingredients together in bowl.

Pat .... into loaf pan.

Bake .... covered, at 350 degrees for 1 hour.

Combine .... remaining ingredients in bowl.

Pour .... over meat loaf.

Bake .... uncovered, for 15 minutes longer.

Debbie Matz
Arapaho H. S., Arapaho, Oklahoma

HEARTY ALL-STAR LOAF

2 env. Lipton Beefy Onion Soup Mix
3 1/2 lb. ground beef
1 c. mashed potato flakes
1 1/2 c. beer
2 eggs
3/4 tsp. caraway seed
4 c. hot mashed potatoes

Combine .... first 6 ingredients in large bowl mixing well.

Pack .... into 9 x 13-inch baking dish.

Chill .... for several hours.

Bake .... at 350 degrees for 1 hour.

Drain ...... off excess drippings.

Frost .... with hot mashed potatoes.

Garnish ..... with cheese strip "field markings" and carrot strip "goal posts."

May .... substitute water for beer.

Photograph for this recipe on page 35.

CHEESE MEATBALLS WITH NOODLES

1 egg
1/2 tsp. ground nutmeg
1 1/4 tsp. salt
1/2 tsp. pepper
1 tbsp. finely chopped parsley
1 1/2 lb. ground chuck
1/3 c. dry bread crumbs
6 oz. Swiss cheese, cut in 1/2-inch cubes
2 tbsp. oil
3 med. onions, chopped
1 46-oz. can tomato juice
8 oz. medium egg noodles
1/4 tsp. thyme (opt.)

Beat .... first 3 ingredients and 1/4 teaspoon pepper together in bowl.
Add .... parsley, ground chuck and crumbs, mixing well.
Shape ...... 2 tablespoonfuls around each cheese cube to form balls.
Brown ...... 1/2 at a time in oil in 4-quart saucepan.
Remove .... meatballs and set aside.
Saute ...... onions in pan drippings until brown.
Add .... tomato juice.
Bring .... to a boil.
Stir .... in noodles gradually.

Add .... meatballs, thyme and 1/4 teaspoon pepper.
Simmer ..... covered, for 10 minutes, stirring occasionally.
Yields ...... 6 servings.

Photograph for this recipe on this page.

MEATBALL CASSEROLE

1 1/2 lb. ground beef
2 tsp. salt
1 c. condensed tomato soup
1 tbsp. flour
1/4 tsp. pepper
2 tbsp. oil
1 lg. onion, chopped
2 c. diced celery
4 med. potatoes, peeled, diced

Mix .... first 5 ingredients together in bowl.
Shape ...... into 1 1/2-inch balls.
Brown ...... in oil in skillet.
Place .... in 3-quart casserole.
Combine .... remaining ingredients in bowl.
Arrange ..... over meatballs.
Bake .... covered, at 350 degrees for 50 minutes or until potatoes are tender.

Stacie Long
Ryan H. S., Ryan, Oklahoma

BACHELOR HAMBURGER STEAK

2 lb. ground beef
Salt and pepper to taste
6 1/4-in. slices onion
6 slices Cheddar cheese
1 can tomato soup

Shape ...... ground beef into 6 patties.
Place .... in baking dish.
Season ..... with salt and pepper to taste.
Top .... each patty with 1 slice onion and 1 slice cheese.
Dilute ...... soup with 1/2 cup water in bowl.
Pour .... over patties.
Bake .... covered, at 350 degrees for 1 3/4 hours or until done.

Sue Weber
Pioneer Area Vo-Tech School, Ponca City, Oklahoma

Recipes on pages 12, 23 and 33.

RICE-A-BURGERS

1 lb. ground beef
2 eggs, slightly beaten
3 c. cooked rice
2 tsp. seasoned salt
3/4 c. catsup
1/2 tsp. oregano
4 slices Cheddar cheese, cut into
    triangles

Combine .... first 4 ingredients in large bowl;
    mix well.
Spread ..... on eight 8-inch triple-thickness
    foil circles.
Crimp ...... foil edges as for pizza crust.
Spread ..... with catsup.
Sprinkle .... with oregano.
Bake .... at 450 degrees for 10 minutes.
Top .... with cheese.
Bake .... for 5 minutes longer.

Photograph for this recipe on page 70.

UNUSUAL HAMBURGERS

1 lb. lean ground round
1/8 tsp. margarine
1/8 tsp. basil
1/4 tsp. thyme
1/4 tsp. garlic powder
2 tbsp. lemon juice
Grated rind of 1 lemon
1 egg, slightly beaten
1 c. skim milk

Combine .... all ingredients in bowl, mixing
    well.
Shape ...... into patties on rack in broiler
    pan.
Broil .... to desired degree of doneness.

Mary A. Geer
Lindsay H. S., Lindsay, Oklahoma

CORN BREAD PIE

1 lb. hamburger
Chopped green pepper
Chopped onion
1 can chili beans
1 can tomatoes

Recipes on pages 18 and 25.

Salt, pepper, garlic salt to taste
1 pkg. corn bread mix

Saute ...... hamburger, green pepper and
    onion in skillet until tender.
Add .... beans, tomatoes and seasonings.
Pour .... into casserole.
Prepare ..... corn bread using package
    directions.
Spread ..... over meat mixture.
Bake .... at 350 degrees for 30 minutes or
    until brown.
Yields ...... 6 servings.

Roberta Smith
Verden H. S., Verden, Oklahoma

ZESTY MEAT PIES

2 3-oz. packages cream cheese, softened
2/3 c. butter, softened
1 1/3 c. sifted flour
1 1/2 tsp. salt
1 lb. ground round
2 tbsp. oil
Dash of pepper
3/4 c. barbecue relish
1 egg, slightly beaten

Combine .... first 3 ingredients and 1/2 tea-
    spoon salt with pastry blender
    until crumbly.
Shape ...... into ball.
Chill .... until firm.
Saute ...... ground round in oil in skillet un-
    til browned and crumbly.
Drain ...... on paper towels.
Mix .... with 1 teaspoon salt, pepper and
    relish.
Roll .... 1/4 at a time on floured surface
    to 1/8-inch thickness.
Cut .... into fourteen 4 1/2-inch circles.
Spoon ...... 1/4 cup meat mixture onto each
    of 7 circles.
Top .... with remaining circles.
Moisten ..... edges with water and crimp with
    fork to seal.
Combine .... egg with 1 teaspoon water.
Brush ...... over pastry tops.
Place .... on baking sheet.
Bake .... at 400 degrees for 25 minutes.
May .... be chilled or frozen to pack into
    lunch boxes.

Photograph for this recipe on page 39.

GINA'S MEAT PIE

1 1/2 lb. hamburger, cooked
1 tsp. onion powder
1/2 tsp. each seasoned salt, garlic salt
Salt and pepper to taste
1 8-oz. can tomato paste
1 8-oz. can tomato sauce
1 c. shredded Colby cheese
1 c. cooked sm. macaroni (opt.)
Pastry for 2-crust pie
Mozzarella cheese slices

Combine . . . . hamburger, seasonings, tomato paste and tomato sauce in skillet.
Stir . . . . in Colby cheese until melted.
Add . . . . . . macaroni.
Pour . . . . . . into pastry-lined pie plate.
Cover . . . . . with Mozzarella cheese and remaining pastry.
Bake . . . . . . at 450 degrees for 30 minutes or until crust is golden.

Gina J. Meier
Hitchcock Elementary School, Hitchcock, Oklahoma

TAMALE PIE

1 pkg. taco seasoning mix
1 1-lb. can tomatoes
1 12-oz. can corn
1 lb. ground beef, cooked
1 10 or 12-oz. package corn bread mix

Stir . . . . taco seasoning mix, tomatoes and corn into cooked ground beef in skillet.
Bring . . . . . . to a boil, stirring frequently.
Prepare . . . . . corn bread mix according to package directions.
Pour . . . . . . hot meat mixture into 2-quart casserole.
Spoon . . . . . corn bread mixture over top.
Bake . . . . . . at 400 degrees for 15 minutes or until golden brown.
Yields . . . . . . 6 servings.

Sheri Ott
Drummond Public School, Drummond, Oklahoma

ZUCCHINI PIE

1/2 to 2 lb. ground beef
2 tbsp. salad oil
1/2 chopped green pepper
1 tsp. chopped parsley
1/2 tsp. minced dry onion flakes
1/2 tsp. garlic salt
1 tsp. salt
1 tsp. ground oregano
6 med. zucchini, sliced
1/2 c. bread crumbs
1/4 c. grated Cheddar cheese
2 lg. tomatoes, peeled, sliced
2 Tbsp. oil
Pepper

Combine . . . . first 8 ingredients in skillet.
Cook . . . . until brown and crumbly.
Place . . . . layer of zucchini in large casserole.
Cover . . . . . . with half the meat mixture.
Mix . . . . bread crumbs and cheese together in bowl.
Sprinkle . . . . half the cheese mixture over meat mixture.
Repeat . . . . . layers.
Top . . . . with tomato slices and oil.
Sprinkle . . . . with pepper.
Bake . . . . at 350 degrees for 1 hour.
Yields . . . . . . 6 servings.
Note . . . . may microwave on High for 20 minutes.

Virginia Darnell
Apache H. S., Apache, Oklahoma

RICE SABROSIA

1 c. chopped onion
1/2 c. green pepper
1 hot pepper, chopped
1 tbsp. chili powder
1 tsp. each pepper and salt
2 c. tomatoes
1 1/2 lb. ground beef, cooked
1 sm. box rice, cooked

Add . . . . first 7 ingredients to cooked ground beef in skillet.
Cook . . . . over medium-low heat for several minutes.
Add . . . . rice to ground beef mixture.
Simmer . . . . . over low heat for 30 minutes.
Yields . . . . . . 6-8 servings.

Sue Sokolosky
Oklahoma FHA President 1980-81
Stillwater, Oklahoma

SATURDAY NIGHT SPECIAL

1 lb. ground beef
1 1 1/2-lb. can pork and beans
1 16-oz. can tomatoes, drained
1 tsp. salt
1 lg. onion, thinly sliced
2 slices bacon
1/4 c. packed brown sugar

Brown . . . . . . ground beef in skillet; drain.
Add . . . . next 3 ingredients, mixing well.
Pour . . . . half the mixture into baking dish.
Cover . . . . . . with layer of onion.
Add . . . . remaining beef mixture.
Top . . . . with bacon.
Sprinkle . . . . with brown sugar.
Bake . . . . at 350 degrees for 1 hour.
Yields . . . . . . 8 servings.

Fleta Haskins
Sallisaw H. S., Sallisaw, Oklahoma

SHOOTING STARS

1 lb. hamburger
1 lg. green pepper, diced
1 med. onion, chopped
1 pkg. dry onion soup mix
1 can enchilada sauce
1 can cream of chicken soup
Green chiles to taste
1 can Ro-Tel
1 doz. soft tortillas, cut in pieces
1 can sliced black olives
1 jar sliced green olives
12 oz. Cheddar cheese, grated
1 c. chopped pecans

Cook . . . . first 3 ingredients together in skillet; drain.
Add . . . . 1/2 cup water and soup mix.
Combine . . . . enchilada sauce, soup, green chiles and Ro-Tel in bowl, mixing well.
Alternate . . . layers of tortillas, hamburger mixture, sauce, olives, cheese and pecans in large casserole.
Bake . . . . at 350 degrees for 1 hour.
Yields . . . . . . 8 servings.

Ann Knopfel
Waukomis H. S., Waukomis, Oklahoma

CHEESE ENCHILADAS

1 1/2 lb. ground meat
1/4 tsp. garlic salt
1 tsp. salt
1 c. chopped onions
3/4 lb. longhorn cheese grated
24 tortillas
1 can cream of chicken soup
1 lg. can evaporated milk
1 lb. Velveeta cheese
1 pkg. dry onion dip mix
1 sm. jar diced pimento
1 sm. can chopped green chiles

Cook . . . . first 4 ingredients together in skillet; drain.
Stir . . . . in longhorn cheese.
Dip . . . . tortillas in hot oil to soften.
Fill . . . . each with ground meat mixture, rolling up to enclose filling.
Place . . . . in large shallow baking pan.
Combine . . . . soup, milk and Velveeta cheese in saucepan.
Heat . . . . until cheese melts.
Add . . . . remaining ingredients.
Pour . . . . over tortillas.
Bake . . . . covered, at 350 degrees for 30 minutes.
Yields . . . . . . 24 enchiladas.

Kim Kay
Drummond H. S., Drummond, Oklahoma

CROWD-SIZED TACO SALAD

2 c. cooked macaroni swirls
1 green pepper, chopped
1 sm. onion, chopped
1 pkg. taco seasoning mix
1 lb. ground beef, cooked, drained
1 lg. head lettuce, torn into
   bite-sized pieces
2 lg. tomatoes, chopped
1 can garbanza beans, drained
1 can Mexican-style beans, drained
1 1/2 c. shredded Cheddar cheese
1/2 sm. bag Fritos, crushed
1 lg. bottle Catalina dressing

Combine . . . . macaroni, green pepper and onion in bowl; chill, covered.

Mix . . . . taco seasoning mix with ground beef in skillet.

Cook . . . . according to seasoning package directions.

Mix . . . . lettuce, tomatoes, macaroni mixture, cooled ground beef mixture, beans and cheese in large bowl.

Add . . . . crushed Fritos and dressing just before serving.

Yields . . . . . . 8-12 servings.

Jean Giesecke
Locust Grove H. S., Locust Grove, Oklahoma

NAVAJO TACOS

4 c. canned pinto beans
1 15-oz. can tomato sauce
1 sm. jar picante sauce
1 to 1 1/2 lb. ground beef, cooked
2 c. flour
4 tsp. baking powder
1/4 tsp. salt
Shortening

Combine . . . . first 4 ingredients in saucepan.

Simmer . . . . . for 30 minutes.

Mix . . . . flour, baking powder, salt, 1 tablespoon (rounded) shortening and 1 to 1 1/4 cups water in bowl; cover.

Let . . . . stand for 15 minutes.

Divide . . . . . . dough into 6 portions.

Knead . . . . . . each on floured surface, pressing into circle.

Punch . . . . . . hole in center of each.

Fry . . . . in 1-inch hot shortening until done; drain.

Spoon . . . . . . meat mixture over bread.

Garnish . . . . . with cheese, lettuce, tomatoes, onions and green chiles.

Angie McKinnon
Wilson H. S., Wilson, Oklahoma

TACO CASSEROLE

1 sm. package taco seasoning mix
1 lb. ground beef, cooked, drained
1 16-oz. package Dorito chips, crushed
1 16-oz. can Mexican beans, drained
1 16-oz. can tomatoes, chopped
1 4-oz. can green chiles, chopped
2 c. grated Cheddar cheese

Add . . . . taco seasoning mix to cooked ground beef in skillet; heat.

Layer . . . . . . half the chips, half the ground beef mixture, beans, tomatoes, chiles, remaining meat mixture, cheese and remaining chips in 9 x 13-inch baking dish.

Bake . . . . at 350 degrees for 25 to 30 minutes.

Wanda Lippe
Picher-Cardin H. S., Picher, Oklahoma

OVEN PORCUPINES

1 lb. ground beef
1/2 c. rice
1/3 c. chopped onion
1 tsp. salt
1/2 tsp. celery salt
1/8 tsp. garlic powder
1/8 tsp. pepper
1 15-oz. can tomato sauce
2 tsp. Worcestershire sauce

Combine . . . . first 7 ingredients with 1/2 cup water in bowl.

Shape . . . . . . by rounded tablespoonfuls into balls.

Place . . . . in 8-inch square baking dish.

Mix . . . . remaining ingredients with 1 cup water in bowl.

Pour . . . . over meatballs.

Bake . . . . covered, for 45 minutes; remove lid.

Bake . . . . for 15 minutes longer.

Lorinda Dannan
Waynoka Public School, Waynoke, Oklahoma

SHERRIE'S LASAGNA

1 box lasagna noodles
1 1/2 lb. hamburger
1/2 lb. ground sausage
2 8-oz. cans tomato sauce
1 pkg. spaghetti seasoning mix
1 carton cottage cheese
1 pkg. mozzarella cheese

Cook . . . . noodles according to package directions.
Brown . . . . . . hamburger and sausage together in skillet; drain.
Add . . . . tomato sauce and seasoning mix.
Simmer . . . . . for 10 minutes.
Cover . . . . . . bottom of 9 x 13-inch casserole with noodles.
Alternate . . . layers of sauce, cottage cheese, mozzarella cheese and remaining noodles.
Bake . . . . at 400 degrees for 30 minutes.

Sherrie Haub
Canton H. S., Canton, Oklahoma

PIZZA CASSEROLE

2 lb. ground beef
1 lg. onion, chopped
1/4 tsp. oregano
1 15-oz. can tomato sauce
1 pkg. spaghetti sauce mix
Mozzarella cheese
2 eggs
1 c. milk
1 tbsp. oil
1 c. flour
1/2 tsp. salt

Brown . . . . . . ground beef and onion in skillet.
Add . . . . next 3 ingredients with 1/2 cup water; simmer.
Pour . . . . into greased 9 x 13-inch pyrex dish.
Top . . . . with mozzarella.
Bake . . . . at 400 degrees for 10 minutes.
Mix . . . . remaining ingredients with wire whip.
Pour . . . . over cheese.
Bake . . . . for 30 minutes longer.

Patricia Hudson, Advisor
Maysville H. S., Maysville, Oklahoma

PIZZA-IN-A-BURGER

1 1/2 lb. ground chuck
1 1/3 c. grated Parmesan cheese
1/4 c. finely chopped onion
1/4 c. chopped pitted ripe olives
1 tsp. salt
1 tsp. oregano
Dash of pepper
1 6-oz. can tomato paste
4 slices mozzarella cheese,
    cut in strips
8 cherry tomatoes, halved
8 slices French bread, toasted

Combine . . . . first 8 ingredients in bowl, mixing well.
Shape . . . . . . into 8 oval patties.
Broil . . . . over medium coals for 10 minutes; turn.
Top . . . . each with cheese and tomatoes.
Broil . . . . for 5 minutes longer or to desired doneness.
Serve . . . . on French bread slices.

Cheryl Allen
Springer H. S., Springer, Oklahoma

PIZZA POTATO BAKE

1 lb. hamburger, cooked
4 c. sliced potatoes
1 med. onion
1 can Cheddar cheese soup
1 soup can milk
1 15-oz. can pizza sauce
6 oz. mozzarella cheese, sliced

Spread . . . . . hamburger in large casserole.
Alternate . . . layers of potatoes and onion over hamburger.
Mix . . . . cheese soup and milk together in bowl.
Pour . . . . over potato mixture, stirring to mix.
Cover . . . . . . with pizza sauce.
Bake . . . . at 350 degrees for 1 hour.
Place . . . . cheese over top.
Heat . . . . until melted.
Yields . . . . . . 6 servings.

Traci Clester
Okeene H. S., Okeene, Oklahoma

POPOVER PIZZA

1 lb. ground beef
1 lg. onion, chopped
1 1.5-oz. bottle spaghetti sauce
1 15-oz. can tomato sauce
2 c. shredded mozzarella cheese
2 eggs
1 c. milk
1 tbsp. oil
1 c. flour
1/2 tsp. salt
1/2 c. Parmesan cheese

Brown . . . . . . ground beef and onion in skillet; drain.
Add . . . . spaghetti sauce, tomato sauce and 1/2 cup water.
Cook . . . . for 10 minutes.
Pour . . . . into 9 x 13-inch pan.
Sprinkle . . . . with mozzarella.
Beat . . . . eggs, milk and oil in bowl until foamy.
Stir . . . . in flour and salt, beating until smooth.
Pour . . . . over meat mixture.
Sprinkle . . . . with Parmesan cheese.
Bake . . . . at 400 degrees for 30 minutes or until puffy and brown.

Jetta Nowakowski
McLoud FHA

TACO PIZZA

2 16-oz. cans tomato sauce
1 can refried beans
1 onion, chopped
2 lb. hamburger, browned, drained
1 can crescent rolls
8 oz. cheese, shredded
Lettuce, shredded
Tomatoes, diced

Add . . . . first 3 ingredients to hamburger in skillet.
Arrange . . . . . crescent rolls in pizza pan to form crust.
Spread . . . . . with meat mixture.
Bake . . . . according to roll package directions or until brown.
Sprinkle . . . . with cheese.
Heat . . . . until cheese melts.
Top . . . . with lettuce and tomatoes.

Diana Bailey, FHA Pres.
Bristow H. S., Bristow, Oklahoma

ITALIAN SPAGHETTI

2 lb. ground beef
1 med. onion, finely chopped
1 green pepper, finely chopped
2 15-oz. cans tomato sauce
2 12-oz. cans tomato paste
1 7 1/2-oz. can pitted ripe olives, drained, sliced
2 env. Italian-style sauce mix
1 tbsp. sugar
1 tsp. oregano leaves
2 cloves of garlic, crushed
1 bay leaf
1 1-lb. box spaghetti, cooked
16 oz. grated Parmesan cheese

Saute . . . . . . ground beef, onion and green pepper in skillet.
Stir . . . . in remaining ingredients except spaghetti and cheese with 3 cups water.
Simmer . . . . . covered, for 1 1/2 hours, stirring occasionally.
Spread . . . . . sauce over hot spaghetti.
Serve . . . . with Parmesan cheese.
Yields . . . . . . 8 servings.

Sheila Patrick
Springer Public Schools, Springer, Oklahoma

TEXAS SPAGHETTI

2 lb. ground beef
1 onion, chopped
Salt and pepper to taste
2 cans tomato soup
1/2 green pepper, chopped
4 oz. egg noodles
Mozzarella cheese, thinly sliced
1 can mushroom soup
1 4.2-oz. can chopped olives (opt.)
Grated Parmesan cheese

Saute . . . . . . ground beef, onion, salt and pepper in skillet.
Add . . . . tomato soup, green pepper and noodles.
Simmer . . . . . covered, for 10 minutes.
Spoon . . . . . . half the mixture into casserole.
Layer . . . . . . mozzarella cheese, mushroom soup and remaining noodle mixture on top.
Sprinkle . . . . with olives and Parmesan cheese.

Bake . . . . at 350 degrees for 30 minutes or until heated through.

Let . . . . stand for 10 minutes before serving.

Yields . . . . . . 6-8 servings.

Note . . . . May microwave for 20 minutes.

Donna Soutee
Choctaw H. S., Choctaw, Oklahoma

HOT SHOT HOT DOG LOAF

1/4 c. finely chopped onion
2 tbsp. butter, melted
1/2 c. hamburger relish
1/2 c. chili sauce
1 tbsp. Worcestershire sauce
1 tbsp. brown sugar
1   16-inch long loaf Italian bread
1   8-oz. package cheese, grated
10 frankfurters, cut in half crosswise

Saute . . . . . . onion in butter in small sauce-pan for about 5 minutes until tender.

Add . . . . next 4 ingredients, mixing well.

Cut . . . . 1-inch slices from end of loaf.

Slice . . . . into ten 1 1/2-inch slices, cutting to but not through bottom.

Spread . . . . . relish mixture between slices.

Spoon . . . . . . half the cheese between slices.

Place . . . . 2 frankfurter halves cut side down and upright between each slice.

Spoon . . . . . . in remaining relish mixture.

Top . . . . with remaining cheese.

Fasten . . . . . . with long skewers to reassemble loaf.

Wrap . . . . tightly with foil.

Bake . . . . at 400 degrees for 20 minutes.

Remove . . . . skewers and serve with additional relish.

Photograph for this recipe below.

HAM AND FRESH VEGETABLE MEDLEY

1   1-lb. cooked boneless ham slice,
      cut into 1/4 x 3-inch slices
1 sm. green pepper, cut into
      1/2-inch slices
1 sm. red pepper, cut into
      1/2-inch slices
1 yellow squash, sliced
1 med. zucchini, sliced
1 onion, sliced
3 tbsp. oil
1 env. chicken bouillon
2 tsp. basil
1/2 tsp. salt
1/4 tsp. pepper
2 lg. tomatoes, cut into 8 wedges

Stir-fry . . . . . first 6 ingredients in oil in skillet
             over high heat for 5 minutes.
Add . . . . bouillon, seasonings and 1/2 cup
             water.
Cook . . . . . . over medium heat for 5 minutes
             or until vegetables are tender-
             crisp, stirring occasionally.
Add . . . . tomatoes.
Cook . . . . . . until heated through.
Yields . . . . . . 4 servings.

Carol Baustert
Union City H. S., Union City, Oklahoma

GLAZED LOUISIANA YAMS AND MINI HAM LOAVES

1 lb. each ground ham, pork sausage
1/3 c. soft bread crumbs
2 tbsp. each finely chopped celery,
      onion, parsley
1/4 tsp. each nutmeg, thyme
1/2 tsp. salt
1/4 tsp. pepper
3/4 c. milk
1 egg, slightly beaten
1   16-oz. can whole cranberry sauce
1/2 c. dark corn syrup
1/8 tsp. ground cloves
4 med. Louisiana yams, cooked,
      peeled, sliced

Combine . . . . ham, sausage, bread crumbs, cel-
             ery, onion, parsley, next 4 sea-
             sonings, milk and egg in bowl,
             mixing well.

Shape . . . . . . into 6 round loaves.
Place . . . . in individual baking pans.
Bake . . . . at 350 degrees for 1/2 hour.
Mix . . . . cranberry sauce, corn syrup and
             cloves in saucepan.
Cook . . . . over low heat until cranberry
             sauce melts, stirring constantly.
Add . . . . yams, stirring to coat.
Pour . . . . off excess drippings from ham
             loaves.
Spoon . . . . . . glazed yams over top of each.
Bake . . . . for 5 to 10 minutes longer.

Photograph for this recipe on page 26.

MICROWAVE SWISS HAM ROLL-UPS

Tater Tots
2 2-oz. slices Swiss cheese, cut in half
4 1-oz. slices boiled ham
1/4 c. sour cream

Microwave . . Tater Tots on paper plate on De-
             frost until thawed.
Place . . . . cheese on ham slices.
Spread . . . . . with sour cream.
Top . . . . each slice with 3 Tater Tots.
Roll . . . . up to enclose filling; secure with
             toothpicks.
Place . . . . on serving plate.
Microwave . . uncovered, for 2 minutes or un-
             til hot.

Connie Miller
Del City H. S., Del City, Oklahoma

MEXICAN SKILLET DINNER

1 lb. ground pork
1/2 c. chopped onion
1 clove of garlic, minced
2 tsp. chili powder
1/4 tsp. salt
1   16-oz. can cut green beans, drained
1   15-oz. can red kidney beans
1/2 lb. Velveeta cheese, cubed
4 c. finely shredded lettuce
1 lg. tomato, chopped
8 pitted ripe olives
1/2 c. French dressing (opt.)

Brown . . . . . . ground pork in electric skillet at
             400 degrees.

Pour . . . . off excess drippings.
Add . . . . next 4 ingredients, mixing well.
Stir . . . . combined beans into pork mixture.
Simmer . . . . . on medium for 10 minutes.
Add . . . . cheese, mixing well.
Turn . . . . off skillet.
Arrange . . . . . lettuce around edges of pork mixture.
Sprinkle . . . . with tomato and olives.
Drizzle . . . . . dressing over lettuce.

Dana Lynn Scott
Cyril H. S., Cyril, Oklahoma

SAUSAGE AND NOODLE CASSEROLE

1/2 lb. sausage
1/4 c. chopped green pepper
1 env. French's cheese sauce mix
1 1/2 c. milk
8 oz. noodles, cooked
1/4 c. fine dry bread crumbs
1 tbsp. melted butter
1/2 tsp. paprika

Saute . . . . . . sausage and green pepper in skillet until light brown.
Drain . . . . . . off excess drippings.
Stir . . . . in sauce mix and milk.
Bring . . . . to a boil, stirring constantly.
Add . . . . noodles.
Pour . . . . into 1 1/2 quart casserole.
Combine . . . . remaining ingredients.
Sprinkle . . . . over top.
Bake . . . . at 400 degrees for 20 minutes.
Yields . . . . . . 4-6 servings.

Photograph for this recipe on page 55.

VICKIE'S SAUSAGE CASSEROLE

1 6-oz. package Ramen beef noodles
1 8-oz. box long grain and wild rice
1 lb. sausage
6 tbsp. chopped onion
1/2 c. chopped green pepper
1 1/2 c. chopped celery
1 sm. can sliced water chestnuts
1 sm. jar sliced mushrooms

Prepare . . . . . noodles and rice using package directions.

Saute . . . . . . sausage in skillet until brown; drain.
Combine . . . . with noodles, rice and remaining ingredients.
Pour . . . . into 9 x 13-inch greased casserole.
Bake . . . . at 350 degrees for 30 minutes.
Yields . . . . . . 16 servings.

Vickie Thompson
Marietta H. S., Marietta, Oklahoma

SHIRLEY'S SPARERIBS

4 lb. spareribs
2 tbsp. oil
2 med. onions, chopped
1 15-oz. can tomato sauce
1/2 tsp. salt
1/4 c. packed brown sugar
1/4 c. vinegar
1 tsp. dry mustard
1 tsp. Worcestershire sauce

Brown . . . . . . spareribs in oil in Dutch oven.
Combine . . . . remaining ingredients and 1 cup water in bowl, mixing well.
Pour . . . . over ribs.
Bake . . . . covered, at 350 degrees for 2 to 2 1/2 hours or until tender.

Shirley Porter
Reydon H. S., Reydon, Oklahoma

BAKED CHICKEN NUGGETS

7 or 8 chicken breasts, boned
2 c. crushed Ritz crackers
1 c. grated Parmesan cheese
1 1/2 tsp. salt
2 tsp. Italian seasoning
1 c. melted butter

Cut . . . . chicken into 1 1/2-inch pieces.
Combine . . . . cracker crumbs, cheese, salt and Italian seasoning, mixing well.
Dip . . . . chicken in butter and coat with crumb mixture.
Place . . . . on baking sheet.
Bake . . . . at 400 degrees for 20 minutes or until golden brown.
Yields . . . . . . 4 servings.

Betsy Wright, H. E. Tchr.
Sequoyah H. S., Claremore, Oklahoma

PANCAKE CHICKEN NUGGETS

2 whole chicken breasts, skinned, boned
1 c. pancake mix
2/3 c. milk
1 tsp. salt
1/4 tsp. pepper
Oil for deep frying
Maple syrup

Cut .... chicken breasts into eight 1 1/2-inch square chunks.
Combine .... next 4 ingredients in bowl, mixing well.
Dip .... chicken into batter.
Fry .... in 350-degree deep fat for 5 minutes or until golden brown.
Serve .... with maple syrup.
Yields ...... 4 servings.

Photograph for this recipe above.

BARBEQUED CHICKEN

1 3-lb. frying chicken, cut up
1/2 c. catsup
3 tbsp. margarine
1 tbsp. lemon juice
2 tbsp. Worcestershire sauce
1 tbsp. chili powder
4 tbsp. vinegar
1 tbsp. liquid smoke
3 tbsp. brown sugar
1 tsp. salt
1 tsp. prepared mustard
1 tsp. paprika
1/2 tsp. pepper

Place .... chicken in 9 x 13-inch casserole.
Combine .... remaining ingredients in saucepan.
Simmer ..... for 15 minutes.

Bake . . . . at 350 degrees for 1/2 hour.
Pour . . . . sauce over chicken.
Bake . . . . until browned, turning once.

Charla Wood
Cyril H. S., Cyril, Oklahoma

BRUNSWICK STEW

1 c. sliced onions
3 tbsp. oil
2 16-oz. cans tomatoes
1/2 c. Sherry
1 env. beef stew seasoning mix
1 10-oz. package frozen whole
    kernel corn
1 10-oz. package frozen lima beans
1 tbsp. Worcestershire sauce
1/2 tsp. salt
3 1/2 to 4 c. chopped cooked chicken
1 10-oz. package frozen okra
1 sm. zucchini, sliced

Saute . . . . . . onions in oil in skillet until
            tender.
Add . . . . next 7 ingredients and 1/2 cup
            water.
Simmer . . . . . covered, for 15 minutes.
Add . . . . chicken, okra and zucchini.
Simmer . . . . . for 10 minutes longer.
Yields . . . . . . 6 servings.

Oaks FHA
Oaks H. S., Oaks, Oklahoma

CHICKEN MARINADA

1/3 c. oil
2 tbsp. lemon juice
1/2 tsp. each oregano, seasoned salt,
    onion salt, garlic salt, paprika
3 lb. chicken pieces, skinned

Combine . . . . oil, lemon juice and seasonings
            in bowl, mixing well.
Pour . . . . over chicken in bowl.
Marinate . . . . for 2 hours or longer.
Place . . . . chicken in broiler pan.
Broil . . . . 9 inches from heat source for 20
            to 30 minutes.
Turn . . . . chicken.

Baste . . . . with marinade.
Broil . . . . for 20 to 30 minutes.

Chris Crow
Ringwood H. S., Ringwood, Oklahoma

HONIED CHICKEN

1/4 c. butter, melted
1/2 c. honey
1/4 c. prepared mustard
1 tsp. salt
1 tsp. curry powder
1 3-lb. chicken, cut up

Combine . . . . first 5 ingredients, mixing well.
Dip . . . . chicken in honey mixture.
Place . . . . in shallow casserole.
Pour . . . . remaining sauce over chicken.
Bake . . . . at 350 degrees for 1 hour.
Yields . . . . . . 4 servings.

Lisa Carter
Smithville H. S., Smithville, Oklahoma

LUSCIOUS LEMON CHICKEN

2 lb. chicken parts
2 tbsp. shortening
1 can cream of chicken soup
2 tbsp. lemon juice
1/2 tsp. paprika
1/2 tsp. salt
1/8 tsp. tarragon leaves
Dash of pepper
Lemon slices

Brown . . . . . . chicken in shortening in skillet.
Pour . . . . off excess drippings.
Add . . . . remaining ingredients except
            lemon.
Cook . . . . covered, over low heat for 45
            minutes or until tender, stirring
            occasionally.
Chill . . . . overnight.
Reheat . . . . . covered, for 15 minutes or until
            heated through, stirring
            occasionally.
Top . . . . with lemon.
Yields . . . . . . 6 servings.

Pat Romine
Byng H. S., Ada, Oklahoma

NOT-THE-SAME-OLD-CHICKEN

1 chicken, cut up
1/4 c. mayonnaise
1 pkg. dry onion soup mix
1/2 c. Russian dressing
1 c. apricot preserves

Arrange . . . . . chicken in 9 x 13-inch glass baking dish with largest pieces around edges.
Combine . . . . remaining ingredients in bowl, mixing well.
Spread . . . . . over chicken, covering each piece.
Microwave . . covered, on High for 10 minutes.
Turn . . . . dish 180 degrees.
Microwave . . for 8 to 12 minutes longer.
Let . . . . stand for 5 to 10 minutes.

Traci Foshee
McLoud School, McLoud, Oklahoma

CHICKEN WAIKIKI

Breasts and legs of 2 chickens
1/2 c. flour
1 tsp. salt
1/4 tsp. pepper
1/3 c. oil
1 lg. can pineapple chunks
1 c. sugar
2 tbsp. cornstarch
3/4 c. vinegar
1 tbsp. soy sauce
1 chicken bouillon cube
1/4 tsp. ginger
1 lg. green pepper, chopped

Coat . . . . chicken with flour seasoned with salt and pepper.
Brown . . . . . . in hot oil in skillet.
Place . . . . . . chicken in baking dish.
Drain . . . . . . pineapple, reserving juice.
Combine . . . . juice with next 6 ingredients in saucepan.
Boil . . . . for 2 minutes, stirring constantly.
Pour . . . . over chicken.
Bake . . . . for 1/2 hour.
Add . . . . pineapple and green pepper.
Bake . . . . for 1/2 hour longer.

Mrs. Albert Clester
Okeene Public School, Okeene, Oklahoma

MICROWAVE CHICKEN CORDON BLEU

4 chicken breasts, boned
4 slices boiled ham
4 slices mozzarella cheese
1 egg white, beaten
1 c. fresh bread crumbs
1 stick butter, melted
1 tsp. salt
1/4 tsp. paprika

Pound . . . . . . chicken breasts with meat mallet until thin.
Place . . . . 1 slice ham and cheese on each chicken breast.
Roll . . . . up and secure with toothpicks.
Dip . . . . in egg white.
Roll . . . . in crumbs.
Place . . . . . . in buttered glass baking dish.
Pour . . . . butter over top.
Sprinkle . . . . with remaining crumbs, salt and paprika.
Microwave . . on Medium for 10 minutes.
Microwave . . on High for 5 minutes, turning dish 1 time during cooking.
Yields . . . . . . 4 servings.

Merritt H. S.
Elk City, Oklahoma

MICROWAVE CHICKEN DIVAN

2 10-oz. packages frozen chopped broccoli
1 chicken, cooked, chopped
1 can cream of chicken soup
2 c. grated Cheddar cheese
1 can French-fried onion rings

Place . . . . broccoli in 9 x 13-inch baking dish.
Microwave . . on High for 3 minutes.
Arrange . . . . . chicken on top.
Sprinkle . . . . with cheese.
Cover . . . . . . with soup.
Microwave . . covered, on High for 7 minutes.
Turn . . . . dish 180 degrees.
Microwave . . for 8 minutes longer.
Top . . . . with onion rings.
Microwave . . for 1 minute longer.
Yields . . . . . . 4-6 servings.

Juli Hadfield
Noble Jr. H. S., Noble, Oklahoma

MICROWAVE FIESTA CHICKEN KIEV

2 lg. chicken breasts, halved,
   boned, skinned
3 tbsp. butter, softened
2 tbsp. Old English sharp cheese
   spread, softened
2 tsp. instant minced onion
1 tsp. salt
1 tsp. monosodium glutamate
2 tbsp. chopped green chiles
2/3 c. butter, melted
1 1/2 c. crushed Cheddar cheese crackers
2 1/2 tbsp. taco seasoning mix

Pound . . . . . . chicken with meat mallet.
Blend . . . . . . butter and cheese spread together in bowl.
Stir . . . . in next 4 ingredients, mixing well.
Spoon . . . . . . onto chicken pieces.
Roll . . . . up to enclose filling and secure with toothpicks.
Dip . . . . in butter and coat with cracker crumbs and taco mix.
Place . . . . in glass 2-quart casserole.
Microwave . . on High for 3 to 4 minutes.
Turn . . . . dish 180 degrees.
Microwave . . for 3 minutes longer.

Tammie Bierig
Okeene Public Schools, Okeene, Oklahoma

CHICKEN BREAST EDEN

6 chicken breasts, boned
White pepper
Bacon slices
1 jar dried beef
2 cans cream of chicken soup
1 1/2 c. sour cream
1 8-oz. package cream cheese, softened

Season . . . . . chicken with pepper.
Wrap . . . . with bacon and secure with toothpicks.
Place . . . . dried beef in baking dish.
Arrange . . . . . chicken breasts over top.
Combine . . . . soup, sour cream and cream cheese in bowl, mixing well.
Pour . . . . over chicken.
Bake . . . . tightly covered, at 325 degrees for 2 hours.

Bake . . . . uncovered, until brown.
Serve . . . . with rice.

Loretta Evans
Binger H. S., Binger, Oklahoma

CHICKEN-CHILE CASSEROLE

1/2 med. onion, chopped
2 to 3 tbsp. margarine
1 can cream of mushroom soup
1 chicken bouillon cube
1/2 sm. can chopped green chiles
1 8-oz. can chicken
1 lb. grated longhorn cheese
1 pkg. fluffy dumplets, cooked
Several slices Velveeta

Saute . . . . . . onion in margarine in skillet.
Add . . . . next 5 ingredients and 1 cup water.
Cook . . . . over low heat for 10 minutes.
Stir . . . . in dumplets.
Pour . . . . into casserole.
Top . . . . with Velveeta.
Bake . . . . at 350 degrees for about 20 minutes or until bubbly.

Carrie Randolph
Hydro H. S., Hydro, Oklahoma

CHICKEN DIVAN FOR EIGHT

2 pkg. frozen broccoli
6 chicken breasts, boned
1 can cream of chicken soup
1/2 c. mayonnaise
1 tsp. lemon juice
1/4 tsp. curry powder
5 slices bread, cubed
1 c. grated longhorn cheese

Cook . . . . broccoli for 4 minutes; drain.
Place . . . . in bottom of large baking dish.
Arrange . . . . . chicken on top.
Combine . . . . next 4 ingredients in bowl.
Pour . . . . over chicken.
Sprinkle . . . . with bread cubes and cheese.
Bake . . . . at 350 degrees for 20 minutes.
Yields . . . . . . 8 servings.

Nell Sullivan
Wilson, Oklahoma

CHICKEN-NOODLE DIVAN

2   10-oz. packages broccoli spears
8 oz. egg noodles
1 can cream of mushroom soup
1 c. milk
2 tbsp. grated Parmesan cheese
2 1/2 lb. chicken thighs
1 env. seasoned coating mix for chicken

Thaw . . . . . . broccoli until spears can be separated.
Cook . . . . noodles in boiling salted water in saucepan for 3 minutes and drain.
Combine . . . . soup and milk in bowl.
Add . . . . noodles, mixing well.
Spread . . . . . in 9 x 13-inch baking dish.
Top . . . . with broccoli and cheese.
Coat . . . . chicken with coating mix using package directions.
Arrange . . . . . on top of casserole.
Bake . . . . at 400 degrees for 50 minutes.
Yields . . . . . . 4 servings.

Jacki Crow
Ringwood H. S., Ringwood, Oklahoma

HOT CHICKEN SALAD

4 c. chopped cooked chicken
2 tbsp. lemon juice
3/4 c. mayonnaise
1 tsp. salt
1/2 tsp. monosodium glutamate
2 c. chopped celery
4 hard-boiled eggs, sliced
3/4 c. cream of chicken soup
1 tsp. finely minced onion
2 pimentos, finely chopped
1 c. grated cheese
2/3 c. finely chopped toasted almonds
1 1/2 c. crushed potato chips

Combine . . . . first 10 ingredients in large baking dish, mixing well.
Sprinkle . . . . with cheese, almonds and chips.
Chill . . . . in refrigerator overnight.
Bake . . . . at 400 degrees for 20 to 25 minutes.
Yields . . . . . . 8 servings.

Sheila D. Stevenson
Duncan Sr. H. S., Duncan, Oklahoma
Myrtle Stevens
Gracemont, Oklahoma

RITA'S CHICKEN CASSEROLE

2 c. chopped celery
2 c. sliced water chestnuts
1 lg. onion, chopped
Mushrooms (opt.)
1 stick butter
2 chickens, cooked, chopped
1 c. mayonnaise
3 c. cream of chicken soup
Black olives, sliced
Potato chips, crushed

Saute . . . . . . first 4 ingredients in butter in skillet.
Mix . . . . in remaining ingredients except chips.
Spread . . . . . half the chips in bottom of casserole.
Spoon . . . . . . chicken mixture into casserole.
Top . . . . with chips.
Garnish . . . . . with paprika.
Bake . . . . at 350 degrees for 30 to 35 minutes or until bubbly.

Martha Driever
Hitchcock, Oklahoma

CHICKEN TETRAZZINI

1 lg. onion, finely chopped
1 lg. green pepper, finely chopped
1 can mushrooms, drained
3 tbsp. butter
1 can cream of chicken soup
1 can cream of mushroom soup
1/2 c. chicken broth
1 lb. Velveeta cheese, chopped
5 lb. chicken breasts, cooked, chopped
2 boxes cut spaghetti noodles, cooked
1 sm. jar pimentos (opt.)
Sliced almonds (opt.)
1/2 lb. American cheese, grated (opt.)

Saute . . . . . . first 3 ingredients in butter in skillet until tender.
Stir . . . . in soups, broth and Velveeta.
Simmer . . . . . until cheese melts.
Add . . . . chicken, noodles, pimento and almonds.
Pour . . . . into casseroles.
Sprinkle . . . . with American cheese.
Bake . . . . at 300 degrees until cheese melts.

Serve . . . . immediately.
Yields . . . . . . 8-10 servings.

Rita Dickey
Tipton H. S., Tipton, Oklahoma

THREE-CHEESE CHICKEN BAKE

1/2 c. chopped onion
1/2 c. chopped green epper
3 tbsp. butter
1 can cream of chicken soup
1 6-oz. can sliced mushrooms, drained
1/2 c. chopped pimento, drained
1/3 c. milk
1/2 tsp. crushed dried basil
8 oz. lasagna noodles, cooked
1 1/2 c. cream-style cottage cheese
2 c. diced cooked chicken
2 c. shredded American cheese
1/2 c. grated Parmesan cheese

Saute . . . . . . onion and green pepper in butter in skillet until tender.
Stir . . . . in next 5 ingredients.
Layer . . . . . . half the noodles, sauce, cottage cheese, chicken, and cheeses in 9 x 13-inch baking dish.
Repeat . . . . . layers excet for American and Parmesan cheeses.
Bake . . . . at 350 degrees for 45 minutes.
Sprinkle . . . . with reserved cheeses.
Bake . . . . for 2 minutes longer.
Yields . . . . . . 8-10 servings.

Debbie Vincent
Past State President, Stillwater, Oklahoma

CHICKEN AND RICE WITH SAUSAGE

1 lg. chicken, cooked, chopped
1/4 lb. smoked sausage, sliced
1 1/4 c. rice
3 tbsp. shortening
3 c. chicken broth
1/2 c. chopped onion
1 clove of garlic
1/2 c. tomato sauce
1 tsp. salt

Place . . . . chicken and sausage in casserole.
Brown . . . . . . rice in shortening in skillet, stirring constantly and drain.
Spread . . . . . over meats.
Combine . . . . remaining ingredients.
Pour . . . . over top.
Bake . . . . covered, at 325 degrees for 1 hour.

Cynthia Clampet
Sulphur H. S., Sulphur, Oklahoma

CHICKEN CONTINENTAL

1 3 to 4-lb. chicken, cut up
Flour
1/4 c. butter
1 can cream of chicken soup
2 1/2 tbsp. grated onion
1 tsp. salt
Dash of pepper
1 tbsp. chopped parsley
1/2 tsp. celery flakes
1/8 tsp. thyme
1 1/3 c. minute rice

Coat . . . . chicken with flour.
Brown . . . . . . in butter in skillet.
Remove . . . . chicken.
Stir . . . . next 7 ingredients and 1 1/3 cups water into pan drippings.
Bring . . . . to a boil, stirring constantly.
Spread . . . . . rice in shallow 1 3/4-quart casserole.
Pour . . . . soup mixture, reserving 1/3 cup, over rice.
Arrange . . . . . chicken on top.
Drizzle . . . . . with remaining soup.
Bake . . . . covered at 375 degrees for 1/2 hour or until tender.
Yields . . . . . . 6-8 servings.

June Lovelace
Elk City H. S., Elk City, Oklahoma

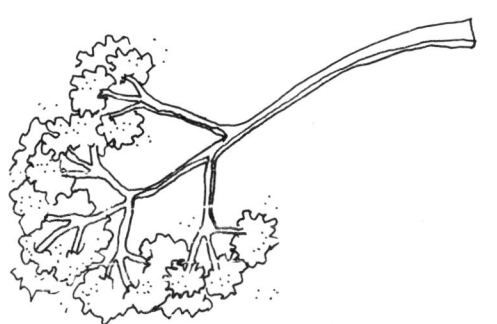

EASY CHICKEN AND RICE CASSEROLE

1 c. rice
1 chicken, cut up
1 can mushroom soup
1 can celery soup
1 env. dry onion soup mix

Sprinkle . . . . rice in baking dish.
Arrange . . . . . chicken on top.
Combine . . . . canned soups with 1 soup can water.
Pour . . . . over chicken.
Top . . . . with onion soup mix.
Bake . . . . at 300 degrees for 3 hours.

Mildred Klein
Oakwood, Oklahoma

TAMMY'S CHICKEN-RICE CASSEROLE

2 c. minute rice
1 can cream of chicken soup
1 can cream of mushroom soup
1/2 soup can milk
1/2 soup can milk
1 fryer, cut up
1 env. dry onion soup mix

Spread . . . . . rice in greased 9 x 13-inch baking dish.
Heat . . . . soups, milk and 1 soup can water in saucepan until blended.
Pour . . . . over rice.
Arrange . . . . . chicken over top.
Sprinkle . . . . with onion soup mix.
Bake . . . . covered, at 350 degrees for 1 1/2 hours.

Tammy Smith
Meeker H. S., Meeker, Oklahoma

CRUNCHY CHICKEN CASSEROLE

1 whole chicken, cooked, boned
2 c. chicken broth
1 can cream of chicken soup
1 can cream of mushroom soup
1 onion, chopped
1 hot pepper, chopped
1 3/4-lb. bag Tostitos, crushed
1 lb. grated cheese

Combine . . . . first 7 ingredients in bowl, mixing well.
Spread . . . . . in 9 x 13-inch baking dish.

Top . . . . with cheese.
Bake . . . . at 325 degrees until cheese melts.
Yields . . . . . . 10 servings.

Rhonda Cothran
Marietta H. S., Marietta, Oklahoma

KING RANCH CHICKEN

1 6 1/4-oz. package tortilla chips, crushed
1 fryer, cooked, chopped
3/4 c. chopped onion
1/2 c. chopped green pepper
1 tbsp. chili powder
1 c. milk
1 can cream of chicken soup
1 can cream of mushroom soup
1 10-oz. can Ro-Tel
1/2 lb. fresh mushrooms, sliced (opt.)
1/2 lb. sharp Cheddar cheese, grated

Place . . . . tortilla chips in 2-quart casserole.
Top . . . . with chicken.
Mix . . . . next 8 ingredients in bowl.
Pour . . . . over chicken.
Top . . . . with cheese.
Bake . . . . at 350 degrees until bubbly and lightly browned.

Glenda Cobb
Verden H. S., Verden, Oklahoma

SHERRY'S MEXICAN CHICKEN

1 pkg. flour tortillas
Chicken broth
1 fryer, cooked, chopped
1 tsp. garlic salt
1 tsp. chili powder
1 onion, chopped
2 cans cream of chicken soup
1 can Ro-Tel
1/2 lb. grated Cheddar cheese

Soften . . . . . . tortillas in broth.
Combine . . . . remaining ingredients except cheese in bowl, mixing well.
Alternate . . . layers of tortillas, sauce and cheese in 9 x 13-inch baking dish until all ingredients are used ending with cheese.

Bake . . . . at 350 degrees for 35 minutes.
Yields . . . . . . 8 servings.

Sherry Wood
Dickson School, Ardmore, Oklahoma

MICHELLE'S MEXICAN CHICKEN

1 doz. corn tortillas
Chicken broth
1 chicken, cooked, chopped
1 onion, chopped
1 tsp. chili powder
1 tsp. garlic salt
1 can cream of mushroom soup
1 can chicken soup
1/2 lb. Cheddar cheese
1 can Ro-Tel

Dip . . . . tortillas in chicken broth.
Layer . . . . . . tortillas, chicken and onion in baking pan.
Mix . . . . chili powder and garlic salt with soups in bowl.
Spread . . . . . over layers.
Top . . . . with cheese and Ro-Tel.
Bake . . . . at 350 degrees for 30 minutes.
Yields . . . . . . 4-6 servings.

Michelle Mackey
Bray-Doyle H. S., Bray, Oklahoma

SOUR CREAM-CHICKEN ENCHILADES

2 cans cream of chicken soup
1/2 c. chopped onion
1 4-oz. can chopped green chiles
1 c. sour cream
1/2 tsp. salt
1 pkg. flour tortillas
4 or 5 chicken breasts, cooked, shredded
2 c. grated Monterey Jack cheese

Combine . . . . first 5 ingredients in saucepan, mixing well.
Heat . . . . until warm, do not boil.
Spoon . . . . . . a small amount sauce into bottom of 9 x 12-inch baking dish.
Fill . . . . tortillas with chicken, sauce and cheese.
Roll . . . . up to enclose filling.
Arrange . . . . . in prepared dish.
Top . . . . with remaining sauce and cheese.

Bake . . . . at 350 degrees for 1/2 hour.
Yields . . . . . . 6-8 servings.

Jane Lingo
Sapulpa H. S., Sapulpa, Oklahoma

TACO CHICKEN PIE

1 chicken, cooked, chopped
1 c. chicken broth
1 can cream of chicken soup
1 can cream of mushroom soup
1 can Ro-Tel
1 onion, chopped
1 bag taco-flavored Dorito chips

Combine . . . . first 6 ingredients in bowl, mixing well.
Alternate . . . layers of chicken mixture and chips in large casserole.
Bake . . . . at 350 degrees for 30 to 45 minutes.

Darla Holderfield
Bristow H. S., Bristow, Oklahoma

SWISS TURKEY QUICHE

1 unbaked pie shell
1 c. shredded Swiss cheese
2 tbsp. flour
1 tbsp. instant chicken bouillon
2 c. cubed turkey
1 c. milk
3 eggs, well beaten
1/4 c. chopped onion
2 tbsp. chopped green pepper
2 tbsp. chopped pimento
1 can French-fried onions

Bake . . . . pie shell at 425 degrees for 8 minutes.
Toss . . . . cheese with flour and bouillon in bowl.
Stir . . . . in next 6 ingredients, mixing well.
Pour . . . . into pie shell.
Bake . . . . at 350 degrees for 45 minutes.
Top . . . . with onions.
Bake . . . . for 5 minutes longer.
Let . . . . stand for 10 minutes before cutting.

Jannie Barrington
Okemah H. S., Okemah, Oklahoma

SCALLOPS AMANDINE

1/3 c. flour
1/4 tsp. salt
3/4 lb. scallops
1/4 c. butter
3 tsp. slivered almonds
1 tsp. lemon juice
1 tsp. snipped parsley

Mix . . . . flour and salt in bowl.
Coat . . . . scallops with flour mixture.
Cook . . . . in half the butter in electric skillet at 350 degrees until golden.
Remove . . . . to warm platter.
Saute . . . . . . almonds in remaining butter in skillet until golden.
Stir . . . . in lemon juice and parsley.
Pour . . . . over scallops.
Yields . . . . . . 4 servings.

Susan Cusamano
Ryan Public School, Ryan, Oklahoma

SALMON CROQUETTES

1 can pink salmon, boned, shredded
2 eggs, slightly beaten
2 tbsp. flour
1/2 c. bread crumbs
3 tbsp. finely chopped onions
2 tbsp. sweet pickle juice
1/3 c. cornmeal
1/3 c. flour

Mix . . . . first 6 ingredients in bowl.
Shape . . . . . . into patties.
Combine . . . . cornmeal and flour in bowl.
Roll . . . . each patty in cornmeal mixture.
Place . . . . in waxed paper-lined dish.
Chill . . . . covered, for 2 hours or longer.
Fry . . . . in oil in skillet, turning once.

Mary Barnes
Wilson H. S., Wilson, Oklahoma

SPAGHETTI WITH TUNA SAUCE

2 tbsp. flour
1/2 tsp. salt
2 tbsp. butter, melted
2 c. milk
1/4 c. prepared mustard
2 7-oz. cans tuna, drained
8 oz. spaghetti, cooked
2 tbsp. grated Parmesan cheese

Blend . . . . . . flour and salt into butter in saucepan.
Stir . . . . in milk.
Bring . . . . to a boil, stirring constantly.
Cook . . . . until thick, stirring occasionally.
Add . . . . mustard and tuna.
Pour . . . . over spaghetti.
Top . . . . with cheese.

Photograph for this recipe on opposite page.

TUNA RING WITH CHEESE SAUCE

1 egg
2 7-oz. cans tuna, drained
1/2 c. chopped onion
1 1/2 c. shredded sharp Cheddar cheese
1/2 c. snipped parsley
1 tsp. celery salt
1/4 tsp. pepper
2 c. biscuit mix
1/4 c. butter
1/4 tsp. each salt and pepper
2 c. milk

Beat . . . . egg in bowl, reserving 2 tablespoons.
Stir . . . . in tuna, onion, 1/2 cup cheese, parsley, celery salt and pepper.
Combine . . . . biscuit mix and 1/2 cup cold water in bowl.
Knead . . . . . . 5 times on floured surface.
Roll . . . . into 10 x 15-inch rectangle.
Spread . . . . . with tuna mixture.
Roll . . . . as for jelly roll.
Shape . . . . . . into ring on greased baking pan, pinching ends together.
Cut . . . . 2/3 of the way through ring at 1-inch intervals with scissors.
Turn . . . . each section on its side.
Brush . . . . . . top with remaining beaten egg.
Bake . . . . at 375 degrees for 25 to 30 minutes.
Combine . . . . remaining ingredients and 1 cup cheese in saucepan.
Heat . . . . until cheese melts.
Serve . . . . over tuna ring.

Connie Welch
Barnsdall H. S., Barnsdall, Oklahoma

TUNA SPECIAL

    1   7-oz. can tuna, drained
    1/4 c. shelled sunflower seeds
    1/2 sm. red onion
    1/4 c. chopped apple
    1/4 tsp. dried basil
    2 tbsp. mayonnaise
    2 tbsp. yogurt
    3 pita breads
    6 tbsp. shredded carrots
    3/4 c. alfalfa sprouts

Combine . . . . first 7 ingredients in bowl, mixing well.

Fill . . . . each pita bread with 1/3 of the tuna mixture.

Top . . . . with carrots and alfalfa sprouts.

Yields . . . . . . 3 sandwiches.

Karona Conkling
Ryan Public School, Ryan, Oklahoma

EGG SALAD CASSEROLE

    6 to 8 hard-boiled eggs, chopped
    1 1/2 c. chopped celery
    1/4 c. broken pecans
    1 tsp. minced onion
    1/4 tsp. pepper
    2 tbsp. snipped parsley
    1/2 tsp. salt
    2/3 c. mayonnaise
    1 c. grated sharp American cheese
    1 c. crushed potato chips

Combine . . . . first 8 ingredients in bowl, mixing well.

Spoon . . . . . . into 4 small casseroles.

Top . . . . with cheese and potato chips.

Bake . . . . at 375 degrees for 25 minutes.

Becky Ann Ellis
Pawhuska H. S., Pawhuska, Oklahoma

BAKED EGG AND CHEESE DISH

5 slices bread, buttered, cubed
4 oz. sharp Cheddar cheese, shredded
4 eggs
2 c. milk
1 tsp. salt
1 tsp. dry mustard
Dash of pepper

Alternate ... layers of bread cubes and cheese in buttered baking dish until all ingredients are used.
Combine .... remaining ingredients in bowl, beating well.
Pour .... over layers.
Bake .... covered, at 350 degrees for 45 minutes to 1 hour or until knife inserted in center comes out clean.

Jennifer Harmon
Moore West Mid-H. S., Moore, Oklahoma

HEALTH NUT OMELET

3 soft corn tortillas, cut up
Butter
1 sm. onion, diced
6 eggs, beaten
1/2 green pepper, chopped
1/4 c. grated cheese
1 tomato, chopped
1 tbsp. sunflower seeds
1 tbsp. bacon bits
2 tbsp. alfalfa sprouts

Brown ...... tortillas in butter in skillet.
Add .... onion.
Saute ...... until slightly cooked.
Pour .... eggs over top.
Sprinkle .... with green pepper and cheese.
Cook .... over low heat until partially set.
Top .... with remaining ingredients.
Cook .... until set.

Stanley A. McDaniel, Principal
Okeene H. S., Okeene, Oklahoma

QUICHE LORRAINE

12 slices crisp-cooked bacon, crumbled
1 c. shredded Swiss cheese
1/3 c. minced onion
1 unbaked 9-inch pie shell

4 eggs, beaten
2 c. whipping cream
3/4 tsp. salt
1/4 tsp. sugar
1/8 tsp. cayenne pepper

Spread ..... first 3 ingredients in pie shell.
Combine .... remaining ingredients in bowl, beating well.
Pour .... into pie shell.
Bake .... at 425 degrees for 15 minutes.
Bake .... at 300 degrees for 30 minutes longer or until quiche tests done.
Let .... stand for 10 minutes before serving.

Brenda Barnes
Duncan H. S., Duncan, Oklahoma

GINGER'S MICROWAVE MANICOTTI

1 c. cottage cheese
1/2 c. grated mozzarella cheese
1/2 c. Parmesan cheese
1 egg
1/2 c. bread crumbs
1 tsp. Italian seasoning
1/2 c. grated Cheddar cheese
1 box manicotti noodles, cooked
3/4 c. tomato sauce

Combine .... first 6 ingredients with 1/4 cup Cheddar cheese in bowl, mixing well.
Stuff .... manicotti with mixture.
Place .... in greased 11 x 14-inch glass baking dish.
Top .... with tomato sauce and remaining Cheddar cheese.
Microwave .. on Medium for 8 minutes.

Ginger Goble
Chandler H. S., Chandler, Oklahoma

MEATLESS SPAGHETTI PIE

6 oz. spaghetti, cooked
5 tbsp. butter
1/3 c. grated Parmesan cheese
2 eggs, beaten
1 c. cottage cheese
1 c. chopped onion
1/3 c. chopped celery
1/3 c. chopped green pepper

1 8-oz. can tomatoes, chopped
1 6-oz. can tomato paste
1 tsp. sugar
3/4 tsp. Italian seasoning
1/2 tsp. garlic salt
2 c. 1/4 inch thick sliced zucchini
1/2 c. shredded mozzarella cheese

Rinse	spaghetti with hot water, draining well.
Combine	with 2 tablespoons butter in bowl, stirring until butter melts.
Stir	in Parmesan cheese and eggs.
Spread	in buttered 10-inch pie plate.
Spoon	cottage cheese over bottom.
Saute	onion, celery and green pepper in 3 tablespoons butter in skillet for 5 minutes or until tender.
Add	tomatoes, tomato paste, sugar and seasonings.
Simmer	for 15 minutes, stirring occasionally.
Add	zucchini.
Simmer	covered, for 5 minutes longer.
Spoon	over cottage cheese.
Bake	at 350 degrees for 20 minutes.
Remove	from oven.
Sprinkle	with mozzarella.
Bake	for 5 minutes longer or until cheese melts.
Serve	immediately.

Photograph for this recipe on page 2.

CHILI RELLENO CASSEROLE

3 7-oz. cans whole green chiles
1 lb. Monterey Jack cheese, shredded
4 corn tortillas, cut into wide strips
5 eggs, beaten
1/2 c. milk
1/2 tsp. each salt, pepper, ground
   cuminseed, garlic
1/4 tsp. onion salt
Paprika to taste
1 lg. tomato, sliced

Layer	chiles, cheese and tortilla strips in greased baking dish.
Beat	eggs, milk and seasonings except paprika together in bowl.
Pour	over layers.
Sprinkle	with paprika.
Arrange	tomato slices over top.

Bake	at 350 degrees for 40 minutes.
Let	stand for several minutes before serving.

Carol Purvine Sanchez
Seiling, Oklahoma

MEXI-CHILI CASSEROLE

1 c. chopped onions
1 tbsp. butter
1 15-oz. can chili without beans
1 10-oz. can enchilada sauce
1/4 c. sour cream
1 tsp. ground cuminseed
3 c. cooked rice
1 1/2 c. grated Cheddar cheese
1 c. corn chips

Saute	onions in butter in skillet.
Add	remaining ingredients except cheese and chips, mixing well.
Spoon	into greased 2-quart casserole.
Top	with cheese and chips.
Bake	at 350 degrees for 20 minutes.

Beverly Bierig
Okeene Public Schools, Okeene, Oklahoma

MEXICAN MEAL-IN-ONE CASSEROLE

12 4-inch flour tortillas, quartered
2 16-oz. cans ranch-style chili beans
1 12-oz. jar mild taco sauce
6 oz. mozzarella cheese, shredded
6 oz. Cheddar cheese, shredded

Spread	tortillas in 9 x 13-inch baking dish.
Bake	at 350 degrees until golden brown.
Combine	beans and half the taco sauce in blender container.
Process	to consistency of refried beans.
Alternate	layers of bean mixture and cheese over tortillas until all ingredients are used ending with cheese.
Garnish	with sliced black olives, mushrooms, or tomatoes or browned sausage or ground beef.
Bake	at 350 degrees until bubbly.
Serve	with remaining taco sauce.

Laura Rusika
Cyril H. S., Cyril, Oklahoma

Vegetables

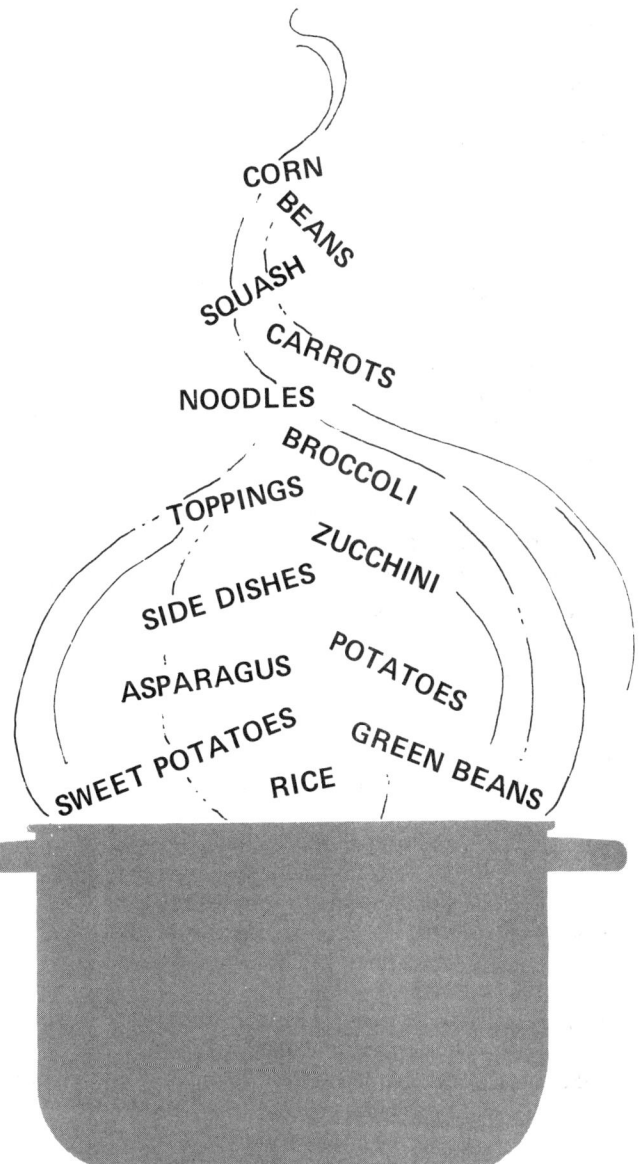

CORN

BEANS

SQUASH

CARROTS

NOODLES

BROCCOLI

TOPPINGS

ZUCCHINI

SIDE DISHES

ASPARAGUS

POTATOES

SWEET POTATOES

RICE

GREEN BEANS

ASPARAGUS CASSEROLE

2 cans asparagus, drained
1 1/4 c. crushed crackers
3 eggs, beaten
2 hard-boiled eggs, chopped
1/2 tsp. pepper
1 sm. can mushrooms
1 c. milk
1 1/2 tsp. salt
1 c. grated cheese
2 tbsp. butter, melted

Combine .... first 9 ingredients in bowl, mixing well.
Pour .... into greased casserole.
Drizzle ..... with butter.
Bake .... at 350 degrees for 20 to 30 minutes or until bubbly.

Melissa Hodges
Wilson H. S., Wilson, Oklahoma

CHEESE-ASPARAGUS CASSEROLE

1 20-oz. can asparagus
2 tbsp. margarine, melted
1 tbsp. flour
1 tsp. salt
1/4 tsp. pepper
Evaporated milk
1/2 c. fine cracker crumbs
2 hard-boiled eggs, chopped
1/2 c. grated cheese

Drain ...... asparagus reserving liquid.
Blend ...... next 4 ingredients in saucepan.
Add .... enough evaporated milk to reserved asparagus liquid to measure 1 1/2 cups.
Blend ...... into flour mixture.
Cook .... for 2 minutes, stirring constantly.
Spread ..... asparagus in shallow greased 1 1/2-quart casserole, reserving several spears for top.
Layer ...... half the crumbs, eggs, half the sauce and remaining crumbs over asparagus.
Top .... with reserved asparagus, remaining sauce and cheese.
Bake .... at 350 degrees for 30 minutes or until bubbly.

Mary Ann Rogers
Okeene H. S., Okeene, Oklahoma

WALNUT-MUSHROOM ASPARAGUS

4 sm. green onions, chopped
1 c. sliced fresh mushrooms
3 tbsp. butter
1/4 c. toasted California walnuts
Salt to taste
1 1/2 lb. asparagus, cooked

Saute ...... onions and mushrooms in butter in skillet until tender.
Add .... walnuts and salt.
Spoon ...... over lightly buttered asparagus.
Yields ...... 4 servings.

Photograph for this recipe on page 58.

BOSTON BAKED BEANS

2 1/2 c. dried navy beans
1 tbsp. mustard
3 tbsp. molasses
4 oz. bacon, chopped

Combine .... beans and cold water to cover in saucepan.
Let .... stand for 6 hours or longer.
Drain ...... water from beans.
Add .... mustard, molasses and 3 1/4 cups water.
Boil .... for 3 minutes.
Pour .... into bean pot.
Stir .... in bacon.
Bake .... at 250 degrees for 8 hours or until beans are tender.
Yields ...... 12 servings.

Jamie Selby
Ryan Public School, Ryan, Oklahoma

STOVE TOP BAKED BEANS

1 med. onion, chopped
1 tbsp. shortening
1 med. can pork and beans
1/2 c. packed brown sugar
1/2 c. catsup

Saute ...... onion in shortening in skillet.
Add .... remaining ingredients and 1/4 cup water, mixing well.
Cook .... over low heat for 10 to 15 minutes or until bubbly.

Kristy Roberts
Wilson H. S., Wilson, Oklahoma

TONNA'S BAKED BEANS

2 slices bacon, chopped
1 onion, chopped
3/4 c. packed brown sugar
1 c. catsup
2 tsp. vinegar
2 tbsp. liquid smoke
1 tsp. salt
1 tsp. chili powder
1 2-lb. can pork and beans

Saute ...... bacon and onion in skillet until brown.
Add .... remaining ingredients, mixing well.
Simmer ..... for 30 to 60 minutes.

Tonna Coffey
Hinton H. S., Hinton, Oklahoma

GREEN BEANS DELICIOUS

1 lg. onion, sliced
2 tbsp. margarine
1 can chopped pimentos
1 can mushroom pieces
1 jar Old English cheese
1 can mushroom soup
1 can French-cut green beans, drained
Crushed Ritz crackers

Saute ...... onion in margarine in skillet.
Stir .... in pimentos and mushrooms.
Simmer ..... for 10 minutes.
Blend ...... in cheese and soup.
Stir .... in beans.
Pour .... into buttered casserole.
Top .... with crumbs and a small amount of additional butter.
Bake .... at 350 degrees until brown.

Julie Boone
Pawhuska H. S., Pawhuska, Oklahoma

FAVORITE GREEN BEAN CASSEROLE

1 lg. can green beans
2 tbsp. melted butter
2 tbsp. flour
1 can mushroom soup
1/2 tsp. Worcestershire sauce
2 oz. grated cheese
1/2 c. buttered bread crumbs

Drain ...... beans reserving 2 tablespoons liquid.
Blend ...... butter and flour in saucepan.
Add .... next 3 ingredients with reserved bean liquid.
Cook .... over medium heat until thick, stirring constantly.
Combine .... with beans in casserole.
Top .... with crumbs.
Bake .... at 350 degrees for 30 minutes.

Glenda Tharp
Verden H. S., Verden, Oklahoma

GREEN BEANS AND RICE

1 c. finely chopped onions
1 tbsp. butter
1 can cream of mushroom soup
2 c. cooked rice
1 16-oz. can green beans, drained
1 12-oz. can luncheon meat, chopped
1 tsp. salt
1 c. grated Cheddar cheese

Saute ...... onions in butter in skillet until tender.
Stir .... in soup.
Cook .... for 2 minutes.
Stir .... in remaining ingredients except cheese.
Pour .... into 2-quart casserole.
Top .... with cheese.
Bake .... at 350 degrees for 20 minutes.

Evelyn Shaw
Okeene H. S., Okeene, Oklahoma

DELUXE GREEN BEAN CASSEROLE

2 cans julienne green beans, drained
1 4-oz. can mushrooms, drained
1 1-lb. can bean sprouts, drained
1 8-oz. can sliced water chestnuts, drained
1/2 tsp. salt
1 can mushroom soup
1 c. grated Cheddar cheese

Combine .... all ingredients except cheese in casserole, mixing well.
Top .... with cheese.
Bake .... at 350 degrees for 25 minutes.

Phyllis K. Sams
Muskogee H. S., Muskogee, Oklahoma

FRESH BROCCOLI WITH MILD CHEESE SAUCE

1 bunch broccoli
1 tsp. salt
Pinch of pepper
2 tbsp. butter, melted
2 tbsp. flour
1 c. milk
1 c. shredded American cheese

Separate .... broccoli into spears, removing large leaves and tough stalks.
Place .... in large saucepan with 1/2 inch boiling water, salt and pepper.
Simmer ..... covered, for 10 to 12 minutes or until tender.
Blend ...... butter and flour in saucepan.
Stir .... in milk.
Cook .... until thickened, stirring constantly.
Add .... cheese.
Cook .... until cheese melts, stirring constantly.
Serve .... over drained broccoli.
Yields ...... 4-6 servings.

Photograph for this recipe on page 69.

HOLIDAY BROCCOLI WITH RICE

1/2 c. finely chopped celery
1 med. onion, finely chopped
1/4 c. margarine
1 can cream of chicken soup
1/4 tsp. salt
1 tsp. soy sauce
Dash each of nutmeg, cayenne pepper
1 4-oz. jar pimento cheese spread
1 c. rice, cooked
1 10-oz. package frozen broccoli spears, partially cooked, drained

Saute ...... celery and onion in margarine in skillet until lightly browned.
Blend ...... in remaining ingredients except rice and broccoli.
Reserve ..... 4 tablespoons sauce.
Stir .... in rice.
Pour .... into shallow buttered baking dish.
Arrange ..... broccoli over rice.
Spread ..... with reserved sauce.

Bake .... at 350 degrees for 35 to 40 minutes.

Marlin Isaacs
Wilson H. S., Wilson, Oklahoma

LINDA'S BROCCOLI CASSEROLE

1 c. chopped onions
1 c. chopped celery
Butter
1 can cream of chicken soup
1 can cream of mushroom soup
1 8-oz. jar Cheez Whiz
1 pkg. chopped broccoli, cooked
2 c. rice, cooked

Saute ...... onions and celery in a small amount of butter in skillet.
Stir .... in remaining ingredients with 1 soup can water.
Pour .... into buttered casserole.
Bake .... at 350 degrees for 35 minutes.

Linda Jackson
McAlester H. S., McAlester, Oklahoma

REGINA'S BROCCOLI CASSEROLE

2 pkg. frozen chopped broccoli, cooked, drained
1 can cream of chicken soup
1 c. minute rice
3/4 c. Cheez Whiz
2 tbsp. butter, melted
1/2 c. milk
3 tbsp. minced onions

Combine .... all ingredients in large bowl, mixing well.
Pour .... into 9 x 13-inch baking dish.
Bake .... at 350 degrees for 30 minutes.

Regina Hudson
Barnsdall H. S., Barnsdall, Oklahoma

FAMILY FAVORITE RICE-BROCCOLI CASSEROLE

1/2 c. chopped onion
1/2 c. chopped celery
1 pkg. frozen chopped broccoli, cooked
1 can cream of chicken soup
1 sm. jar Cheez Whiz
Salt to taste

1 c. rice, cooked
Paprika

Saute ...... onion and celery in skillet.
Stir .... in broccoli, soup, Cheez Whiz and salt.
Spread ..... rice over bottom and up sides of casserole.
Spoon ...... broccoli mixture over rice.
Sprinkle .... with paprika.
Bake .... at 375 degrees for 30 minutes.

Eletha Gayle Penham
Ryan Public School, Ryan, Oklahoma

MRS. BERNARD'S RICE AND BROCCOLI CASSEROLE

1 10-oz. package frozen chopped broccoli
1 c. chopped onion
1 c. chopped celery
2 (or more) tbsp. margarine
1 c. minute rice, cooked
1 can mushroom soup
4 slices American cheese, grated

Cook .... broccoli according to package directions until tender-crisp.
Saute ...... onion and celery in margarine in skillet until tender-crisp.
Combine .... broccoli, rice, soup, and sauteed vegetables, mixing well.
Pour .... into greased 9 x 12-inch baking dish.
Top .... with cheese.
Bake .... at 350 degrees until cheese melts.

Vivian Bernard
Oklahoma Lt. Governor's Wife
Rush Springs, Oklahoma

ELEGANT CARROTS

6 med. carrots, peeled, sliced
2 tbsp. butter
3/4 tsp. salt
1 tsp. brown sugar
1/2 c. chicken broth
1/3 c. cream
1 egg yolk
2 tsp. lemon juice
1/2 c. toasted California walnuts

Combine .... first 5 ingredients in saucepan.
Simmer ..... covered, until tender.
Mix .... cream and egg yolk until blended in saucepan.
Stir .... in carrots and cooking liquid.
Cook .... until heated through.
Add .... lemon juice and walnuts.

Photograph for this recipe on page 58.

SCALLOPED CARROTS

10 carrots, pared, sliced
1 med. onion, minced
2 tbsp. butter
3 tbsp. flour
1/2 tsp. salt
1/4 tsp. dry mustard
1/8 tsp. each pepper, celery salt
1 c. milk
6 oz. Cheddar cheese, sliced
3 tbsp. bread crumbs

Cook .... carrots in a small amount of water in saucepan until tender-crisp; drain, reserving liquid.
Saute ...... onion in butter in skillet for 2 to 3 minutes.
Blend ...... in flour and seasonings.
Stir .... in milk gradually.
Cook .... until smooth, stirring constantly and adding 1/4 cup reserved carrot liquid if necessary.
Alternate ... layers of carrots and cheese in 1-quart casserole until all ingredients are used.
Pour .... sauce over layers.
Sprinkle .... with crumbs.
Bake .... at 350 degrees for 25 minutes.
Yields ...... 12-15 servings.

Tina Kimble
Hydro H. S., Hydro, Oklahoma

MICROWAVE TANGY MUSTARD-CAULIFLOWER

1/2 med. head cauliflower
1/4 c. mayonnaise
Salt and pepper to taste
1/2 tsp. onion, chopped
1/2 tsp. mustard
1/2 tsp. lemon juice
1/4 c. shredded Cheddar cheese

Place .... cauliflower in 1 1/2-quart glass casserole with 1 tablespoon water.
Microwave .. covered, on High for 4 to 5 minutes or until tender.
Combine .... remaining ingredients except cheese in small bowl, blending well.
Pour .... over cauliflower.
Top .... with cheese.
Microwave .. on Medium for 1 1/2 to 2 minutes.
Let .... stand for 2 minutes.
Yields ...... 5-6 servings.

Peggy Haynes
El Reno H. S., El Reno, Oklahoma

HOT CORN CASSEROLE

3 cans yellow cream-style corn
2 eggs, beaten
3/4 c. yellow cornmeal
1/2 tsp. garlic salt
1/2 c. oil
1/2 tsp. baking powder
1 sm. can chopped chili pepper
1/2 lb. mild Cheddar cheese, shredded

Combine .... first 7 ingredients with 2/3 of the cheese in bowl, mixing well.
Pour .... into greased baking dish.
Top .... with remaining cheese.
Bake .... at 350 degrees for 45 minutes.
Yields ...... 12-15 servings.

Candy Gray, H. E. District Supervisor
State Dept. Vo-Tech Ed.
Stillwater, Oklahoma

MEXICAN CORN

1 8-oz. package cream cheese, softened
1/2 c. milk
2 cans whole kernel corn
1 tsp. salt
1/2 tsp. red pepper
1 2-oz. can chopped green chiles

Blend ...... cream cheese with milk in bowl.
Stir .... in remaining ingredients.
Pour .... into greased baking dish.
Bake .... at 350 degrees for 30 minutes.
Yields ...... 6-8 servings.

Jeannie Laubach
Okeene Public School, Okeene, Oklahoma

CORN PUDDING

3/4 c. cornmeal
Salt to taste
1 3/4 c. milk, scalded
2 tbsp. margarine
1 can cream-style corn
3/4 tsp. baking powder
3 eggs, separated

Beat .... cornmeal and salt into milk in saucepan.
Cook .... over low heat until very thick, stirring constantly.
Stir .... in margarine, corn and baking powder.
Add .... beaten egg yolks, mixing well.
Fold .... in stiffly beaten egg whites.
Pour .... into greased 2-quart baking dish.
Bake .... at 350 degrees until brown and fluffy.

Eva Doris Richardson
Kiowa H. S., Kiowa, Oklahoma

MICROWAVE EGGPLANT CASSEROLE

1 med. eggplant, peeled, cubed
2 eggs, beaten
1/4 c. margarine, melted
1 c. bread crumbs
1/4 c. chopped pimentos
1 onion, chopped
2 c. cream-style corn
1 c. grated Colby cheese
Salt and pepper to taste
1/2 c. grated sharp Cheddar cheese

Cook . . . . eggplant in a small amount of boiling water in saucepan for 10 minutes; drain.

Combine . . . . with next 7 ingredients and seasonings in greased 2-quart glass casserole, mixing well.

Microwave . . covered, on High for 4 to 5 minutes.

Turn . . . . casserole 1/4 turn.

Microwave . . on High for 3 to 4 minutes.

Top . . . . with Cheddar cheese.

Microwave . . on High for 1 minute longer or until cheese melts.

May . . . . bake at 350 degrees for 1 hour.

Marcy Carrick, H. E. Tchr.
Cleveland Middle School, Cleveland, Oklahoma

DEVILED BLACK-EYED PEAS AND RICE WITH SAUTEED TOMATOES

1 10-oz. package frozen black-eyed peas
1 sm. clove of garlic, chopped
1 sm. onion, chopped
1/2 sm. green pepper, chopped
1/2 c. finely chopped celery
1 bouillon cube
Salt
1 4 1/2-oz. can deviled ham
2 c. fluffy hot rice
1 tbsp. butter
Pepper to taste
1/4 c. grated Parmesan cheese
1/2 c. packaged seasoned crumbs
4 med. firm ripe tomatoes
Tabasco sauce to taste

Combine . . . . first 6 ingredients with 1/2 teaspoon salt in saucepan.

Add . . . . 2 cups boiling water.

Cook . . . . covered, over medium heat for 20 to 25 minutes or until peas are tender, stirring frequently.

Drain . . . . . . vegetables.

Stir . . . . in deviled ham.

Toss . . . . with rice, butter and salt and pepper to taste.

Combine . . . . cheese and crumbs, mixing well.

Cut . . . . each tomato into 3 slices.

Coat . . . . with crumb mixture.

Sprinkle . . . . with Tabasco sauce.

Saute . . . . . . in skillet.

Arrange . . . . . around edges of serving platter with rice mixture in center.

Photograph for this recipe below.

POTATO CASSEROLE

6 med. potatoes, cooked, peeled, grated
1/4 c. butter, melted
2 c. shredded Cheddar cheese
2 c. sour cream
1/3 c. chopped green onions
1 1/2 tsp. salt
1/4 tsp. pepper

Combine .... all ingredients in large bowl, mixing well.
Pour .... into casserole.
Bake .... covered, at 350 degrees for 45 minutes.
Yields ...... 12 servings.

Karen Epperly
Washita Heights School, Corn, Oklahoma

CHEESE POTATOES

6 lg. potatoes, peeled, cubed
4 tbsp. finely chopped onion
4 tbsp. margarine
4 tbsp. flour
1 tsp. salt
1 tsp. Worcestershire sauce
1 tsp. prepared mustard
Milk
1/2 lb. Velveeta cheese, cubed
1 c. corn flakes

Cook .... potatoes in boiling water in saucepan until nearly tender; drain.
Saute ...... onion in margarine in skillet until tender.
Blend ...... in flour and seasonings.
Cook .... for 1 minute.
Add .... enough milk to make medium white sauce.
Cook .... until thick, stirring constantly.
Add .... cheese.
Cook .... until cheese melts, stirring constantly.
Combine .... potatoes and sauce in casserole.
Top .... with corn flakes.
Bake .... at 350 degrees for 15 to 20 minutes.

Eva Doris Richardson, Advisor
Kiowa H. S., Kiowa, Oklahoma

HEAVENLY POTATOES

10 potatoes, cooked, mashed
1 lg. package cream cheese, softened
1 8-oz. carton sour cream
2 tbsp. minced onion
2 tsp. garlic salt
Parsley flakes
Paprika
1/2 stick margarine, melted

Combine .... first 5 ingredients in large bowl, beating well.
Spoon ...... into buttered casserole.
Sprinkle .... with parsley and paprika.
Drizzle ..... with margarine.
Chill .... for 24 hours.
Bake .... at 325 degrees until heated through.

Hollis FHA
Hollis, Oklahoma

SPINACH PIE CASSEROLE

1 pkg. frozen chopped spinach, thawed
3 eggs, beaten
2 tbsp. butter, softened
1/4 lb. Velveeta cheese, shredded
3 tbsp. flour
1 sm. carton cottage cheese
Dash of salt

Combine .... all ingredients in large bowl, mixing well.
Pour .... into large deep baking dish.
Bake .... at 350 degrees for 1 hour or until brown around edges.

Willene Walsh
Union City H. S., Union City, Oklahoma

SQUASH PATTIES

Squash, cooked, drained, mashed
Salt and pepper to taste
Brown sugar to taste
Corn bread, crumbled
1 egg
Chopped pecans

Combine .... squash and seasonings in bowl.
Add .... remaining ingredients to make of thick consistency.
Shape ...... into patties.

Saute ......in oil in skillet until golden brown.

Rhonda Jernigan
Pryor Jr. H. S., Pryor, Oklahoma

SPAGHETTI SQUASH

1 spaghetti squash
3 to 5 tbsp. butter, softened
2 to 8 tbsp. diced onion
Velveeta cheese, grated

Cut ....squash in half crosswise and remove seeds.
Place ....cut side up in baking dish.
Spread .....cavities with butter and sprinkle with onion.
Bake ....covered, at 325 degrees for 1 hour.
Fill ....cavities with cheese.
Bake ....uncovered, until cheese melts.
Stir ....with fork to make spaghetti-like strands.
Yields ......4 servings.

Jewel Felder
Okeene, Oklahoma

SQUASH PIE

1 3/4 c. mashed cooked squash, strained
1 c. sugar
3 eggs, beaten
1 1/2 c. milk
1 tbsp. butter, melted
1 tsp. each salt, cinnamon
1/2 tsp. each nutmeg, ginger
1 unbaked pie shell (opt.)

Combine ....first 5 ingredients and seasonings in bowl, mixing well.
Pour ....into pie shell.
Bake ....at 400 degrees for 50 minutes.

Martha Henderson
Mooreland H. S., Mooreland, Oklahoma

STACY'S SQUASH CASSEROLE

3 c. cooked drained yellow squash
1 c. milk
2 eggs, beaten
1 c. grated cheese
1/2 c. chopped onion

1 c. cracker crumbs
Butter

Combine ....first 5 ingredients with 1/2 cup crumbs in bowl, mixing well.
Pour ....into buttered casserole.
Top ....with remaining crumbs.
Dot ....with butter.
Bake ....at 350 degrees for 40 minutes.

Stacy Wallis
Wilson H. S., Wilson, Oklahoma

BAKED STUFFED TOMATOES DOTHAN

6 med. ripe tomatoes
1/2 c. peanut butter
3/4 c. soft bread crumbs
1 tsp. salt
1/8 tsp. freshly ground pepper
1/2 tsp. oregano
2 tbsp. finely chopped onion
1/4 c. finely diced celery

Remove ....stem end from tomatoes.
Cut ....thin slice from bottom.
Remove ....pulp with spoon and chop.
Combine ....pulp with remaining ingredients in bowl, mixing well.
Spoon ......into tomato shells.
Place ....in greased baking dish.
Bake ....at 400 degrees for 1/2 hour.

Photograph for this recipe below.

CANDIED YAMS

4 med. yams, peeled
3/4 c. sugar
1/4 c. packed light brown sugar
Dash of salt
1 tsp. cinnamon
1 tbsp. flour
1 stick butter
2 slices lemon
1/2 can crushed pineapple

Cut .... yams as for French-fries.
Spread ..... in 8 x 12-inch baking dish.
Mix .... next 5 ingredients in bowl.
Sprinkle .... over yams.
Top .... with butter and lemon slices.
Spread ..... with pineapple and add 1 cup water.
Bake .... covered, at 400 degrees for 1 hour or until tender.

Terri Chandler
Wilson H. S., Wilson, Oklahoma

MICROWAVE-BAKED SWEET POTATOES

3 c. mashed sweet potatoes
1 c. sugar
1/4 c. Milnot
2 eggs, beaten
1 tsp. vanilla extract
1/2 c. coconut
1 1/2 sticks margarine, softened
1 c. nuts
1 c. packed brown sugar
1/2 c. flour

Combine .... first 6 ingredients with 1/2 stick margarine in bowl, mixing well.
Spread ..... in 9 x 13-inch glass baking pan.
Combine .... remaining ingredients and 1 stick margarine in bowl, mixing well.
Sprinkle .... over sweet potato mixture.
Microwave .. on High for 7 minutes or bake at 325 degrees for 15 to 20 minutes.

Diane Stephens
Guymon H. S., Guymon, Oklahoma

SWEET POTATO PIE

1 1/2 c. cooked mashed sweet potatoes
3/4 c. sugar
1/4 tsp. salt
Dash of cinnamon
Dash of nutmeg
2 eggs, slightly beaten
1 c. milk
1/2 c. evaporated milk
Butter to taste
1 unbaked 9-in. pie shell

Combine .... first 9 ingredients in bowl, mixing until smooth.
Pour .... into pie shell.
Bake .... at 400 degrees for 50 minutes or until pie tests done.

Mrs. Lorean Droke
Okeene, Oklahoma

AUTUMN SWEET POTATO BAKE

3 med. sweet potatoes
Salt to taste
1   10-oz. can apricots
3 tbsp. brown sugar
1 tbsp. cornstarch
Cinnamon to taste
1/2 c. light raisins
3 tbsp. dry Sherry
1/2 tsp. grated orange rind

Cook .... whole sweet potatoes in boiling salted water in saucepan for 30 to 40 minutes or until tender.
Drain ...... peel and cut into halves lengthwise.
Place .... in 6 x 10-inch baking dish.
Sprinkle .... with salt.
Drain ...... apricots, reserving syrup.
Arrange ..... apricots over potatoes.
Add .... enough water to reserved syrup to measure 1 cup.
Combine .... brown sugar, cornstarch, salt and cinnamon in saucepan.
Stir .... in syrup mixture and raisins.
Bring .... to a boil over high heat.
Add .... Sherry and orange rind, mixing well.
Pour .... over potatoes.
Bake .... at 350 degrees for 20 minutes, basting occasionally.

Diane Brown
Pryor Jr. H. S., Pryor, Oklahoma

Recipes on pages 13, 24 and 62.

ZUCCHINI FRITTERS

1 egg, beaten
1 c. grated zucchini
1/2 c. grated onion
1/4 c. grated cheese
3 tsp. (rounded) flour
1/4 tsp. each pepper, salt,
    baking powder
1/2 c. each oil, margarine

Combine .... all ingredients except oil and margarine in bowl, mixing well.
Let .... stand for 5 minutes.
Drop .... by spoonfuls into mixture of hot oil and margarine in skillet.
Fry .... until brown, turning once.

Mrs. Ed Metzler
Okeene, Oklahoma

ZUCCHINI QUICHE

Zucchini slices
Chopped onions to taste
1/4 lb. Swiss cheese, shredded
1/2 pkg. bacon, crisp-fried, crumbled
1 unbaked 9-in. pie shell
3 eggs, beaten
1 1/2 c. milk
Salt and pepper to taste
Dash of nutmeg

Saute ...... zucchini and onions in skillet until tender.
Layer ...... with cheese and bacon in pie shell.
Beat .... eggs with remaining ingredients in bowl.
Pour .... over filled pie shell.
Bake .... at 425 degrees for 15 minutes.
Reduce ..... temperature to 325 degrees.
Bake .... for 20 minutes longer or until quiche tests done.

Kelly Blair
Assistant City Editor, Enid Daily Eagle
Enid, Oklahoma

PEANUT BUTTER CHANTILLY

1/4 c. peanut butter
1/2 pt. sour cream
1 tbsp. horseradish
1 tsp. salt

Recipe on page 37.

Dash of pepper
1 tbsp. lemon juice

Blend ...... peanut butter and sour cream in bowl.
Fold .... in remaining ingredients.
Serve .... with cooked vegetables.
Yields ...... 1 1/4 cups.

Photograph for this recipe on page 67.

SAVORY WALNUT CRUMBS FOR VEGETABLES

1/2 c. coarsely chopped California
    walnuts
1/4 c. butter, melted
1 c. soft bread crumbs
1/4 tsp. dried herb

Saute ...... walnuts in butter in skillet until lightly toasted.
Add .... bread crumbs and herb tossing to mix.
May .... use as topping for baked tomatoes or cooked vegetables and for stuffed mushrooms.

Photograph for this recipe on page 60.

CHEESE-GRITS CASSEROLE

1 1/2 c. grits
3 eggs, beaten
1 1/2 sticks butter, softened
1 lb. Cheddar cheese, shredded
3 tsp. savory salt
2 tsp. salt
1 tsp. paprika
Tabasco sauce to taste

Cook .... grits in 6 cups boiling water in saucepan for 30 minutes, stirring frequently.
Combine .... remaining ingredients in bowl, mixing well.
Stir .... into grits.
Pour .... into casserole.
Bake .... at 325 degrees for 1 hour. This is excellent served with a roast.
Yields ...... 8-10 servings.

Sue Caldwell Smith
Bartlesville H. S., Bartlesville, Oklahoma

HOMINY CASSEROLE

1 lg. can hominy
1 4-oz. can chopped chiles
1 can Cheddar cheese soup
1/2 tsp. garlic salt

Combine .... all ingredients in buttered casserole, mixing well.
Bake .... at 350 degrees for 30 minutes.
Yields ...... 4-6 servings.

Oaks FHA, Wanda Kimbrell, Advisor
Oaks H. S., Oaks, Oklahoma

EGG GLOB NOODLES

2 eggs, beaten
2 dashes of salt
2 dashes of pepper
1 c. flour
2 tbsp. milk
Hot soup or broth

Combine .... first 4 ingredients in bowl, beating until thick.
Add .... milk and a small amount of additional flour if necessary.
Drop .... by small spoonfuls into soup. Be sure spoon is warm and moistened with soup to prevent sticking.
Cook .... covered, until noodles test done.
Yields ...... 10 servings.

Butch Farrand
Ringwood H. S., Ringwood, Oklahoma

HOMEMADE EGG NOODLES

6 eggs, beaten
1 tsp. salt
1 tsp. pepper
2 to 3 c. flour
Broth

Combine .... first 3 ingredients, beating well.
Add .... flour, 1/2 cup at a time, mixing until stiff.
Divide ...... dough into halves.
Roll .... very thin on floured waxed paper into long strips.
Cut .... as desired.
Place .... waxed paper on cookie sheet.
Chill .... for 2 hours or longer.

Drop .... into boiling broth.
Cook .... for 20 minutes or until tender.

Windi Buck
Wilson H. S., Wilson, Oklahoma

CASE NOODLE CASSEROLE

1 pkg. medium noodles
2 c. yogurt
2 c. cottage cheese
1/4 to 1/2 c. melted butter
3/4 tsp. salt
1/4 tsp. pepper
2 eggs, beaten
1/4 c. chopped onion, sauteed
Onion powder to taste (opt.)
Buttered bread crumbs

Cook .... noodles using package directions until just tender.
Rinse ...... with cold water; drain.
Combine .... with next 8 ingredients in bowl, mixing well.
Pour .... into casserole.
Top .... with crumbs.
Bake .... at 300 degrees for 1 hour.

Kittie Keith
Oklahoma City, Oklahoma

CHINESE-FRIED RICE

2 eggs, slightly beaten
Dash of pepper
1 to 2 tbsp. chopped green onion
4 c. cooked rice
2 tbsp. soy sauce
1/2 tsp. sugar
1 c. chopped cooked pork

Mix .... eggs and pepper.
Pour .... into nonstick skillet.
Cook .... until partially set.
Stir .... in remaining ingredients.
Cook .... until heated through, stirring gently.

Melanie Byrd
Ringwood H. S., Ringwood, Oklahoma

KATRINIA'S HONEY RICE

3 c. cooked rice
1/2 c. seedless raisins

2 1/2 c. milk
1/2 c. honey
2 tbsp. butter
1 tsp. grated lemon rind
1 tbsp. lemon juice

Combine .... first 5 ingredients in saucepan.
Bring .... to a boil.
Simmer ..... for 15 minutes, stirring occasionally.
Stir .... in lemon rind and juice.
Yields ...... 6 servings.

Katrinia Crenshaw
Geary FHA, Geary, Oklahoma

MUSHROOM-RICE CASSEROLE

1 1/2 c. rice
6 tbsp. margarine
1 sm. can mushrooms, drained
2 cans onion soup

Saute ...... rice in margarine in skillet until lightly brown.
Add .... mushrooms.
Saute ...... for 3 minutes.
Stir .... in soup and 1 soup can water.
Pour .... into casserole.
Dot .... with additional margarine.
Bake .... at 350 degrees for 45 minutes to 1 hour.
Yields ...... 8 servings.

Judy Queen, H. E. Tchr.
Braman H. S., Braman, Oklahoma

QUICK AND EASY SPANISH RICE

1/2 tsp. salt
1 1/2 c. minute rice
1 green pepper, chopped
1 onion, chopped
1 lb. hamburger
1 tsp. seasoned salt
1 15-oz. can tomato sauce
1/4 c. picante sauce

Bring .... 1 1/2 cups water and salt to a boil in saucepan.
Stir .... in rice.
Let .... stand, covered, for 5 minutes.
Saute ...... green pepper, onion, hamburger and seasoned salt in skillet until hamburger is brown.

Add .... drained rice with tomato and picante sauces, mixing well.
Cook .... until heated through.
Yields ...... 6 servings.

Dianne Roberts
Pryor Jr. H. S., Pryor, Oklahoma

VEGETABLE-RICE CASSEROLE

1 lg. onion, chopped
2 green peppers, chopped
1 lb. fresh mushrooms, sliced
2 tbsp. margarine
1 can chicken-mushroom soup
2 c. cooked rice
3/4 c. grated cheese

Saute ...... onion, green peppers and mushrooms in margarine in skillet until tender.
Blend ...... in soup.
Combine .... with rice and cheese in casserole.
Garnish ..... with additional cheese.
Bake .... at 350 degrees for 20 minutes.
Yields ...... 8-10 servings.

Jane Frudy
Tahlequah Jr. H. S., Tahlequah, Oklahoma

SAN FRANCISCO TREAT

1 pkg. chicken-flavored Rice-A-Roni
2 6-oz. jars artichoke hearts
1/3 c. mayonnaise
1/4 tsp. curry powder
8 stuffed green olives, thinly sliced
1 c. chopped water chestnuts
2 green onions, chopped

Cook .... Rice-A-Roni using package directions.
Drain ...... artichokes reserving marinade.
Chop .... artichokes and add to rice mixture.
Blend ...... reserved marinade with mayonnaise and curry powder.
Stir .... in remaining ingredients.
Add .... to artichoke mixture, tossing to mix.
Chill .... for 3 hours or longer.
Yields ...... 8 servings.

Betty Lynn True
State Dept. of Vo-Tech Ed., Stillwater, Oklahoma

Breads

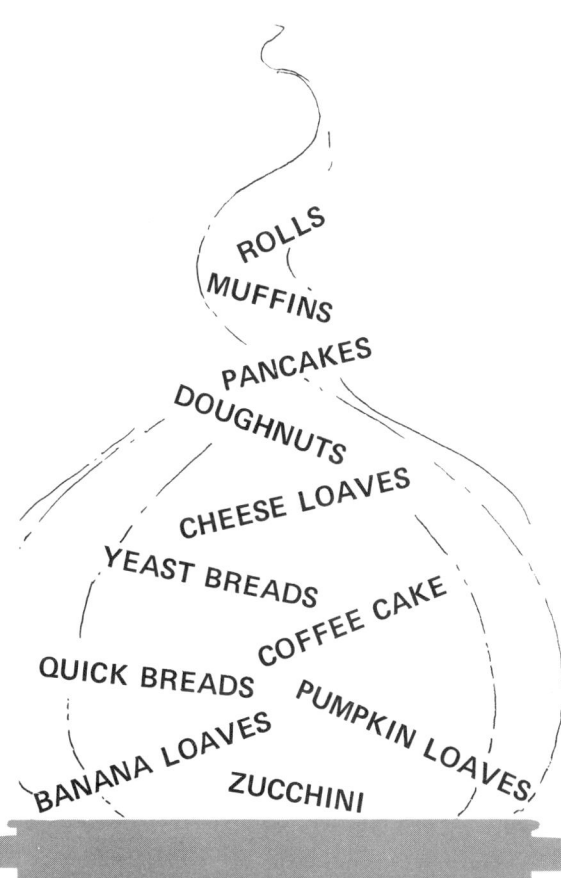

ROLLS
MUFFINS
PANCAKES
DOUGHNUTS
CHEESE LOAVES
YEAST BREADS
COFFEE CAKE
QUICK BREADS
PUMPKIN LOAVES
BANANA LOAVES
ZUCCHINI

CHEESE TWIST BISCUITS

1 1/2 c. flour
1/2 c. cornmeal
1 tbsp. baking powder
1 tsp. salt
1/4 c. shortening
1/2 c. milk
Butter, melted
1/4 c. Parmesan cheese

Sift . . . . dry ingredients together in bowl.
Cut . . . . in shortening until crumbly.
Add . . . . milk gradually, mixing lightly.
Knead . . . . . . on floured surface for several seconds.
Roll . . . . out into 10 x 12-inch rectangle.
Brush . . . . . . with butter.
Sprinkle . . . . with cheese.
Fold . . . . in half.
Cut . . . . into 1/2-inch wide strips.
Twist . . . . . . strips, pinching ends together to seal.
Place . . . . on baking sheet.
Bake . . . . at 400 degrees for 10 to 12 minutes.
Yields . . . . . . 2 dozen.

Jeanette Brainard
Oklahoma Wheat Growers' Exec. Sec.
Enid, Oklahoma

CINNAMON-SUGAR BOWKNOTS

1 can Hungry Jack Flaky biscuits
1/2 stick butter, melted
1/2 c. sugar
1/2 tsp. cinnamon
1/4 tsp. nutmeg
4 tbsp. honey

Separate . . . . each biscuit into 2 thin biscuits.
Pull . . . . each into long strip; pinch in center and twist.
Dip . . . . 1 side in butter then in mixture of sugar, cinnamon and nutmeg.
Place . . . . sugared side up on baking sheet.
Bake . . . . at 425 degrees for 8 to 10 minutes or until brown.
Mix . . . . remaining butter with honey.
Brush . . . . . . over bowknots.

Kim Remington
Nowata H. S., Nowata, Oklahoma

CRUNCHY BREAKFAST BARS

2 c. oats
2/3 c. shredded coconut
1/2 c. chopped nuts
1/3 c. wheat germ
1/3 c. packed brown sugar
1/4 c. soft margarine
2 tbsp. honey

Combine . . . . first 4 ingredients in bowl, mixing well.
Blend . . . . . . remaining ingredients in small bowl.
Add . . . . to oatmeal mixture, mixing well.
Press . . . . into greased 9 x 13-inch baking dish.
Bake . . . . at 325 degrees for 20 minutes.
Cut . . . . into bars when cool.

Bobbie Rogers
Duncan H. S., Duncan, Oklahoma

DIET BREAKFAST BARS

1/2 c. butter
3 c. miniature marshmallows
1/2 c. peanut butter
1/2 c. instant nonfat dry milk
1/4 c. orange-flavored breakfast drink
1 c. raisins
4 c. Cheerios

Melt . . . . butter and marshmallows over low heat in large saucepan, stirring constantly.
Blend . . . . . . in peanut butter, dry milk and breakfast drink.
Stir . . . . in raisins and Cheerios until evenly coated.
Press . . . . into buttered 9 x 9-inch pan.
Cut . . . . into bars when cool.
Yields . . . . . . 12 bars/about 145 calories each.

Robin Robison
Moore West Mid-H. S., Oklahoma City, Oklahoma

CRUNCHY APRICOT COFFEE CAKE

2 c. crisp rice cereal,
crushed
1/8 tsp. ground ginger
1/2 c. butter, softened
Sugar

2 tsp. baking powder
1 1/2 c. flour
1/2 tsp. salt
1 egg
1/2 c. apricot syrup
1 17-oz. can apricot halves,
   drained, chopped

Mix . . . . cereal, ginger, 1/4 cup butter and 3 tablespoons sugar in bowl until crumbly; set aside.
Mix . . . . next 3 dry ingredients together; set aside.
Beat . . . . 1/4 cup butter and 3/4 cup sugar in bowl until well blended.
Add . . . . egg, beating well.
Stir . . . . in apricot syrup.
Blend . . . . . . in flour mixture.
Spread . . . . . in greased 8-inch square baking pan.
Spoon . . . . . . 3/4 of the apricots over dough.
Sprinkle . . . . with cereal mixture.
Top . . . . with remaining apricots.
Bake . . . . at 350 degrees for 45 minutes.
Yields . . . . . . 9 servings.

Kim Hodges
Okeene Public Schools, Okeene, Oklahoma

BUBBLE BREAD

24 frozen dinner rolls
1 c. packed brown sugar
1 sm. box butterscotch pudding mix
1/4 c. sugar
1 tbsp. cinnamon
1/2 c. chopped nuts
1 stick butter, melted

Arrange . . . . . frozen rolls in greased tube pan.
Combine . . . . brown sugar and pudding mix in bowl.
Sprinkle . . . . over rolls.
Mix . . . . sugar and cinnamon in bowl.
Sprinkle . . . . . on top.
Top . . . . with nuts.
Drizzle . . . . . with butter.
Let . . . . rise, covered, overnight.
Bake . . . . at 350 degrees for 30 minutes.
Cool . . . . for 15 minutes.
Turn . . . . out on serving plate.
Do . . . . not use instant pudding.

Shirley Teske
State Dept. of Vo-Tech Ed., Stillwater, Oklahoma

CRANBERRY-NUT COFFEE CAKE

2 c. Bisquick
2 tbsp. sugar
1 egg
Milk
1/4 c. packed brown sugar
1/2 c. chopped walnuts
1/4 tsp. cinnamon
1 8-oz. can cranberry sauce
1 c. confectioners' sugar
1 tsp. vanilla extract

Combine . . . . first 3 ingredients and 2/3 cup milk in bowl.
Beat . . . . vigorously for 1/2 minute.
Spread . . . . . in greased 9 x 13-inch baking dish.
Mix . . . . brown sugar, walnuts and cinnamon in bowl.
Sprinkle . . . . over batter.
Spoon . . . . . . cranberry sauce over top.
Bake . . . . at 400 degrees for 20 to 25 minutes.
Combine . . . . confectioners' sugar, vanilla and enough milk to make of icing consistency in bowl.
Spread . . . . . over warm cake.

Julie Thorn
Ryan H. S., Ryan, Oklahoma

FAVORITE COFFEE CAKE

1/4 c. sugar
2 1/2 tsp. baking powder
3/4 tsp. salt
1/4 c. shortening
3/4 c. milk
1 egg
Flour
1/3 c. packed brown sugar
1/2 tsp. cinnamon
3 tbsp. butter

Combine . . . . first 6 ingredients and 1/2 cup flour in bowl.
Beat . . . . vigorously for 1/2 minute.
Spread . . . . . in greased 9-inch layer cake pan.
Mix . . . . remaining ingredients with enough flour to make crumbly topping.
Sprinkle . . . . over batter.
Bake . . . . at 375 degrees for 25 to 30 minutes or until cake tests done.

Rennee Williams
Moore West Mid-H. S., Moore, Oklahoma

CREAM CHEESE COFFEE CAKE

2 1/2 c. flour
1 tsp. salt
1 c. butter
Sugar
5 egg yolks
2 pkg. dry yeast
1   8-oz. packages cream cheese,
      softened
1 egg white, slightly beaten
1/2 c. finely chopped nuts

Combine .... flour, salt, butter, 1 tablespoon sugar and 4 egg yolks in bowl.
Mix .... with pastry blender.
Dissolve .... yeast in 1/4 cup warm water for 3 to 5 minutes; stir.
Add .... to dough, mixing well.
Chill .... for 2 hours.
Mix .... cream cheese, 1 cup sugar and remaining egg yolk in bowl, beating until smooth.
Roll .... out half the chilled dough on floured surface to fit 10 x 15-inch baking pan.
Spread ..... with cream cheese mixture.
Roll .... out remaining dough to fit over top.
Pinch ...... edges to seal.
Brush ...... with egg white.
Sprinkle .... with nuts.
Let .... rise for 1 hour.
Bake .... at 350 degrees for 30 minutes.

Mrs. Weldon Geis
Okeene, Oklahoma

MONKEY BREAD

4 cans buttermilk biscuits
3 tsp. cinnamon
1 3/4 c. sugar
3/4 c. margarine
1/4 c. packed brown sugar
1/4 c. sweetened condensed milk

Cut .... each biscuit into fourths.
Combine .... 1 1/2 teaspoons cinnamon and 3/4 cup sugar in bag.
Add .... biscuits, shaking to coat.
Arrange ..... biscuits in greased bundt pan.
Mix .... margarine, brown sugar, condensed milk, 1 cup sugar and 1 1/2 teaspoons cinnamon in saucepan.

Bring .... to a boil.
Pour .... over biscuits.
Bake .... at 350 degrees for 30 minutes.

Stephany Sanders
Moore West Mid-H. S., Oklahoma City, Oklahoma

PEACH KUCHEN

1 3/4 c. flour
1/2 tsp. salt
1 c. sugar
1/2 c. butter
8 sm. ripe peaches, peeled, sliced
1 tsp. cinnamon
2 egg yolks, beaten
1 c. heavy cream, sour cream or yogurt

Combine .... flour, salt and 1/4 cup sugar in bowl.
Cut .... in butter until crumbly.
Press .... into 9 x 9-inch baking dish.
Arrange ..... peaches over crust.
Sprinkle .... with 3/4 cup sugar and cinnamon.
Bake .... at 400 degrees for 15 minutes.
Mix .... egg yolks and cream in bowl.
Pour .... over peaches.
Bake .... for 30 minutes longer.

Saundra Purvine Butorovich
Seiling, Oklahoma

PLUCKET BREAD

2 sticks margarine, melted
2 sm. packages butterscotch pudding mix
1 c. packed brown sugar
2 pkg. frozen dinner rolls,
    sliced in half

Combine .... first 3 ingredients in bowl, mixing well.
Alternate ... layers of rolls and pudding mixture in greased tube pan.
Let .... rise, covered, until doubled in bulk.
Bake .... at 375 degrees for 15 to 20 minutes.
Do .... not use instant pudding.

Cathy Lindsey
Ringwood H. S., Ringwood, Oklahoma

STACKED MAPLE-WALNUT RINGS

1/3 c. finely chopped walnuts
2 tbsp. brown sugar
2 tbsp. sugar
1 tsp. cinnamon
1   10-oz. package refrigerator buttermilk
     biscuits
1/4 c. maple syrup
Cherry-Caramel Ring

Combine . . . . first 4 ingredients in small bowl, mixing well; set aside.
Coat . . . . biscuits with maple syrup.
Dip . . . . into walnut mixture.
Arrange . . . . . overlapping in greased 8-inch glass tube pan.
Microwave . . on Medium for 4 minutes.
Rotate . . . . . dish 180 degrees.
Microwave . . on Medium for 2 to 4 minutes longer or until biscuits test done.
Let . . . . stand for 5 minutes.
Invert . . . . . . onto serving plate.
Sprinkle . . . . with remaining walnut mixture.
Top . . . . with Cherry-Caramel Ring.

Cherry-Caramel Ring

1/4 c. butter
1/2 c. packed brown sugar
2 tbsp. light corn syrup
1/2 c. pecan halves
1/4 c. maraschino cherries, quartered
1   10-oz. package refrigerator
     buttermilk biscuits
1 c. confectioners' sugar
1 to 2 tbsp. milk

Microwave . . butter on High in 8-inch glass tube pan for 1/2 to 1 minute.
Stir . . . . in brown sugar and corn syrup with fork.
Arrange . . . . . pecans and cherries over sugar mixture.
Place . . . . biscuits over top, overlapping to fit.
Microwave . . on Medium for 3 minutes.
Rotate . . . . . dish 180 degrees.
Microwave . . on Medium for 3 to 5 minutes longer or until biscuits test done.
Invert . . . . . . on top of maple-walnut layer.
Combine . . . . remaining ingredients in bowl, mixing well.
Drizzle . . . . . glaze over top.

Photograph for this recipe on page 103.

APPLESAUCE DOUGHNUTS

2 c. flour
1/2 c. sugar
2 tsp. baking powder
1 tsp. cinnamon
1/2 tsp. salt
1 egg
1/2 c. applesauce
1/2 c. milk
1 1/2 tbsp. melted shortening
Oil for deep frying

Sift . . . . dry ingredients together into bowl.
Beat . . . . egg, applesauce and milk together in small bowl.
Stir . . . . into dry ingredients, mixing well.
Mix . . . . in shortening.
Drop . . . . by teaspoonfuls into 375-degree deep fat.
Fry . . . . until brown.
Dip . . . . in confectioners' sugar glaze and cool on rack.
Yields . . . . . . 2 dozen.

Barbara Bedwell
Okeene Public Schools, Okeene, Oklahoma

CAKE DOUGHNUTS

4 c. sifted flour
4 tsp. baking powder
1 tsp. salt
1 c. sugar
2 tbsp. margarine
2 eggs, well beaten
1 c. milk
Oil for deep frying

Sift . . . . first 3 ingredients together 3 times.
Cream . . . . . . sugar and margarine in bowl.
Add . . . . eggs, milk and flour mixture, mixing well.
Roll . . . . 1/2 inch thick on floured surface.
Cut . . . . with doughnut cutter and let stand for 5 minutes.
Fry . . . . in hot deep fat until brown.
Drain . . . . . . on paper towels.
Frost . . . . or sugar as desired.

Dawn Danks
Reydon H. S., Reydon, Oklahoma

OVERNIGHT DOUGHNUTS

1 qt. milk, scalded
1 c. sugar
1 c. shortening
1 c. mashed potatoes
1 pkg. yeast
1 tsp. each soda, baking powder
1 tbsp. salt
12 c. flour
Oil for deep frying

Combine .... first 4 ingredients in large bowl, mixing well.
Stir .... yeast, soda, baking powder, salt and 4 cups flour into cooled milk mixture.
Let .... rise until light.
Mix .... in remaining 8 cups flour.
Chill .... overnight or longer.
Roll .... on floured surface, cutting with doughnut cutter.
Let .... rise for 30 to 40 minutes or until very light.
Fry .... in hot deep fat until brown.
Note .... dough may also be used for dinner rolls.
Yields ...... 4 dozen.

Holly Herring
Thomas H. S., Thomas, Oklahoma

RAISED DOUGHNUTS

1 pkg. dry yeast
3/4 c. milk, scalded
1/4 c. shortening
1/4 c. sugar
1 tsp. salt
3 1/2 to 3 3/4 c. sifted flour
1 egg
Oil for deep frying

Soften ...... yeast in 1/4 cup warm water.
Combine .... milk, shortening, sugar and salt in bowl, mixing well.
Beat .... 1 cup flour into lukewarm milk mixture.
Add .... yeast, egg and enough flour to make soft dough, beating well.
Knead ...... on floured surface for 8 minutes or until smooth and elastic.
Place .... in greased bowl, turning to coat surface.

Let .... rise for 1 1/4 hours or until doubled in bulk.
Punch ...... dough down.
Let .... rise for 55 minutes or until doubled in bulk.
Roll .... 1/3 inch thick on floured surface.
Cut .... with doughnut cutter.
Let .... rise for 30 to 40 minutes or until very light.
Fry .... in hot deep oil until brown.
Drain ...... on paper towels.

Carol Droke
Okeene H. S., Okeene, Oklahoma

BECKY'S FRY BREAD

1 c. self-rising flour
1/4 c. buttermilk
Oil for frying
Confectioners' sugar

Combine .... flour and buttermilk in bowl, mixing well with fork.
Drop .... by spoonfuls into 1-inch deep hot oil in skillet.
Fry .... until brown, turning once.
Sprinkle .... with confectioners' sugar.
Yields ...... 6-8 servings.

Becky Sloan
Moore West Mid-H. S., Oklahoma City, Oklahoma

NAVAJO TACO FRY BREAD

3 c. flour
1 tbsp. baking powder
1 tsp. salt
Oil for deep frying

Combine .... first three ingredients with 1 cup warm water in bowl, mixing well.
Let .... stand for 10 minutes.
Knead ...... 10 times on floured surface.
Divide ...... dough into 1/2-cup portions.
Pat .... into 6 to 8-inch circles.
Make .... small hole in center of each circle.
Fry .... 1 at a time in 375-degree oil until brown.
Yields ...... 6-8 servings.

Jerry Burkey
Cyril H. S., Cyril, Oklahoma

NORWEGIAN LEFSE

1 qt. cold mashed potatoes
1 tsp. salt
1/4 c. shortening
1/4 c. heavy cream
2 1/2 c. flour

Combine . . . . all ingredients in bowl, mixing well.
Divide . . . . . . into 36 to 48 portions.
Roll . . . . each on very lightly floured surface to 10-inch diameter circle.
Cook . . . . on hot griddle over medium-high heat for 45 seconds or until pancake starts to bubble; turn.
Cook . . . . . . for 45 seconds longer.
Serve . . . . . . rolled up with butter and sugar.
Yields . . . . . . 3-4 dozen.

Kandy Flikeid
Drummond School, Drummond, Oklahoma

DIET APPLE PANCAKE

1 slice bread, crumbled
1 egg
1/3 c. instant nonfat milk
Artificial sweetener equal to
  2 tsp. sugar
Cinnamon to taste
1 apple, grated

Combine . . . . all ingredients except apple with 1 teaspoon water in bowl, mixing well.
Stir . . . . in apple.
Spoon . . . . . . onto hot griddle.
Cook . . . . until brown, turning once.
Serve . . . . . . with diet margarine and diet syrup.
Yields . . . . . . 10 pancakes.

Terri Wattie
Moore West H. S., Oklahoma City, Oklahoma

ROBERTA'S PANCAKES

2 c. sifted flour
3 tsp. baking powder
1 tsp. salt
2 eggs, beaten
2 c. milk
1/4 c. melted shortening

Combine . . . . dry ingredients in bowl, mixing well.
Add . . . . remaining ingredients, mixing well.
Pour . . . . onto hot greased griddle.
Cook . . . . until bubbly and edges are brown.
Turn . . . . and cook until brown.
Yields . . . . . . 16 pancakes.

Roberta Bondurant
Springer H. S., Springer, Oklahoma

SOUTHERN PEANUT PANCAKES

1 3/4 c. milk
1 egg
3 tbsp. Planters oil
1 1/2 c. flour
2 tbsp. sugar
2 tsp. baking powder
1/2 tsp. salt
1 1/4 c. whole kernel corn
1/4 c. chopped Planters Cocktail
peanuts

Mix . . . . first 3 ingredients in bowl.
Add . . . . flour, sugar, baking powder and salt.
Beat . . . . with rotary beater until smooth.
Stir . . . . in corn and peanuts.
Pour . . . . 3 tablespoons batter onto hot greased griddle.
Bake . . . . until brown on both sides, turning once.
Yields . . . . . . 20 pancakes.

Photograph for this recipe below.

RAISIN BREAKFAST PUFFS

3 tbsp. packed brown sugar
1/2 tsp. cinnamon
3/4 c. dark seedless raisins
2 c. biscuit mix
2/3 c. milk
2 tbsp. shortening, melted

Mix . . . . brown sugar and cinnamon.
Combine . . . . raisins and biscuit mix in bowl.
Blend . . . . . . in milk and shortening.
Drop . . . . by tablespoonfuls into cinnamon sugar.
Place . . . . sugared side up on greased baking sheet.
Bake . . . . at 400 degrees for 15 minutes.
Yields . . . . . . 12 puffs.

Photograph for this recipe above.

YUMMY FRIED TOAST

Bread, sliced, buttered both sides
Cinnamon-sugar
Maple syrup

Brown . . . . . . 1 side of bread in skillet over medium heat.
Turn . . . . over, sprinkling with cinnamon-sugar and perforating several times with fork.
Pour . . . . syrup over bread.
Cook . . . . until brown on both sides.

Peggy Hendricks
Chouteau School, Chouteau, Oklahoma

CORN BREAD RING

1 c. yellow cornmeal
1 c. flour

2 tbsp. sugar
4 tsp. baking powder
1/2 tsp. salt
1 egg
1 c. milk
1/2 c. oil
1/2 c. finely crushed French-fried
   onions
1 tbsp. Parmesan cheese

Combine .... first 5 ingredients in mixing bowl.
Add .... egg, milk and oil.
Beat .... for 1 minute or until smooth.
Coat .... greased 8-inch glass tube pan with onion crumbs and cheese, reserving excess crumbs.
Pour .... batter into prepared pan.
Sprinkle .... with reserved crumbs.
Microwave .. on Low for 6 minutes.
Turn .... dish 180 degrees.
Microwave .. on High for 3 to 5 minutes or until bread tests done.
Invert ...... on wire rack to cool.

Photograph for this recipe on page 103.

JALAPENO CORN BREAD

1 1/4 c. cornmeal
1/2 c. flour
1 tsp. soda
1 tsp. sugar
2 tsp. baking powder
1/2 tsp. each basil, salt, allspice
1/4 tsp. each pepper, chili powder,
   coriander
1 jalapeno pepper, chopped
1 lg. green pepper, chopped
1 med. onion, chopped
1/2 stick margarine, melted
1 c. sour cream
3 eggs, beaten
1 c. milk
1 lb. sausage, cooked
1 c. grated Cheddar cheese

Sift .... dry ingredients into large bowl.
Add .... peppers, onion, margarine, sour cream, eggs and milk, mixing well.

Pour .... half the batter into greased 9 x 12-inch baking pan.
Spread .... sausage and cheese over top.
Spoon ...... remaining batter over all.
Bake .... at 350 degrees for 45 to 50 minutes or until bread tests done.
Let .... stand for 10 minutes before cutting.

Katie Marcoux
Okeene, Oklahoma

TENNESSEE MOUNTAIN CORN BREAD

1 tbsp. (heaping) shortening
8 tbsp. (heaping) self-rising
   cornmeal
Buttermilk

Cut .... shortening into cornmeal in bowl until crumbly.
Add .... enough buttermilk to make thick batter, mixing well.
Spread .... in hot greased iron skillet.
Bake .... at 475 degrees until golden brown.
Yields ...... 4-6 servings.

Dr. Hope Ross
Enid, Oklahoma

GRAHAM CRACKERS

4 c. whole wheat flour
1 c. butter
2 tsp. baking powder
1/2 c. honey
1 egg, beaten

Combine .... all ingredients in bowl, mixing well.
Roll .... 1/4 inch thick on floured surface.
Cut .... into crackers.
Place .... on baking sheet.
Bake .... at 350 degrees for 15 to 20 minutes or until lightly browned.
Yields ...... 2 dozen.

Janice Bates
Wilson H. S., Wilson, Oklahoma

HUSH PUPPIES

2 1/4 c. yellow cornmeal
1 tsp. salt
2 tbsp. chopped onions
3/4 tsp. soda
1 1/2 c. buttermilk
Oil for deep frying

Combine .... first 5 ingredients in bowl, mixing well.
Drop .... by spoonfuls into 375-degree deep fat.
Fry .... for 2 minutes or until brown.
Yields ...... 2 dozen.

Barbara Padilla
Guymon H. S., Guymon, Oklahoma

GLORIA'S HUSH PUPPIES

1/3 c. flour
3 tsp. baking powder
1 tsp. salt
1 3/4 c. cornmeal
1/4 c. finely chopped onion (opt.)
1 egg, slightly beaten
1 c. buttermilk
Oil for deep frying

Sift .... first 3 ingredients together into bowl.
Stir .... in cornmeal and onion.
Add .... egg and buttermilk, mixing well.
Drop .... by spoonfuls into 350-degree deep fat.
Fry .... until golden brown, turning once.
Drain ...... on paper towels.
Yields ...... 18-24 servings.

Gloria Jean Entz
Lookeba-Sickles School, Lookeba, Oklahoma

BEER MUFFINS

4 1/2 c. biscuit mix
3/4 c. sugar
1 12-oz. can beer

Combine .... all ingredients in bowl, mixing well. Batter will be slightly lumpy.
Spoon ...... into 12 greased and floured muffin cups.

Bake .... at 375 degrees for 20 to 30 minutes or until brown.
Yields ...... 24-36 muffins.

Teresa Helton
Waynoka Public H. S., Waynoka, Oklahoma

BLUEBERRY MUFFINS

1 3/4 c. flour
2 1/2 tsp. baking powder
3/4 tsp. salt
4 tbsp. sugar
1 egg, well beaten
1/2 c. milk
1/3 c. oil
1 can whole blueberries

Sift .... first 3 ingredients with 2 tablespoons sugar into bowl.
Add .... combined egg, milk and oil, mixing well.
Drain ...... 3/4 cup liquid from blueberries; discard.
Mix .... 2 tablespoons sugar with blueberries and remaining liquid.
Stir .... into batter.
Spoon ...... into 12 greased muffin cups.
Bake .... at 400 degrees for 20 to 25 minutes.
Yields ...... 12 muffins.

Teri Douglas
Lindsay H. S., Lindsay, Oklahoma

BLUEBERRY-CREAM CHEESE MUFFINS

2 c. whole wheat flour
1 c. sugar
1 1/2 tsp. baking powder
1 tsp. salt
1/2 tsp. soda
3/4 c. orange juice
2 tbsp. oil
1 egg
1 to 2 c. fresh blueberries
1 3-oz. package cream cheese, softened

Combine .... first 5 ingredients in bowl, mixing well.
Beat .... orange juice, oil and egg together.

Stir . . . . into flour mixture until just moistened.
Fold . . . . in blueberries.
Fill . . . . 16 greased muffin cups 1/2 full.
Cut . . . . cream cheese into 16 pieces, placing 1 piece in each cup.
Top . . . . with remaining batter.
Bake . . . . at 400 degrees for 15 to 20 minutes.
Yields . . . . . . 16 muffins.

Jayne Detten
Wellston H. S., Wellston, Oklahoma

BLUEBERRY-OATMEAL MUFFINS

3 c. biscuit mix
1/2 c. packed dark brown sugar
3/4 c. quick-cooking oatmeal
1 tsp. cinnamon
2 eggs, well beaten
1 1/2 c. milk
1/4 c. melted butter
2 c. fresh or dry-pack frozen
    blueberries, rinsed, drained

Combine . . . . first 4 ingredients in bowl.
Mix . . . . eggs, milk and butter in small bowl, mixing well.
Stir . . . . into dry ingredients until just moistened.
Fold . . . . in blueberries.
Fill . . . . greased muffin cups 2/3 full.
Bake . . . . at 400 degrees for 15 to 20 minutes or until browned.
Yields . . . . . . 18 muffins.

Photograph for this recipe on page 6.

MAKE-AHEAD BRAN MUFFIN BATTER

2 c. 100% bran cereal
1 c. shortening
2 c. sugar
4 eggs, well beaten
1 qt. buttermilk
4 c. Bran Buds
5 c. sifted flour
5 tsp. soda
2 tsp. salt

Pour . . . . 2 cups boiling water over cereal in bowl; set aside.

Cream . . . . . . shortening and sugar in 6-quart bowl until light.
Beat . . . . in eggs, buttermilk, Bran Buds and soaked cereal.
Mix . . . . in sifted dry ingredients.
Store . . . . tightly covered, in refrigerator for up to 6 weeks.
Fill . . . . muffin cups 2/3 full.
Bake . . . . at 400 degrees for 20 minutes.
Yields . . . . . . 5 dozen.

Karen Ensminger
Okeene Public School, Okeene, Oklahoma

FRENCH BREAKFAST MUFFINS

1/3 c. shortening
1 c. sugar
1 egg
1 1/2 c. flour
1 1/2 tsp. baking powder
1/2 tsp. salt
1/2 tsp. nutmeg
1/2 c. milk
1/2 c. butter, melted
1 tsp. cinnamon

Combine . . . . shortening, 1/2 cup sugar and egg in bowl, mixing well.
Add . . . . next 4 ingredients alternately with milk, mixing well after each addition.
Fill . . . . 15 greased muffin cups 2/3 full.
Bake . . . . at 350 degrees for 20 to 25 minutes or until brown.
Roll . . . . muffins in butter, then in mixture of cinnamon and 1/2 cup sugar.
Yields . . . . . . 15 muffins.

Lynnette Ingersoll
Locust Grove H. S., Locust Grove, Oklahoma

OATMEAL MUFFINS

1 c. quick-cooking oats
1 c. milk
1 c. sifted flour
1/3 c. sugar
3 tsp. baking powder
1/2 tsp. salt
1 egg, well beaten
1/4 c. oil

Combine .... oats and milk in bowl.
Let .... stand for 15 minutes.
Combine .... sifted dry ingredients, egg and oil with oats mixture, mixing well.
Fill .... greased muffin cups 2/3 full.
Bake .... at 425 degrees for 20 to 25 minutes.
Yields ...... 12 muffins.

Leslie Gregg
Moore West H. S., Oklahoma City, Oklahoma

PEANUT-BACON MUFFINS

2 tbsp. soft Fleischmann's margarine
1 c. milk
1 egg, beaten
1/2 c. chopped Planters Cocktail Peanuts
1/4 c. crumbled crisp-cooked bacon
1 3/4 c. flour
1/4 c. packed light brown sugar
1 tbsp. baking powder

Stir .... margarine and milk into egg.
Add .... peanuts and bacon.
Sift .... in dry ingredients.
Mix .... for 15 strokes or until just moistened.
Fill .... greased muffin cups 2/3 full.
Bake .... at 400 degrees for 25 minutes or until golden brown.
Yields ...... 10 muffins.

Photograph for this recipe on page 81.

POPPY SEED MUFFINS

1 1/2 c. biscuit mix
1/2 c. sugar
1 tbsp. poppy seed
3/4 c. raisins, chopped

1 egg, beaten
3/4 c. sour cream
1 tsp. vanilla extract

Mix .... first 3 ingredients in bowl.
Make .... a well in center of mixture.
Add .... remaining ingredients, stirring until just moistened.
Fill .... greased muffin cups 1/2 full.
Bake .... at 400 degrees for 20 minutes.
Yields ...... 12 muffins.

Betty Lowrance
Paden H. S., Paden, Oklahoma

BRAN-NUT MUFFINS

2 c. flour
1 c. sugar
5 tsp. baking powder
1 1/2 tsp. salt
2 c. whole bran cereal
1 c. chopped nuts
2 eggs, beaten
1 1/2 c. milk
1/2 c. oil
1/4 c. crushed bran cereal

Combine .... first 6 ingredients in large mixing bowl.
Mix .... eggs, milk and oil in small bowl.
Stir .... into dry mixture until just mixed.
Fill .... paper-lined plastic muffin cups 1/2 full.
Sprinkle .... with crushed cereal.
Microwave .. 6 muffins at a time on Medium for 3 1/2 to 5 1/2 minutes or until muffins test done, rotating muffin pan after several minutes.

Photograph for this recipe on page 103.

FRESH APPLE BREAD

1 c. oil
1 c. sugar
3 eggs, beaten
1 c. pecans
1 tbsp. cinnamon
1 tsp. soda
1 tsp. salt
3 c. flour
4 c. coarsely chopped apples

2 c. raisins (opt.)
3 tsp. vanilla extract
1 stick margarine, softened
1 6-oz. package cream cheese,
    softened
1 lb. confectioners' sugar

Combine .... first 10 ingredients with 2 teaspoons vanilla, mixing well. Bat-
ter will be very thick.
Pour .... into greased loaf pan.
Bake .... at 300 degrees for 35 to 40 minutes or until loaf tests done.
Combine .... remaining ingredients with 1 teaspoon vanilla in bowl, blending
until smooth.
Spread ..... over loaf.

Wendy Agnew
Skiatook H. S., Skiatook, Oklahoma

DONNA'S APPLE BREAD

1 1/4 c. oil
2 c. sugar
2 eggs
1 tsp. vanilla extract
3 c. flour
1 tsp. salt
1 1/2 tsp. soda
3 c. shredded apples
1 c. nuts

Combine .... first 4 ingredients in bowl, beat-
ing well.
Mix .... in flour, salt and soda.
Stir .... in apples and nuts.
Pour .... into 2 greased loaf pans.
Bake .... at 350 degrees for 45 minutes or
until loaf tests done.

Donna Holub
Ringwood H. S., Ringwood, Oklahoma

FRUIT AND NUTTY APRICOT LOAF

1 c. finely chopped dried California
    apricots
2 c. flour
1 c. sugar
2 tsp. baking powder
1 tsp. salt
1/4 tsp. soda
2 tbsp. butter

1 egg, beaten
1/2 c. orange juice
1/2 c. chopped walnuts
1/2 c. confectioners' sugar
2 tbsp. milk

Soak .... apricots in 1 cup warm water in
bowl for 15 minutes.
Drain ...... reserving 1/4 cup liquid.
Combine .... next 5 dry ingredients in large
bowl.
Cut .... in butter until crumbly.
Mix .... egg, reserved apricot liquid and
orange juice in bowl.
Add .... to flour mixture with apricots
and walnuts.
Stir .... until just moistened.
Spoon ...... into greased 5 x 9-inch loaf pan.
Bake .... at 350 degrees for 55 minutes or
until bread tests done.
Cool .... for 10 minutes before removing
from pan.
Let .... stand on wire rack until cool.
Combine .... remaining ingredients in bowl,
mixing well.
Spread ..... over top of loaf.

Photograph for this recipe on page 74.

TAMIE'S BANANA-PECAN BREAD

1/2 c. shortening
1 c. sugar
2 eggs
2 c. flour
1 tsp. soda
1 tsp. salt
2 or 3 bananas, mashed
5 tbsp. buttermilk
1 tsp. vanilla extract
1 c. chopped pecans

Cream ...... shortening and sugar in bowl.
Add .... eggs, 1 at a time, beating well
after each addition.
Add .... sifted dry ingredients, mixing
well.
Mix .... in remaining ingredients.
Pour .... into greased loaf pan.
Bake .... at 300 degrees for 60 to 65 min-
utes or until loaf tests done.

Tamie McCabe
Washita Heights School, Corn, Oklahoma

DELICIOUS BANANA-NUT LOAF

1 c. sugar
2 tbsp. shortening
1 egg
1 c. milk
1 c. mashed bananas
3 c. sifted flour
3 1/2 tsp. baking powder
1 tsp. salt
3/4 c. chopped nuts

Blend . . . . . . first 3 ingredients in bowl.
Stir . . . . in milk and bananas.
Add . . . . sifted dry ingredients, mixing well.
Stir . . . . in nuts.
Pour . . . . into greased loaf pan.
Let . . . . stand for 20 minutes.
Bake . . . . at 350 degrees for 1 hour and 10 minutes or until loaf tests done.

Daviell Baustert
Union City H. S., Union City, Oklahoma

JULIE'S BANANA-NUT BREAD

1/2 c. butter, softened
1 c. sugar
2 eggs
3 or 4 bananas, mashed
2 c. flour
1 tsp. soda
1/4 tsp. salt
1 c. nuts

Cream . . . . . . butter and sugar in bowl.
Add . . . . eggs, beating well.
Mix . . . . in bananas and sifted dry ingredients, blending well.
Stir . . . . in nuts.
Pour . . . . into greased loaf pan.
Bake . . . . at 325 degrees for 1 hour or until loaf tests done.

Julie O'Hair
Medford H. S., Medford, Oklahoma

STACY'S BANANA-NUT BREAD

3/4 c. margarine, softened
1 1/2 c. sugar
4 bananas, mashed
2 eggs, well beaten
1 tsp. vanilla extract
2 c. sifted flour

1 tsp. soda
3/4 tsp. salt
1/2 c. buttermilk
3/4 c. pecans

Cream . . . . . . margarine and sugar in bowl.
Stir . . . . in bananas, eggs and vanilla.
Sift . . . . flour, soda and salt together.
Add . . . . alternately with buttermilk to banana mixture, beating well after each addition.
Stir . . . . in pecans.
Pour . . . . into greased and floured loaf pan.
Bake . . . . at 325 degrees for 1 1/4 hours or until loaf tests done.

Stacy Eichelberger
Hydro H. S., Hydro, Oklahoma

BRAN-BANANA BREAD

2 c. flour
1 tsp. soda
1 tsp. baking powder
1/2 tsp. salt
1 1/2 c. mashed bananas
2 1/2 c. 40% bran flakes
1/2 c. margarine, softened
3/4 c. sugar
2 eggs
1/2 c. coarsely chopped nuts

Combine . . . . first 4 ingredients, mixing well.
Stir . . . . bananas and bran flakes together in bowl.
Let . . . . stand for 2 minutes.
Beat . . . . margarine and sugar in large bowl until fluffy.
Add . . . . eggs and banana mixture, beating well.
Stir . . . . in flour mixture and nuts.
Spread . . . . . in greased 5 x 9-inch loaf pan.
Bake . . . . at 350 degrees for 1 hour or until loaf tests done.
Cool . . . . for 10 minutes before removing from pan.

Tracy Lee Collins
Nowata H. S., Nowata, Oklahoma

CARROT BREAD

1 c. sugar
3/4 c. oil

2 eggs
1 tsp. vanilla extract
1 1/2 c. flour
1 tsp. cinnamon
1/4 tsp. salt
1 tsp. soda
1 c. finely grated carrots
1/2 c. chopped nuts

Combine .... first 4 ingredients in bowl, mixing well.
Add .... dry ingredients, mixing well.
Stir .... in carrots and nuts.
Pour .... into 2 small greased and floured loaf pans.
Bake .... at 325 degrees for about 1 hour and 30 minutes or until loaves test done.

Billie Moore
State Dept. of Vo-Tech Ed, Stillwater, Oklahoma

CHEDDAR-NUT BREAD

1 egg, slightly beaten
1 c. evaporated milk
1/4 tsp. salt
3 3/4 c. buttermilk baking mix
1 1/2 c. shredded sharp Cheddar cheese
1/2 c. chopped nuts

Combine .... all ingredients with 1/2 cup water in bowl, mixing well.
Spoon ...... into buttered 5 x 9-inch loaf pan.
Bake .... at 350 degrees for 55 to 60 minutes or until loaf tests done.

Lisa Smith
Wilson H. S., Wilson, Oklahoma

SPICY PUMPKIN BREAD

3 c. sugar
4 eggs
1 c. oil
3 1/2 c. flour
2 tsp. soda
1 tsp. baking powder
1 1/2 tsp. salt
1 tsp. each cinnamon, nutmeg
1 tbsp. pumpkin pie spice
2 c. mashed pumpkin

Beat .... sugar and eggs together in bowl.
Blend ...... remaining ingredients and 2/3 cup water in bowl.
Combine .... all ingredients, mixing well.
Pour .... into 3 oiled loaf pans.
Bake .... at 325 degrees for 1 to 1 1/2 hours or until loaves test done.

La Fonda Johnson
Sentinel H. S., Sentinel, Oklahoma

STRAWBERRY BREAD

1 can strawberry pie filling
2 eggs
1/3 c. oil
2 1/2 c. flour
1 tbsp. baking powder
1/2 tsp. salt
1/2 c. sugar
1/2 c. chopped nuts
Strawberry Butter
Strawberry Cream Cheese

Reserve ..... 1/2 cup pie filling.
Combine .... remaining pie filling with eggs, mixing well.
Add .... next 6 ingredients, stirring until just moistened.
Pour .... into oiled waxed paper-lined loaf pan.
Bake .... at 350 degrees for 1 1/2 hours or until loaf tests done.
Cool .... for 5 minutes before removing from pan.
Serve .... with Strawberry Butter or Strawberry Cream Cheese

Strawberry Butter

1/2 c. strawberry pie filling
1 stick butter, softened
1/4 c. confectioners' sugar

Blend ...... all ingredients in bowl.

Strawberry Cream Cheese

1/2 c. strawberry pie filling
1 3-oz. package cream cheese, softened

Blend ...... all ingredients in bowl.

Dana Coughran
Nowata H. S., Nowata, Oklahoma

SUMMER SQUASH BREAD

2 eggs, beaten
3/4 c. sugar
1/2 c. oil
2 tsp. vanilla extract
1 1/3 c. coarsely shredded summer
squash
1 1/2 c. flour
2 tsp. cinnamon
1 tsp. baking powder
1/2 tsp. soda
1/4 tsp. salt

Combine . . . . eggs, sugar, oil and vanilla in bowl, beating until lemon colored.
Stir . . . . in squash and combined dry ingredients, mixing well.
Pour . . . . into greased loaf pan.
Bake . . . . at 350 degrees for 40 minutes or until loaf tests done.
Cool . . . . for 10 minutes before removing from pan.

Cherry Couley
Coyle Public Schools, Coyle, Oklahoma

ZUCCHINI-NUT BREAD

3 eggs, beaten
2 c. sugar
1 c. oil
2 c. grated zucchini
1 tsp. lemon juice
2 tsp. vanilla extract
2 c. chopped nuts
3 c. sifted flour
1 tsp. each salt, baking powder,
soda
1 tbsp. cinnamon

Combine . . . . first 7 ingredients in bowl, beating well.
Add . . . . remaining ingredients, mixing lightly.
Spoon . . . . . . into 2 greased loaf pans.
Bake . . . . at 350 degrees for 50 minutes.
Cool . . . . on rack for 10 minutes before removing from pans.

Caroleen J. Clester
Okeene, Oklahoma

CHEESY SUPPER BREAD

2 tsp. baking powder
2 tsp. salt
2 tbsp. sugar
2 pkg. dry yeast
4 3/4 to 5 1/4 c. Shawnees' Best
all-purpose flour
1 1/4 c. buttermilk
2 tbsp. margarine
1 c. coarsely shredded Cheddar
cheese
1 egg, beaten
1 tbsp. milk

Combine . . . . first 4 ingredients and 1 1/2 cups flour in large mixing bowl.
Heat . . . . buttermilk, margarine and 3/4 cup water in saucepan until very warm.
Add . . . . to dry ingredients gradually, mixing well.
Beat . . . . with electric mixer at high speed for 2 minutes.
Stir . . . . in cheese and enough flour to make stiff dough.
Knead . . . . . . on lightly floured surface until smooth and elastic.
Shape . . . . . . into 2 round loaves.
Place . . . . on greased baking sheet.
Let . . . . rise, covered, in warm place until doubled in bulk.
Mix . . . . egg and milk together.
Brush . . . . . . over tops of loaves.
Bake . . . . at 350 degrees for 40 to 45 minutes or until bread tests done.
Cool . . . . on wire rack.

William L. Jord
Shawnee Milling Company, Shawnee, Oklahoma

HERBED CHEESE BRAID

1 pkg. dry yeast
1/4 c. butter
1 c. seasoned mashed potatoes
1 tbsp. sugar
2 tsp. salt
3/4 c. milk, scalded
2 eggs, beaten
1/2 tsp. oregano
1/2 tsp. basil
4 to 4 1/2 c. sifted flour

2 c. shredded Cheddar cheese
Melted butter

Dissolve . . . . yeast in 1/4 cup warm water.

Combine . . . . next 5 ingredients in bowl, mixing well.

Let . . . . stand until lukewarm.

Add . . . . yeast, eggs, herbs, and 1 cup flour, mixing well.

Stir . . . . in cheese and enough remaining flour to make stiff dough.

Knead . . . . . . on floured surface until smooth and elastic.

Place . . . . . . in greased bowl, turning to grease surface.

Let . . . . rise, covered, in warm place until doubled in bulk.

Divide . . . . . . into 6 pieces.

Roll . . . . each piece on floured surface into 15-inch long rope.

Braid . . . . 3 ropes together.

Place . . . . . . in greased baking sheet.

Repeat . . . . with remaining dough.

Brush . . . . . . tops with melted butter.

Let . . . . rise until doubled in bulk.

Bake . . . . at 350 degrees for 45 minutes or until bread tests done.

Cool . . . . on wire racks.

Photograph for this recipe on this page.

SAVORY CHEESE BREAD

1/2 c. butter
2 3/4 c. flour
2 tbsp. sugar
1/2 tsp. salt
1 pkg. dry yeast
1 c. milk
1 egg, beaten
1 pkg. dry onion soup mix
1 c. shredded Cheddar cheese

Cut . . . . butter into flour, sugar and salt in large mixing bowl until crumbly.

Dissolve . . . . yeast in 1/4 cup warm water.

Add . . . . to dry ingredients with milk and egg.

Beat . . . . with spoon until well blended.

Combine . . . . 2 tablespoons soup mix and 1/4 cup cheese, mixing well; set aside.

Stir . . . . remaining soup mix and cheese into batter, mixing well.

Pour . . . . into 2 greased 4 x 8-inch glass loaf pans.

Sprinkle . . . . with reserved soup mixture.

Let . . . . rise, covered, in warm place for 1 1/2 to 2 hours or until puffy.

Microwave . . 1 loaf at a time, on Low for 5 minutes.

Rotate . . . . . dish 180 degrees.

Microwave . . on High for 5 to 7 minutes longer or until bread tests done.

Let . . . . stand for 5 minutes before turning onto wire rack to cool.

Photograph for this recipe on page 103.

DOUBLE-QUICK DINNER ROLLS

1 pkg. dry yeast
2 tbsp. sugar
1 tsp. salt
2 1/4 c. flour
1 egg, beaten
2 tbsp. shortening, melted

Dissolve . . . . yeast in 1 cup warm water in large mixing bowl.

Stir . . . . in sugar, salt and half the flour.

Beat . . . . until smooth.

Add . . . . egg and shortening.

Beat . . . . in remaining flour until smooth.

Let . . . . rise, covered, in warm place until doubled in bulk.

Stir . . . . dough down.

Fill . . . . greased muffin cups 1/2 full.

Let . . . . rise in warm place until doubled in bulk.

Bake . . . . at 400 degrees for 15 to 20 minutes.

Pamela Shanklin
Hinton H. S., Hinton, Oklahoma

GOLDEN HONEY ROLLS

3 1/4 c. flour
1 pkg. dry yeast
1 tsp. salt
1 c. milk
1/2 c. oil
3 tbsp. honey
1 egg
1 egg, separated
1/3 c. sugar
2 tbsp. butter, softened

Combine .... 1 1/2 cups flour, yeast and salt in bowl.
Heat .... milk, oil and 2 tablespoons honey in saucepan until very warm.
Add .... to flour mixture with egg and egg yolk.
Beat .... with electric mixer at low speed until blended.
Beat .... at medium speed for 3 minutes.
Stir .... in remaining 1 3/4 cups flour.
Let .... rise, covered, in warm place for 45 to 60 minutes or until doubled in bulk.
Beat .... for 30 seconds.
Drop .... by tablespoonfuls in single layer into 2 greased 9-inch round cake pans.
Combine .... sugar, butter, remaining 1 tablespoon honey and egg white, mixing well.
Drizzle ..... half over rolls.
Let .... rise for 20 to 30 minutes or until doubled in bulk.
Drizzle ..... remaining sugar mixture over top.
Bake .... at 350 degrees for 25 to 30 minutes or until golden brown.
Remove .... from pan immediately.

Photograph for this recipe above.

MICHELLE'S HOT ROLLS

2 pkg. dry yeast
1 c. sugar
3/4 c. butter, softened
7 c. flour
1/2 c. dry milk powder
1 tbsp. salt

Dissolve .... yeast in 2 1/2 cups water.
Add .... sugar, stirring to dissolve.
Stir .... in butter.

Mix . . . . remaining ingredients together.

Add . . . . to liquid ingredients, mixing well.

Beat . . . . with electric mixer with dough hook until smooth.

Place . . . . in greased bowl, turning to grease surface.

Let . . . . rise, covered, in warm place until doubled in bulk.

Shape . . . . . . into rolls.

Place . . . . in baking pan.

Let . . . . rise until doubled in bulk.

Bake . . . . at 350 degrees for 25 minutes.

Yields . . . . . . 25-30 rolls.

Michelle Cosby
Lindsay H. S., Lindsay, Oklahoma

QUICK YEAST ROLLS

2 tbsp. dry yeast
1/2 c. sugar
1/2 c. dry milk powder
7 c. flour
1/2 tsp. baking powder
1/2 c. shortening
Melted butter

Combine . . . . yeast, sugar and 2 cups lukewarm water.

Let . . . . stand for 10 minutes.

Sift . . . . dry ingredients together into large bowl.

Cut . . . . in shortening.

Add . . . . liquid ingredients, mixing well.

Let . . . . rise in warm place for 1/2 hour.

Roll . . . . out on floured surface.

Shape . . . . . . into rolls.

Place . . . . in baking pan.

Let . . . . rise for 1/2 hour.

Bake . . . . at 425 degrees for 10 minutes.

Brush . . . . . . tops with melted butter.

Bake . . . . for 5 minutes longer.

Kathy Grove
Vanoss School, Ada, Oklahoma

WONDER DOUGH

1 pkg. yeast
5 to 5 1/2 c. self-rising flour
1 tsp. soda
4 tbsp. sugar
1 c. shortening
2 c. buttermilk

Dissolve . . . . yeast in 2 tablespoons lukewarm water.

Sift . . . . dry ingredients together into bowl.

Cut . . . . in shortening until crumbly.

Stir . . . . in yeast and buttermilk.

Knead . . . . . . on floured surface until dough holds together.

Roll . . . . out 1/2 to 3/4 inch thick.

Cut . . . . with biscuit cutter.

Place . . . . on baking sheet.

Bake . . . . at 400 degrees for 15 to 20 minutes or until golden brown.

May . . . . keep dough in refrigerator for several days before using.

Ann Ritchie
Stilwell Jr. H. S., Stilwell, Oklahoma

CAKE MIX CINNAMON ROLLS

1 box yellow cake mix
2 pkg. dry yeast
1 tsp. salt
5 c. flour
Melted butter
3/4 c. sugar
2 tbsp. cinnamon
1 box confectioners' sugar
Milk

Combine . . . . first 3 ingredients and 2 1/2 cups lukewarm water in large bowl.

Stir . . . . in flour, mixing well.

Let . . . . rise for 45 minutes to 1 hour.

Roll . . . . on floured surface into thin rectangle.

Brush . . . . . . with melted butter.

Combine . . . . sugar and cinnamon.

Sprinkle . . . . over buttered surface.

Roll . . . . as for jelly roll.

Cut . . . . into 1/2 to 3/4-inch slices.

Place . . . . in greased baking pan.

Let . . . . rise for 45 minutes.

Bake . . . . at 350 degrees for 15 to 20 minutes.

Mix . . . . confectioners' sugar and a small amount of milk in bowl to make icing of spreading consistency.

Spread . . . . . over warm rolls.

Note . . . . Do not use pudding cake mix.

Kenny Wright
Drummond School, Drummond, Oklahoma
Brenda Oney
Okeene H. S., Okeene, Oklahoma

Desserts and Beverages

ICE CREAM

CHEESECAKES

PECAN PIE

BREAD PUDDING

MILLIONAIRE PIE

BAKED ALASKA

STRAWBERRY PIE

FROZEN DESSERTS

CHOCOLATE PIE

PASTRY

ANGEL FOOD CAKE DESSERT

1/4 lb. margarine, softened
1/2 box confectioners' sugar
2 eggs, separated
1/2 tsp. vanilla extract
1 angel food cake, sliced
1 med. jar maraschino cherries, chopped
1 29-oz. can crushed pineapple, drained
1 pt. whipping cream, whipped
1 3 1/2-oz. can coconut

Cream ...... margarine and confectioners' sugar in bowl.
Add .... egg yolks 1 at a time, beating well after each addition.
Stir .... in vanilla.
Fold .... in stiffly beaten egg whites.
Layer ...... cake slices, creamed mixture, cherries, pineapple, whipped cream and coconut in 9 x 13-inch pan.
Chill .... before cutting into squares.

Sue Taylor
Meeker H. S., Meeker, Oklahoma

APPLE CRISP

4 c. sliced apples
1 tbsp. lemon juice
1/3 c. flour
1/2 c. packed brown sugar
1 c. oatmeal
1 tsp. cinnamon
1/3 c. melted butter

Place .... apples in greased shallow baking dish.
Sprinkle .... with lemon juice.
Combine .... next 4 ingredients in bowl.
Add .... melted butter, mixing until crumbly.
Spread ..... over apples.
Bake .... at 375 degrees for 30 minutes or until apples are tender.
Yields ...... 6 servings.

Violet Freeze
Braman H. S., Braman, Oklahoma

APPLE PIZZA PIE

Pastry for 2-crust pie
6 or 7 tart apples, thinly sliced

1/2 c. sugar
1 tsp. cinnamon
3/4 c. flour
1/2 c. packed brown sugar
1/2 c. butter, softened

Press .... pastry into pizza pan.
Cover ..... with sliced apples.
Blend ..... sugar and cinnamon in bowl.
Sprinkle .... over apples.
Combine .... remaining ingredients in bowl.
Spread ..... over apples.
Bake .... at 350 degrees for 30 to 40 minutes or until apples are tender.

Karen Winn
Verden H. S., Verden, Oklahoma

FRESH APPLE PUDDING

1/4 c. butter, softened
1 c. sugar
1 egg, beaten
2 1/2 c. peeled chopped apples
1 c. chopped pecans
1/4 c. maraschino cherries, chopped
1 tsp. soda
1 tsp. nutmeg
1 c. flour
1/4 tsp. salt
1 tsp. cinnamon

Cream ...... butter and sugar in bowl.
Add .... egg, beating until fluffy.
Stir .... in apples, pecans and cherries.
Sift .... remaining ingredients together.
Add .... to creamed mixture, blending well.
Pour .... into greased and floured 7 x 12-inch pan.
Bake .... at 350 degrees for 35 to 45 minutes.
Cut .... into squares.
Serve .... with whipped cream.
Yields ...... 6-8 servings.

Wanda Babcock
State Dept. of Vo-Tech Ed., Stillwater, Oklahoma

BANANA SPLIT CAKE

2 c. crushed vanilla wafers
1 1/2 c. butter
2 eggs

1 box confectioners' sugar
1 lg. can crushed pineapple, drained
5 bananas, sliced
1 lg. carton Cool Whip
Nuts
Cherries

Mix . . . . wafer crumbs with 1/2 cup melted margarine.
Press . . . . into 9 x 13-inch pan.
Combine . . . . eggs, 1 cup softened butter and confectioners' sugar in bowl.
Beat . . . . with electric mixer for 15 minutes.
Spread . . . . . over crumb mixture.
Cover . . . . . . with crushed pineapple.
Arrange . . . . . banana slices over pineapple.
Top . . . . with Cool Whip.
Decorate . . . . with nuts and cherries.
Chill . . . . until serving time.
Yields . . . . . . 10 servings.

Leah Stine
Drummond H. S., Drummond, Oklahoma

NO-BAKE BANANA PUDDING

1 8-oz. carton sour cream
2 3 1/2-oz. packages instant vanilla pudding mix
3 1/2 c. milk
Vanilla wafers
3 bananas
1 8-oz. carton Cool Whip

Mix . . . . first 3 ingredients together in bowl until thick.
Alternate . . . with layers of vanilla wafers and bananas in large serving dish.
Top . . . . with Cool Whip.
Chill . . . . until serving time.

Tina Pendergraft
Dover H. S., Dover, Oklahoma

CREAMY BANANA PUDDING

12 vanilla wafers
1 8-oz. package cream cheese, softened
1/4 c. sugar
1/2 tsp. vanilla extract
1 c. whipping cream, whipped
2 med. bananas, sliced

Line . . . . bottom and side of 1-quart bowl with vanilla wafers.
Blend . . . . . . cream cheese, sugar and vanilla in bowl.
Fold . . . . in remaining ingredients.
Spoon . . . . . . over vanilla wafers.
Chill . . . . until serving time.
Yields . . . . . . 4-6 servings.

Dalinda McGechie
Sentinel H. S., Sentinel, Oklahoma

FRUIT-TOPPED BREAD PUDDING

3 c. bread cubes
1/4 tsp. nutmeg
1/2 c. seedless raisins
1/2 c. packed light brown sugar
2 tbsp. butter
1 tsp. vanilla extract
1/4 tsp. salt
3 c. milk, scalded
3 lg. eggs, beaten
Strawberry preserves

Place . . . . bread cubes in 2-quart baking dish.
Stir . . . . next 6 ingredients into hot milk.
Add . . . . eggs gradually, stirring constantly.
Pour . . . . over bread.
Bake . . . . at 350 degrees for 25 to 30 minutes or until pudding tests done.
Top . . . . with preserves.
Serve . . . . warm.
Yields . . . . . . 6 servings.

Photograph for this recipe on page 31.

CHERRY-PINEAPPLE DESSERT

1 can sour cherries
1 can crushed pineapple
1 box white cake mix
1 stick melted butter

Mix . . . . cherries and pineapple together in casserole.
Spread . . . . . with cake mix.
Drizzle . . . . . with melted butter.
Bake . . . . at 350 degrees for 30 minutes or until light brown.

Sonseria Williams
Weatherford H. S., Weatherford, Oklahoma

CHERRY STUFF

1 can cherry pie filling
1 sm. box yellow cake mix
1/4 c. margarine
Brown sugar to taste

Spread . . . . . pie filling in 6 x 10-inch glass baking dish.
Sprinkle . . . . with cake mix.
Drizzle . . . . . with butter.
Sprinkle . . . . brown sugar on top.
Bake . . . . at 350 degrees for 30 minutes.
Yields . . . . . . 4 servings.

Christy Hamburger
Paden H. S., Paden, Oklahoma

BAKED FUDGE

1/2 c. sifted flour
1/2 c. cocoa
2 c. sugar
4 eggs, well beaten
1 c. pecans
1 c. melted butter
2 tsp. vanilla extract

Combine . . . . flour, cocoa and sugar in bowl.
Beat . . . . in eggs and remaining ingredients.
Pour . . . . into 8 x 8-inch pan.
Place . . . . in larger pan with 1/2 inch water.
Bake . . . . at 350 degrees for 1 hour.

Lori Kays
Pryor Jr. H. S., Pryor, Oklahoma

CHOCOLATE DELIGHT

1 c. chopped pecans
1 c. flour
1 stick margarine, softened
1 8-oz. package cream cheese, softened
1 lg. container Cool Whip
1 c. confectioners' sugar
1 pkg. each chocolate, vanilla instant pudding mix
1 tsp. vanilla extract
3 c. milk
1 Hershey Bar, grated

Mix . . . . first 3 ingredients in bowl.
Press . . . . into 9 x 13-inch pan.

Bake . . . . at 350 degrees for 20 minutes.
Blend . . . . . . cream cheese, 1 cup Cool Whip and confectioners' sugar in bowl.
Spread . . . . . over cooled crust.
Combine . . . . remaining ingredients except Hershey bar in bowl, mixing well.
Spread . . . . . over cream cheese mixture.
Chill . . . . until firm.
Cover . . . . . . with remaining Cool Whip.
Sprinkle . . . . with grated Hershey bar.

Darla Hightower
Empire H. S., Duncan, Oklahoma

CHOCOLATE AND VANILLA PUDDING DESSERT

1 c. flour
1 stick margarine, softened
1 1/4 c. confectioners' sugar
1 c. nuts
1 8-oz. package cream cheese, softened
4 tsp. vanilla extract
1 9-oz. carton Cool Whip
1 sm. box instant vanilla pudding mix
1 sm. box instant chocolate pudding mix
3 c. milk

Mix . . . . flour, margarine, 1/4 cup confectioners' sugar and nuts in bowl.
Press . . . . into 9 x 13-inch baking pan.
Bake . . . . at 350 degrees for 25 minutes.
Blend . . . . . . cream cheese, 1 cup confectioners' sugar, 3 teaspoons vanilla and 1 cup Cool Whip in bowl.
Spread . . . . . over cooled crust.
Beat . . . . pudding mixes, milk and 1 teaspoon vanilla in bowl until thick.
Spread . . . . . over cream cheese mixture.
Cover . . . . . . with remaining Cool Whip.
Chill . . . . until serving time.

Lori Kliewer
Washita Heights School, Corn, Oklahoma

JANELL'S MISSISSIPPI MUD

1 c. flour
Chopped pecans
1/2 c. margarine, melted
1 8-oz. package cream cheese, softened

Cool Whip
1 c. confectioners' sugar
3 c. milk
2 pkg. instant chocolate pudding mix
1 tsp. vanilla extract

Mix . . . . flour, 1/2 cup pecans and margarine.
Spread . . . . . in 9 x 13-inch baking pan.
Bake . . . . at 350 degrees for 15 minutes.
Combine . . . . cream cheese, 1 cup Cool Whip and confectioners' sugar in bowl, mixing well.
Spread . . . . . over crust.
Beat . . . . milk, pudding mix and vanilla in bowl with electric mixer.
Pour . . . . over cream cheese mixture.
Cover . . . . . . with additional Cool Whip.
Sprinkle . . . . with additional chopped pecans.
Yields . . . . . . 18 servings.

Janell Le Valley
Wakita H. S., Wakita, Oklahoma

COCONUT TORTE

1 pkg. fluffy white frosting mix
1 tsp. vanilla extract
1 c. graham cracker crumbs
1 6-oz. package chocolate chips
1/2 c. flaked coconut
1/2 c. chopped pecans

Prepare . . . . . frosting mix using package directions.
Stir . . . . in vanilla.
Fold . . . . in remaining ingredients.
Pour . . . . into greased 9-inch pie plate.
Bake . . . . at 350 degrees for 30 minutes.
Yields . . . . . . 8 servings.

Marla Cail
Wanette H. S., Wanette, Oklahoma

FRUIT PIZZA

1 8-oz. roll refrigerator sugar cookies, sliced 1/8-in. thick
1 8-oz. package cream cheese, softened
1/3 c. sugar
1/2 tsp. vanilla extract
Grapes, strawberries, banana slices, orange slices, apple wedges, blueberries, kiwi and fresh pineapple
1/2 c. orange marmalade

Line . . . . 14-inch pizza pan with cookie slices, overlapping slightly.
Bake . . . . at 375 degrees for 12 minutes or until golden brown.
Blend . . . . . . cream cheese, sugar and vanilla in bowl.
Spread . . . . . over cooled crust.
Arrange . . . . . fruit over cream cheese layer.
Combine . . . . marmalade and 2 tablespoons water in bowl.
Pour . . . . over fruit.
Chill . . . . in refrigerator.
Cut . . . . into wedges to serve.
Yields . . . . . . 10 servings.

Debbie Hobaugh
Braman H. S., Braman, Oklahoma

LEMON SQUARES

1/2 c. butter, softened
1 c. flour
1/2 c. salted cashews, finely ground
1 c. confectioners' sugar
1 8-oz. package cream cheese, softened
3/4 c. whipping cream, whipped
2 3 3/4-oz. packages instant lemon pudding mix
3 c. milk
Grated lemon rind

Mix . . . . first 3 ingredients in bowl.
Press . . . . into bottom of 9 x 13-inch baking pan.
Bake . . . . at 375 degrees for 15 minutes or until light brown.
Beat . . . . confectioners' sugar and cream cheese in bowl until fluffy.
Fold . . . . 2/3 of the whipped cream into cream cheese mixture.
Spread . . . . . over cooled crust; chill.
Mix . . . . pudding mix, milk and 1 tablespoon lemon rind in bowl until thick.
Pour . . . . over cream cheese mixture.
Chill . . . . up to 24 hours.
Spread . . . . . remaining whipped cream over pudding mixture.
Sprinkle . . . . with grated lemon rind.

Debbie Briske
Weatherford H. S., Weatherford, Oklahoma

DUTCH PEACH KUCHEN

1/2 c. butter, softened
1 c. sugar
1 1/2 c. sifted flour
1 tsp. cinnamon
1/2 tsp. baking powder
1/2 tsp. salt
1/4 tsp. nutmeg
3 c. sliced fresh peaches
1/4 c. chopped raisins

Cream ...... butter and sugar in small bowl until light and fluffy.
Sift .... dry ingredients into creamed mixture gradually, mixing until crumbly.
Reserve ..... 1 cup.
Press .... remaining crumb mixture over bottom and 1/2 inch up sides of 8-inch square baking pan.
Mix .... 1/2 cup reserved crumb mixture with peaches.
Arrange ..... over prepared crust.
Combine .... raisins with remaining crumb mixture.
Sprinkle .... over peaches.
Bake .... at 375 degrees for 45 minutes.
Cut .... into squares to serve hot or cold.

Photograph for this recipe above.

RICE CHANTILLY

1/2 c. sugar
1 env. unflavored gelatin
1/4 tsp. salt
4 egg yolks, slightly beaten
2 c. milk
1 c. whipping cream, whipped
1 c. cooked rice
1 8 1/2-oz. can crushed pineapple, drained
1 tsp. vanilla extract

Mix .... sugar, gelatin and salt in saucepan.
Stir .... in egg yolks and milk gradually.
Bring .... to a boil over medium heat, stirring constantly.
Chill .... until partially congealed, stirring occasionally.
Fold .... in whipped cream, rice, pineapple and vanilla.
Pour .... into 1 1/2-quart mold.
Chill .... for 4 hours or until firm.
Unmold .... on serving plate.
Garnish ..... with lingonberry sauce.

Lisa Cox
Wilson H. S., Wilson, Oklahoma

STRAWBERRY BAVARIAN CROWN

1 6-oz. package strawberry gelatin
2 10-oz. packages frozen strawberries, thawed, drained
2 c. whipping cream, whipped
1 10-in. angel food cake
1 tbsp. cornstarch
1 c. strawberry juice
2 or 3 drops of red food coloring
1 tsp. butter

Dissolve .... gelatin in 1 1/2 cups hot water in bowl.
Add .... 1/2 cup ice water.
Chill .... until partially congealed.
Beat .... until light and fluffy.
Fold .... strawberries and whipped cream into gelatin mixture.
Tear .... cake into pieces, discarding brown edges.
Alternate ... layers of cake with gelatin mixture in 10-inch tube pan.
Chill .... until firm.

Unmold . . . . on serving plate.
Blend . . . . . . cornstarch with small amount of strawberry juice in bowl.
Add . . . . to remaining juice in saucepan.
Cook . . . . for 3 to 5 minutes or until clear.
Remove . . . . from heat.
Add . . . . food coloring and butter.
Drizzle . . . . . cooled glaze over mold.
Chill . . . . until serving time.
Yields . . . . . . 12 servings.

Sherri Miller
Waynoka, Oklahoma

STRAWBERRY DREAM

1 10 1/2-oz. angel food cake
1 lg. box instant vanilla pudding mix
3 1/2 c. milk
1 4-oz. carton Cool Whip
1 8-oz. carton sour cream
1 can sweetened condensed milk
1 8-oz. can crushed pineapple
1 16-oz. package frozen strawberries, thawed

Tear . . . . cake into bite-sized pieces.
Place . . . . in 9 x 13-inch dish.
Mix . . . . pudding mix and milk in bowl.
Pour . . . . over cake.
Combine . . . . Cool Whip, sour cream and condensed milk in bowl.
Blend . . . . . . in pineapple and strawberries.
Pour . . . . over pudding.
Chill . . . . for 1 hour before serving.
Yields . . . . . . 12 servings.

Kathy Dale
State Dept. of Vo-Tech Ed., Stillwater, Oklahoma

STRAWBERRY PIZZA

1 c. flour
1/2 c. butter, softened
1 1/2 c. confectioners' sugar
1 8-oz. package cream cheese, softened
1 pkg. Dream Whip, prepared
1 qt. frozen strawberries, thawed
1/2 c. sugar

Mix . . . . flour and butter with 1/2 cup confectioners' sugar.
Press . . . . onto pizza pan to form crust.
Bake . . . . at 325 degrees for 15 to 20 minutes.
Beat . . . . cream cheese and 1 cup confectioners' sugar with Dream Whip.
Spread . . . . . on warm crust.
Top . . . . with strawberries sweetened with sugar.

Janelle LaVon Miller
Hydro H. S., Hydro, Oklahoma

CHERRY CHEESECAKE

1 c. flour
1/4 c. chopped nuts
Confectioners' sugar
1 stick margarine, melted
1 8-oz. package cream cheese, softened
1 10-oz. carton Cool Whip
1 tsp. vanilla extract
1 lg. can cherry pie filling

Stir . . . . first 2 ingredients and 1/2 cup confectioners' sugar into melted margarine in saucepan.
Pat . . . . into 12 x 13-inch pan.
Bake . . . . at 350 degrees until light brown.
Beat . . . . cream cheese with electric mixer until fluffy.
Add . . . . 1 cup confectioners' sugar, beating well.
Stir . . . . in Cool Whip and vanilla.
Spread . . . . . over cooled crust; chill.
Top . . . . with pie filling.
Cut . . . . into squares to serve.
Yields . . . . . . 16 servings.

Jackie Howell
Cache H. S., Cache, Oklahoma

MILNOT CHEESECAKE

1 pkg. lemon gelatin
4 tbsp. lemon juice
1   8-oz. package cream cheese, softened
1 1/2 c. sugar
1 tsp. vanilla extract
1 lg. can Milnot, chilled, whipped
1   1-lb. box graham crackers, crushed
1/2 c. melted butter

Dissolve . . . . gelatin in 1 cup boiling water.
Stir . . . . in lemon juice; cool.
Beat . . . . cream cheese, 1 cup sugar and vanilla together in bowl.
Mix . . . . in gelatin.
Fold . . . . in whipped Milnot.
Combine . . . . graham cracker crumbs, butter and 1/2 cup sugar, mixing well.
Press . . . . into bottom and sides of 9 x 13-inch pan.
Spread . . . . . cream cheese filling over crust.
Sprinkle . . . . with additional crumbs.
Chill . . . . for several hours before serving.

Kim Walker
Verden H. S., Verden, Oklahoma

WASHINGTON CHEESECAKE

1 c. graham cracker crumbs
3 tbsp. margarine, melted
Sugar
3   8-oz. packages cream cheese, softened
2 tbsp. flour
3 eggs
2 tbsp. milk
1 tsp. vanilla extract
1   21-oz. can cherry pie filling

Combine . . . . first 2 ingredients and 3 table-spoons sugar in saucepan, mixing well.
Press . . . . into 9-inch springform pan.
Bake . . . . at 325 degrees for 10 minutes.
Mix . . . . cream cheese, 3/4 cup sugar and flour in bowl with electric mixer.
Add . . . . eggs 1 at a time, beating well after each addition.
Blend . . . . . . in milk and vanilla.
Pour . . . . over crust.
Bake . . . . at 350 degrees for 10 minutes.

Reduce . . . . . oven temperature to 250 degrees.
Bake . . . . for 25 to 30 minutes longer.
Cool . . . . before removing rim of pan.
Chill . . . . until serving time.
Top . . . . with pie filling.

Chris Croft
Medford H. S., Medford, Oklahoma

HOMEMADE SWEETENED CONDENSED MILK

3 tbsp. margarine, melted
1 c. instant nonfat dry milk
2/3 c. sugar

Combine . . . . all ingredients with 1/2 cup boiling water in bowl.
Mix . . . . with electric mixer until smooth.
Yields . . . . . . amount equal to 1 can sweetened condensed milk.

Helen Ray
Paden H. S., Paden, Oklahoma

STRAWBERRY BAKED ALASKA

2 qt. strawberry ice cream, softened
6 lg. egg whites
1/2 tsp. cream of tartar
1 c. sugar
1   9-in. round sponge cake layer

Pack . . . . ice cream into 8-inch round bowl.
Freeze . . . . . . until firm.
Beat . . . . egg whites and cream of tartar until frothy.
Add . . . . sugar gradually, beating until stiff.
Place . . . . cake on cutting board on baking sheet.
Unmold . . . . ice cream onto cake.
Cover . . . . . . cake and ice cream with meringue, sealing to board.
Bake . . . . in preheated 500-degree oven for 3 to 5 minutes or until browned.
Serve . . . . immediately.
Yields . . . . . . 12 to 16 servings.

Pam Morgaridge
Ringwood H. S., Ringwood, Oklahoma

Recipes on pages 79, 82, 86 and 91.

ORANGE BAKED ALASKAS

1 pt. vanilla ice cream
3 lg. oranges, cut in half
3 egg whites
1/4 tsp. cream of tartar
6 tbsp. sugar

Scoop ...... ice cream into 6 balls.
Freeze ...... for 5 hours or longer.
Cut .... thin slice from bottom of each orange half.
Remove .... fruit and membrane.
Line .... bottoms of shells with fruit.
Chill .... in refrigerator.
Beat .... egg whites and cream of tartar until foamy.
Add .... sugar gradually, beating until stiff.
Place .... orange cups on baking sheet.
Fill .... with ice cream balls.
Cover ...... ice cream with meringue, sealing to edges.
Bake .... in preheated 500-degree oven for 2 to 3 minutes.

Cindy Crider
Ringwood H. S., Ringwood, Oklahoma

CARAMEL DELIGHT

1 1/2 c. flour
1/2 c. packed brown sugar
1 c. rolled oats
1 1/2 c. chopped nuts
1 c. margarine, melted
1 6-oz. jar caramel topping
1/2 gal. vanilla ice cream, softened

Combine .... first 4 ingredients in bowl, mixing well.
Stir .... in margarine.
Spread ..... on baking sheet.
Bake .... at 350 degrees for 20 minutes.
Crumble .... when cool.
Spread ..... half the crumbled mixture in 9 x 13-inch pan.
Spoon ...... topping over crumbs.
Slice .... ice cream over topping.
Top .... with remaining crumbs.
Freeze ...... until firm.

Esther L. Moorhead
Berryhill H. S., Tulsa, Oklahoma

Recipes on pages 113 and 126.

FROZEN FRUIT DESSERT

1 pt. sour cream
3/4 c. sugar
2 tbsp. lemon juice
1 can crushed pineapple, drained
1 jar maraschino cherries, chopped
1/2 c. chopped pecans
4 or 5 bananas, chopped
1 15-oz. carton Cool Whip

Combine .... first 7 ingredients in bowl, mixing well.
Fold .... in Cool Whip.
Spoon ...... into paper-lined muffin cups.
Freeze ...... until firm.

Charlotte Isaacs
Medford H. S., Medford, Oklahoma

BUTTER BRICKLE ICE CREAM PIE

1 c. chopped pecans
1 c. crushed graham crackers
1 c. sugar
1 tsp. baking powder
3 egg whites, stiffly beaten
1 qt. butter brickle ice cream, softened
1 Heath bar, crushed

Combine .... first 4 ingredients in bowl, mixing well.
Fold .... into egg whites.
Spread ..... over bottom and side of buttered pie pan.
Bake .... at 325 degrees for 20 minutes.
Fill .... cooled shell with ice cream.
Sprinkle .... Heath bar over top.
Freeze ...... until firm.

Vallie Jo Lung
Fort Cobb H. S., Fort Cobb, Oklahoma

ORANGE SHERBET

3 qt. milk
2 1/2 c. sugar
2 pkg. orange powdered drink mix
1 sm. can crushed pineapple
1 pt. half and half

Combine .... all ingredients in 1-gallon ice cream freezer container, mixing well.
Freeze ...... using freezer directions.

Laura Bergman
Braman H. S., Braman, Oklahoma

PEANUT CRUNCH ICE CREAM BARS

1/2 c. corn syrup
1/2 c. peanut butter
3 c. crisp rice cereal
2 pt. brick ice cream

Combine .... corn syrup and peanut butter in bowl, mixing well.
Stir .... in cereal.
Press .... into waxed paper-lined 9 x 13-inch pan.
Lift .... out with waxed paper.
Cut .... into twelve 3-inch squares.
Slice .... ice cream into six 3-inch squares.
Place .... between 2 crunch squares.
Cut .... each sandwich into bars.
Freeze ...... wrapped, until firm.

Ice Cream Layer Cake

Press .... half the cereal mixture into 2 waxed paper-lined 8-inch round cake pans.
Pack .... 1 pint softened ice cream into lined 8-inch cake pan.
Freeze ...... until firm.
Unmold .... 1 cereal layer on serving plate.
Top .... with ice cream and remaining cereal layer.

Ice Cream Pie

Press .... cereal mixture onto bottom and side of 9-inch pie plate.
Freeze ...... until firm.
Fill .... with 2 pints ice cream.
Freeze ...... until firm.

Ice Cream Tarts

Press .... cereal mixture into 8 medium tart pans.
Fill .... with ice cream.
Freeze ...... until firm.

Photograph for this recipe on page 94.

SPUMONI

3 c. miniature marshmallows
1/2 c. milk
1 c. heavy cream, whipped
1/2 c. slivered toasted almonds
1/2 c. chopped maraschino cherries
1 tsp. vanilla extract
1/4 tsp. almond extract
2 tbsp. cocoa
1 1/2 tsp. rum flavoring

Melt .... marshmallows in milk in double boiler, stirring until smooth.
Chill .... until slightly thickened, mixing well.
Fold .... in whipped cream.
Combine .... half the marshmallow mixture with almonds, cherries, vanilla and almond flavorings.
Add .... cocoa and rum flavoring to remaining marshmallow mixture.
Alternate ... layers of cherry and chocolate mixtures in serving dishes.
Freeze ...... until firm.

Cathy Hald
Cyril H. S., Cyril, Oklahoma

STRAWBERRY FLUFF

1 c. flour
1/3 c. packed brown sugar
1 stick margarine, melted
1/3 c. chopped nuts
3 egg whites
1 lg. package frozen strawberries, partially thawed
1 c. sugar
1 tsp. lemon juice
1 c. prepared Dream Whip

Combine .... first 4 ingredients in bowl, mixing well.
Spread ..... on cookie sheet.
Bake .... at 350 degrees for 15 to 20 minutes, stirring occasionally.
Cool .... and crumble, reserving 1 cup crumbs.
Spread ..... remaining crumbs in 9 x 13-inch dish.
Place .... egg whites, strawberries, sugar and lemon juice in large mixer bowl.
Beat .... with electric mixer at high speed for 15 minutes.
Fold .... in Dream Whip.
Spread ..... in prepared pan.
Top .... with reserved crumbs.
Freeze ...... until firm.

Cindy Harris
Moore West Mid-H. S., Oklahoma City, Oklahoma

TIFFIN FAMOUS FRENCH PUDDING

2 lb. vanilla wafers, crushed
1 lb. butter, softened
4 c. confectioners' sugar
8 eggs
2 c. chopped walnuts
2 c. chopped maraschino cherries
1 tsp. vanilla extract
Pinch of salt
1 qt. whipping cream, whipped

Line . . . . large buttered 10 x 16-inch pan with half the wafer crumbs.
Cream . . . . . . butter in large bowl.
Add . . . . confectioners' sugar gradually, mixing well after each addition.
Beat . . . . in eggs 1 at a time, beating well after each addition.
Spread . . . . over prepared crust.
Chill . . . . . . until firm.
Fold . . . . walnuts, cherries, vanilla and salt into whipped cream.
Spread . . . . over chilled mixture.
Top . . . . with remaining crumbs.
Freeze . . . . . until firm.
Serve . . . . . . with favorite sauce.

Pat Kellner
Okeene Public Schools, Okeene, Oklahoma

BANANA ICE CREAM

8 eggs, beaten
1 3/4 c. sugar
3 pkg. ice cream mix
2 1/2 pt. whipping cream
1 lg. can Milnot
1 tsp. vanilla extract
3 bananas, mashed
Chopped nuts
Milk

Beat . . . . eggs and sugar together in large container.
Add . . . . remaining ingredients except milk, beating well.
Pour . . . . . . into 1 1/2-gallon ice cream freezer container.
Add . . . . milk to fill line.
Freeze . . . . . following manufacturer's instructions.

Eulalia Cowood
Carver Center, Oklahoma City, Oklahoma

TERESA'S BUTTERFINGER ICE CREAM

6 eggs, beaten
2 c. sugar
2 tbsp. (heaping) crunchy peanut butter
4 1.8-oz. Butterfinger bars, chilled, crushed
1 1/2 tsp. vanilla extract
2 cans Milnot
Milk

Combine . . . . all ingredients except milk in bowl, mixing well.
Pour . . . . into 1-gallon ice cream freezer container.
Fill . . . . to fill line with milk.
Freeze . . . . . . using freezer directions.
Yields . . . . . . 1 gallon.

Teresa Turner
Perkins-Tyron H. S., Perkins, Oklahoma

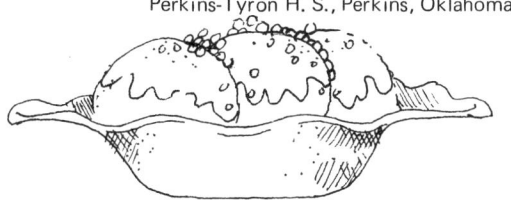

PEACH ICE CREAM

2 c. chopped peaches
1/4 c. sugar
1 or 2 drops of red food coloring
1 or 2 drops of yellow food coloring
1 can sweetened condensed milk
1 c. whipping cream, whipped
1/3 c. slivered toasted almonds

Mash . . . . peaches with sugar, 1/4 cup water and food colorings.
Drain . . . . . . reserving juice.
Add . . . . enough water to juice to measure 3/4 cup liquid.
Combine . . . . peaches, juice mixture and condensed milk, mixing well.
Pour . . . . into freezer trays.
Freeze . . . . . until firm.
Break . . . . . . into chunks in bowl.
Beat . . . . with electric mixer until fluffy.
Fold . . . . in whipped cream and almonds.
Pour . . . . into freezer trays.
Freeze . . . . . until firm.

Sheila Nightengale
Ringwood H. S., Ringwood, Oklahoma

MARILYN'S VANILLA ICE CREAM

2 c. sugar
8 eggs, separated
1 pt. whipping cream
2 tbsp. vanilla extract
1/8 tsp. flour
1/8 tsp. cream of tartar
Dash of salt
Milk

Add . . . . sugar gradually to beaten egg yolks, beating until thick and lemon colored.
Mix . . . . in next 4 ingredients.
Beat . . . . egg whites and salt until stiff.
Fold . . . . into egg yolk mixture.
Pour . . . . into 1-gallon ice cream freezer container.
Add . . . . enough milk to fill container 3/4 full.
Freeze . . . . . . using manufacturer's instructions.
Let . . . . ripen for 1 hour or longer.

Marilyn M. Lamle
Okeene, Oklahoma

COUNTRY VANILLA ICE CREAM

2 1/4 c. sugar
4 eggs, beaten
5 to 6 c. milk
1 pt. half and half
4 1/2 tsp. vanilla extract
1/2 tsp. salt

Beat . . . . sugar into eggs gradually until very stiff.
Add . . . . remaining ingredients, mixing well.
Pour . . . . into 1-gallon ice cream freezer container.
Freeze . . . . . . following freezer directions.

Rene Haffner Haub
West District Vice President 1979-80
Okeene, Oklahoma

OLD-FASHIONED HOMEMADE VANILLA ICE CREAM

2 c. sugar
Pinch of salt
3 tbsp. cornstarch

4 eggs, beaten
4 c. milk, scalded
2 c. cream
2 tbsp. vanilla extract
Milk

Blend . . . . . . sugar, salt and cornstarch in bowl.
Beat . . . . in eggs until smooth, adding a small amount of milk if necessary.
Stir . . . . into scalded milk.
Cook . . . . until thickened, stirring constantly; cool.
Stir . . . . in cream and vanilla.
Pour . . . . into ice cream freezer container.
Add . . . . enough milk to reach fill line.
Freeze . . . . . . using manufacturer's instructions.

Connie Jo Bierig
Okeene Public School, Okeene, Oklahoma

APPLE-MARMALADE PIE

1 10-oz. package pie crust mix
7 c. thinly sliced, pared, tart apples
3/4 tsp. cinnamon
3/4 tsp. ginger
1/2 tsp. nutmeg
1 tbsp. lemon juice
3 tbsp. butter
3/4 c. Smucker's Sweet Orange Marmalade
1 egg yolk, beaten

Prepare . . . . . pie crust mix using package directions.
Roll . . . . 2/3 of the dough on floured surface into 12-inch circle.
Line . . . . 9-inch pie plate.
Chill . . . . remaining dough, covered.
Saute . . . . . . next 5 ingredients in butter in large skillet for 5 minutes or until apples are tender.
Toss . . . . with marmalade.
Spoon . . . . . . into pie shell.
Roll . . . . reserved dough into 10-inch circle.
Cut . . . . into ten 1/2-inch wide strips.
Brush . . . . . . with mixture of egg yolk and 1 teaspoon water.
Place . . . . strips in lattice pattern over apples, trimming and crimping edges.

Bake . . . . at 425 degrees for 35 to 40 minutes or until golden.

Photograph for this recipe on this page.

BUTTERSCOTCH PIE

1/3 c. sifted flour
1 c. packed brown sugar
1/4 tsp. salt
3 egg yolks, slightly beaten
4 tbsp. butter
1/2 tsp. vanilla extract
2 c. milk, scalded
1 baked pie shell

Combine . . . . first 6 ingredients in saucepan.
Add . . . . milk, stirring constantly.
Cook . . . . until thick, stirring constantly.
Pour . . . . into pie shell.
Cool . . . . until serving time.

Connie Thurman
Rattan H. S., Rattan, Oklahoma

BLACK FOREST PIE

1 7-oz. jar marshmallow creme
1 1-oz. squares unsweetened chocolate, melted
1 tsp. vanilla extract
2 tbsp. maraschino cherry juice
1 c. heavy cream, whipped
1/2 c. quartered maraschino cherries
1 chocolate pie crust

Combine . . . . first 3 ingredients in bowl, mixing well.
Blend . . . . . . in cherry juice until smooth.
Fold . . . . in whipped cream and cherries.
Pour . . . . into crust.
Freeze . . . . . . until firm.
Garnish . . . . . with additional cherries.

Betina Dye
Nowata H. S., Nowata, Oklahoma

CHOCOLATE BROWNIE PIE

2 sq. unsweetened chocolate, melted
2 tbsp. butter, melted
3 eggs
1/2 c. sugar
3/4 c. dark corn syrup
3/4 c. chopped pecans
1 unbaked 9-in. pie shell

Combine . . . . first 5 ingredients in bowl, beating well.
Mix . . . . in pecans.
Pour . . . . into pie shell.
Bake . . . . at 350 degrees until pie tests done.

Wanda Carol Belknap
Ryan H. S., Ryan, Oklahoma

CHOCOLATE CHESS PIE

1 1/2 c. sugar
3 tbsp. cocoa
3 eggs, well beaten
5 tbsp. evaporated milk
1 tbsp. white vinegar
1 tbsp. vanilla extract
1/2 stick butter, melted
1 unbaked 9-in. pie crust

Combine . . . . sugar and cocoa in bowl.
Add . . . . eggs, milk, vinegar, vanilla and butter, mixing well.
Pour . . . . into pie crust.
Bake . . . . at 350 degrees for 40 minutes.

Lisa McCurtain
Wilson H. S., Wilson, Oklahoma

MICROWAVE CHOCOLATE PUDDING PIE

1/4 c. butter
1 1/2 c. chocolate cookie crumbs
3 tbsp. sugar
1 sm. package chocolate pudding and
*   pie filling mix*
2 c. milk
1 c. miniature marshmallows

Microwave .. butter in 9-inch glass pie plate on High for 1/2 minute.
Stir .... in cookie crumbs and sugar.
Press .... over bottom and sides of pan.
Microwave .. on High for 2 minutes or until crisp.
Combine .... pudding mix and milk in deep glass casserole.
Microwave .. for 6 minutes or until mixture boils.
Cool .... for 5 minutes.
Stir .... in marshmallows.
Pour .... into prepared crust.
Chill .... until set.

Tina Lumpkin
Ryan Public School, Ryan, Oklahoma

PEANUTTY LEMONADE PIE

7 oz. sweetened condensed milk
3 oz. frozen lemonade concentrate
Peanut butter
1   9-oz. carton whipped topping
1 unbaked 9-in. graham cracker pie crust
1/3 c. margarine
2 1/2 c. quick-cooking oats
1/2 c. packed brown sugar
1/2 c. finely chopped peanuts

Mix .... first 2 ingredients with 1/2 cup peanut butter in bowl.
Stir .... in whipped topping.
Spoon ...... into pie crust.
Melt .... 1/3 cup peanut butter and margarine over low heat in saucepan, stirring occasionally.
Add .... remaining ingredients, mixing well.
Spread ..... in jelly roll pan.
Bake .... at 350 degrees for 15 to 18 minutes or until golden brown, stirring occasionally.

Sprinkle .... cooled topping over lemonade mixture.

Chanin Obermiller
Fairview H. S., Fairview, Oklahoma

FROZEN MILLIONAIRE PIE

1 pkg. Dream Whip
1 can sweetened condensed milk
1/3 c. lemon juice
1/2 c. crushed drained pineapple
Cherries
1/2 c. pecans
1 graham cracker crust

Prepare ..... Dream Whip using package directions.
Combine .... with next 5 ingredients.
Pour .... into crust.
Freeze ...... until firm.

Dena Pritchard
Ninnekah H. S., Ninnekah, Oklahoma

FRESH PEACH PIE

1 c. sugar
1/4 tsp. salt
3 tbsp. peach gelatin
3 tbsp. cornstarch
1 pt. fresh sliced peaches
1 baked 9-in. pie shell
1 sm. container Cool Whip

Combine .... first 4 ingredients and 1 cup hot water in saucepan.
Boil .... for 3 to 5 minutes and set aside to cool.
Arrange ..... peaches in pie shell.
Pour .... gelatin mixture over top.
Top .... with Cool Whip.

Judy Adler, Advisor
Snyder H. S., Snyder, Oklahoma

PEAR PIE WITH HOT CINNAMON SAUCE

4 or 5 fresh pears, sliced
3/4 c. sugar
2 tbsp. flour
1/2 tsp. cinnamon
1 recipe 2-crust pie pastry
1 tbsp. butter
Hot Cinnamon Sauce

Combine .... first 4 ingredients in bowl, tossing to coat.
Arrange ..... in pastry-lined 9-inch pie pan.
Dot .... with butter.
Top .... with remaining pastry, sealing edges.
Cut .... slits in top.
Bake .... at 400 degrees for 45 minutes.
Serve .... warm with Hot Cinnamon Sauce.

Hot Cinnamon Sauce

1/2 c. sugar
1 tbsp. cinnamon
1 tbsp. cornstarch
2 tbsp. butter
1 tsp. vanilla extract

Combine .... first 3 ingredients in saucepan.
Stir .... in 1 cup hot water.
Cook .... until thick and clear, stirring constantly.
Add .... butter and vanilla.
Cook .... for 2 to 3 minutes longer.

Cynthia L. Ward
State Dept. of Vo-Tech Ed., Stillwater, Oklahoma

MICROWAVE SOUTHERN PECAN PIE

1 unbaked 9-in. pie shell
Dried beans
4 tbsp. butter
1 tbsp. flour
3 eggs, beaten
1 c. dark corn syrup
2/3 c. sugar
1/2 tsp. vanilla extract
1 c. pecan halves

Line .... pie shell with plastic wrap.
Fill .... to 1-inch depth with dried beans.
Microwave .. on Medium for 8 minutes, turning 180 degrees once during cooking.
Remove .... wrap and beans.
Microwave .. for 3 minutes longer.
Microwave .. butter in glass mixing bowl on High for 1 minute.
Blend ...... in flour.
Stir .... in eggs, corn syrup and sugar when slightly cooled.

Microwave .. uncovered, on Medium for 10 minutes or until slightly thick, stirring occasionally.
Add .... vanilla, mixing well.
Pour .... into prepared pie shell.
Arrange ..... pecans over top.
Microwave .. on Medium-Low for 8 minutes or until just set, turning 180 degrees once during baking.

Theresa Benson
Ryan H. S., Ryan, Oklahoma

PECAN CUSTARD PIE

3 eggs, well beaten
1 c. sugar
1/4 c. butter
1 c. milk
3 tbsp. flour
1 tsp. vanilla extract
1/4 c. maple syrup
1/4 c. quick-cooking oats
1/4 c. pecans
Coconut
1 unbaked pie shell

Combine .... first 7 ingredients in bowl, mixing well.
Stir .... in oats, pecans, and generous sprinkle coconut.
Pour .... into pie shell.
Bake .... at 350 degrees until set.

Barbie Lamle
Okeene H. S., Okeene, Oklahoma

FRESH STRAWBERRY PIE

1 c. sugar
3 tbsp. cornstarch
Dash of salt
1/2 3-oz. package strawberry gelatin
1 qt. fresh strawberries
1 baked pie shell

Combine .... first 3 ingredients in saucepan.
Add .... 1 cup water, mixing well.
Cook .... until thick and clear, stirring constantly.
Add .... gelatin and set aside to cool.
Fold .... in strawberries.
Pour .... into pie shell.
Chill .... for 1 hour.

Nan Lockhart
Mustang H. S., Mustang, Oklahoma

MARGARET'S PIE CRUST

3 c. flour
1 tsp. salt
1 1/4 c. shortening
1 egg, beaten
1 tbsp. vinegar

Mix . . . . flour and salt in bowl.
Cut . . . . in shortening until crumbly.
Combine . . . . egg, vinegar and 5 tablespoons water, mixing well.
Add . . . . to dry ingredients, mixing well.
Roll . . . . on floured surface to desired size.

Margaret Oney
Okeene, Oklahoma

FRIED PIE CRUST

5 c. flour
1 tsp. baking powder
1 tsp. salt
1 tsp. sugar
1 c. shortening
1 lg. can evaporated milk
1 egg, slightly beaten

Sift . . . . dry ingredients together into bowl.
Cut . . . . in shortening until crumbly.
Combine . . . . remaining ingredients.
Stir . . . . into dry ingredients, mixing well.
Roll . . . . out on floured surface.
Fill . . . . with favorite filling, sealing well.
Fry . . . . in hot deep fat until golden brown.

Dana Hoover
Cement School, Cement, Oklahoma

HOT APPLE CIDER NOG

2 eggs, beaten
1/2 c. sugar
1 c. apple juice
1/4 tsp. salt
1/4 tsp. cinnamon
1/8 tsp. nutmeg
3 c. milk, scalded
1/2 c. whipping cream, whipped

Combine . . . . first 6 ingredients in saucepan, mixing well.
Add . . . . milk gradually.

Cook . . . . until heated, stirring constantly.
Pour . . . . into mugs.
Top . . . . with whipped cream.
Serve . . . . hot or cold.
Yields . . . . . . 6 servings.

Photograph for this recipe above.

APRICOT-PINEAPPLE PUNCH

1 46-oz. can pineapple juice
1 46-oz. can apricot juice
2 6-oz. cans frozen lemonade, thawed
1 6-oz. can frozen limeade, thawed
Red food coloring (opt.)
3 qt. ginger ale

Combine . . . . first 4 ingredients in punch bowl, mixing well.
Add . . . . food coloring, ginger ale and ice.
Yields . . . . . . 35-40 servings.

Darlene Caddell
Central Jr. H. S., Lawton, Oklahoma

BANANA PUNCH

2 c. sugar
5 very ripe bananas, mashed
2 c. orange juice
Juice of 2 lemons
1 46-oz. can pineapple juice
2 bottles of ginger ale

Combine . . . . all ingredients except ginger ale with 6 cups water in large container, mixing well.
Freeze . . . . . . until firm.
Thaw . . . . . . until slushy.
Add . . . . ginger ale and serve.

Jotta Christy
Hammon H. S., Hammon, Oklahoma

BOB-FOR-ORANGE PUNCH

5 Florida oranges
Whole cloves
1 c. sugar
2 2-in. cinnamon sticks
3 qt. Florida orange juice
1 qt. apple juice

Stud . . . . oranges with cloves.
Place . . . . in baking dish.
Bake . . . . at 325 degrees for 3 hours.
Combine . . . . sugar, 12 cloves, cinnamon and 1 cup water in saucepan.
Simmer . . . . . for 10 minutes.
Remove . . . . cloves and cinnamon.
Stir . . . . in juices.
Cook . . . . until heated through.
Pour . . . . into heatproof punch bowl.
Float . . . . baked oranges on top.

Photograph for this recipe on page 104.

SPARKLING BEVERAGE

2 env. unsweetened soft drink mix
2 c. sugar
1 28-oz. bottle of ginger ale, club soda or collins mixer

Dissolve . . . . 1 envelope drink mix and 1 cup sugar in 2 quarts cold water.
Pour . . . . into ice cube trays.
Freeze . . . . . . until firm.
Dissolve . . . . remaining drink mix and 1 cup sugar in 1 quart cold water in pitcher.
Stir . . . . in ginger ale.
Pour . . . . over flavored ice cubes.
Yields . . . . . . 8 servings.

Photograph for this recipe on page 12.

NEW YEAR'S EGGNOG

3/4 c. sugar
6 eggs, separated

1 pt. cream, chilled
1 pt. milk, chilled
1 pt. whiskey
1/4 c. Jamaican rum

Add . . . . sugar to softly beaten egg whites, beating until stiff.
Fold . . . . into well-beaten egg yolks in large bowl.
Add . . . . cream, milk, whiskey and rum gradually, stirring constantly.
Pour . . . . into chilled punch bowl.
Ladle . . . . . . into cups, sprinkling each serving with nutmeg.
Yields . . . . . . 20 servings.

Gail Hodges
Wilson H. S., Wilson, Oklahoma

HOT CRANBERRY PUNCH

3 c. cranberry juice
3 c. pineapple juice
1/2 c. packed brown sugar
1 stick cinnamon
1 tbsp. whole cloves

Combine . . . . first 3 ingredients with 1 1/2 cups water in electric percolator.
Place . . . . cinnamon and cloves in grounds basket.
Percolate . . . . until cycle ends.

Kristi Lamle
Okeene H. S., Okeene, Oklahoma

HOT AND SPICY MILK DRINK

4 c. milk
1/4 c. packed light brown sugar
Several grains of salt
1 6-oz. package butterscotch chips
Whipped cream (opt.)
Ground nutmeg

Heat . . . . first 3 ingredients in 2-quart saucepan over very low heat until lukewarm.
Add . . . . butterscotch chips.
Cook . . . . until chips are melted, stirring constantly.
Pour . . . . into mugs.
Top . . . . with whipped cream.
Sprinkle . . . . with nutmeg.
Yields . . . . . . 4-6 servings.

Photograph for this recipe on page 128.

Cakes

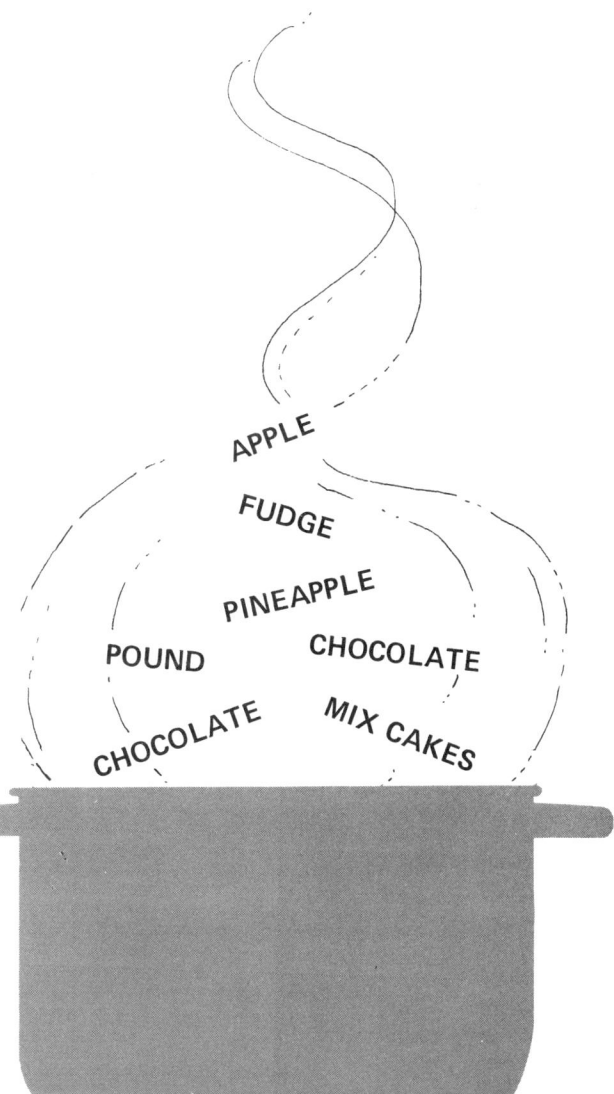

APPLE

FUDGE

PINEAPPLE

POUND   CHOCOLATE

CHOCOLATE   MIX CAKES

APPLE CAKE WITH BUTTERMILK SAUCE

3 c. sifted flour
1 1/2 tsp. soda
1 tsp. cinnamon
3 c. sugar
3 eggs
1 1/4 c. oil
1 tsp. vanilla extract
1/4 c. orange juice
2 c. grated fresh apple
1 c. chopped walnuts
1 c. flaked coconut
1/2 c. margarine
1/2 c. buttermilk

Sift . . . . flour, 1 teaspoon soda and cinnamon together.
Blend . . . . . . 2 cups sugar, eggs, oil, vanilla and orange juice in large bowl.
Mix . . . . in flour mixture.
Fold . . . . in apple, walnuts and coconut.
Spoon . . . . . . into greased and floured 10-inch tube pan.
Bake . . . . at 325 degrees for 1 1/2 hours.
Cool . . . . on rack for 15 minutes.
Turn . . . . out onto serving plate.
Combine . . . . 1 cup sugar, 1/2 teaspoon soda, margarine and buttermilk in saucepan.
Cook . . . . until mixture boils, stirring constantly.
Spoon . . . . . . over warm cake.

Debbie Morriss
Ringling H. S., Ringling, Oklahoma

FROSTED FRESH APPLE CAKE

2 c. flour
2 c. sugar
2 tsp. soda
1/4 tsp. salt
2 tsp. cinnamon
1 1/2 c. oil
4 eggs
3 c. chopped apples
2 1/2 tsp. vanilla extract
1/2 c. butter, softened
1   8-oz. package cream cheese, softened
1   1-lb. box confectioners' sugar
1/2 c. chopped walnuts

Sift . . . . dry ingredients together into bowl.
Mix . . . . in next 3 ingredients with 1/2 teaspoon vanilla.
Pour . . . . into 3 greased and floured 9-inch cake pans.
Bake . . . . at 325 degrees for 25 to 30 minutes or until cakes test done.
Cream . . . . . . butter and cream cheese together in bowl.
Add . . . . confectioners' sugar and remaining 2 teaspoons vanilla, beating well.
Stir . . . . in walnuts.
Frost . . . . cooled cake.

Loretta Greb
Okeene, Oklahoma

ROSEMARY'S FRESH APPLE CAKE

1/2 c. butter, softened
2 c. sugar
2 eggs
2 c. flour
1 tsp. nutmeg
2 tsp. cinnamon
1 tsp. soda
1 tsp. salt
4 1/2 c. grated apples
1/2 c. chopped dates
2 c. chopped nuts

Cream . . . . . . butter and sugar in bowl.
Beat . . . . in eggs.
Sift . . . . dry ingredients together.
Add . . . . to creamed mixture alternately with apples, beating well after each addition.
Fold . . . . in dates and nuts.
Pour . . . . into greased and floured tube pan.
Bake . . . . at 350 degrees for 1 hour or until cake tests done.

Juanita Westfahl
Okeene, Oklahoma

FAVORITE FRESH APPLE CAKE

1 c. oil
2 c. sugar
2 eggs, beaten
3 c. flour
1 tsp. soda

1/2 tsp. salt
1 tsp. cinnamon
3 c. chopped apples
2 tsp. vanilla extract

Combine . . . . first 3 ingredients in bowl, mixing well.
Add . . . . sifted dry ingredients, beating well.
Stir . . . . in apples and vanilla.
Spread . . . . . in greased and floured 9 x 13-inch baking dish.
Bake . . . . at 300 degrees for 55 to 60 minutes or until cake tests done.

Diedna Bennyhill
Moore West-Mid H. S., Oklahoma City, Oklahoma

BANANA-NUT CAKE

Butter, softened
1 c. sugar
3 eggs, beaten
3 c. flour
6 tbsp. buttermilk
1 1/2 tsp. soda
5 bananas, mashed
1 1/4 c. nuts
1 1/2 tsp. vanilla extract
1 1/2 c. confectioners' sugar

Cream . . . . . . 3/4 cup butter and sugar together in bowl.
Add . . . . next 4 ingredients, mixing well.
Beat . . . . in 4 mashed bananas, 3/4 cup nuts and 1 teaspoon vanilla.
Pour . . . . into prepared baking pan.
Bake . . . . at 350 degrees for 35 minutes.
Blend . . . . . . remaining bananas, 1/2 teaspoon vanilla, confectioners' sugar and 1/2 cup nuts in bowl.
Spread . . . . . over cool cake.

Natalie Davis
Geary H. S., Geary, Oklahoma

APPLESAUCE-CHOCOLATE CAKE

2 c. flour
1 1/2 tsp. soda
1 1/2 tsp. salt
2 tbsp. cocoa
1/2 tsp. each cinnamon, nutmeg, allspice
Sugar
1/2 c. shortening
2 eggs

2 c. applesauce
1 c. chopped pecans
2 c. raisins
1 6-oz. package chocolate chips

Combine . . . . first 7 dry ingredients with 1 1/2 cups sugar in large bowl.
Add . . . . shortening, eggs and applesauce, beating well.
Stir . . . . in 1/2 cup pecans and raisins.
Pour . . . . into 10 x 12-inch baking pan.
Sprinkle . . . . with remaining pecans and chocolate chips.
Top . . . . with 2 tablespoons sugar.
Bake . . . . at 350 degrees for 40 minutes.

Connie Guthrie
Whitaker H. S., Pryor, Oklahoma

CHOCOLATE SQUARE CAKE

3 sticks margarine
6 tbsp. cocoa
2 c. flour
2 c. sugar
1/2 c. sour milk
2 eggs, beaten
2 tsp. vanilla extract
1 tsp. soda
1 tsp. cinnamon
6 tbsp. milk
1 box confectioners' sugar
1 c. nuts
1/2 c. coconut

Combine . . . . 2 sticks margarine, 3 tablespoons cocoa and 1 cup water in saucepan.
Bring . . . . to a boil.
Add . . . . flour and sugar, mixing well.
Beat . . . . in sour milk, eggs, 1 teaspoon vanilla, soda and cinnamon.
Pour . . . . into prepared sheet cake pan.
Bake . . . . at 350 degrees for 25 minutes.
Mix . . . . 1 stick margarine, 3 tablespoons cocoa and milk in saucepan.
Bring . . . . to a boil.
Add . . . . confectioners' sugar, beating until creamy.
Stir . . . . in 1 teaspoon vanilla, nuts and coconut.
Spread . . . . . over hot cake.

Wilma Hajek, H. E. Tchr.
Medford H. S., Medford, Oklahoma

DELICIOUS DEVIL'S FOOD CAKE

1 1/2 c. sugar
1/2 c. shortening
1/2 c. cocoa
2 eggs
2 1/2 to 3 c. flour
1 c. buttermilk
2 tbsp. soda

Beat .... first 4 ingredients together in bowl.
Add .... flour and buttermilk.
Stir .... in 1 cup boiling water gradually, mixing well.
Mix .... in soda.
Pour .... into baking pan.
Bake .... at 350 degrees for 30 minutes.

Dovey Peterman
Hennessey H. S., Hennessey, Oklahoma

BLENDER DOUBLE FUDGE CAKE

1 egg
3 tbsp. shortening
1 c. milk
3 1-oz. envelopes premelted unsweetened chocolate
1/2 tsp. vanilla extract
1 1/4 c. flour
1 1/3 c. sugar
1 1/4 tsp. baking powder
1/2 tsp. salt
1/4 tsp. soda
1/2 c. semisweet chocolate chips
1/4 c. nuts, chopped

Place .... all ingtedients except chocolate chips and nuts in blender container.
Blend ...... at high speed for 30 seconds.
Pour .... batter into greased and floured 9-inch square baking pan.
Bake .... at 350 degrees for 35 minutes.
Sprinkle .... chocolate chips and nuts over hot cake.

Kathy Wilson
Moore West H. S., Oklahoma City, Oklahoma

FEATHERY FUDGE CAKE

2/3 c. butter, softened
1 3/4 c. sugar
2 eggs
1 tsp. vanilla extract
2 1/2 oz. unsweetened chocolate, melted, cooled
2 1/2 c. sifted cake flour
1 1/4 tsp. soda
1/2 tsp. salt

Cream ...... first 4 ingredients together in bowl.
Beat .... with electric mixer at high speed for 5 minutes.
Blend ...... in chocolate.
Sift .... dry ingredients together.
Add .... to creamed mixture alternately with 1 1/2 cups ice water, beating well after each addition.
Pour .... into 2 waxed paper-lined 9-inch round pans.
Bake .... at 350 degrees for 30 to 35 minutes or until cakes test done.
Frost .... with desired frosting.

Kim Wiggins
Ringwood, H. S., Ringwood, Oklahoma

LINDA'S GERMAN CHOCOLATE CAKE

4 oz. Hershey's sweet chocolate
2/3 c. butter, softened
Sugar
1 tsp. vanilla extract
3 eggs, separated
1 3/4 c. cake flour
3/4 tsp. soda
1/2 tsp. salt
2/3 c. buttermilk
1 recipe Coconut-Pecan Frosting

Melt .... chocolate in 1/3 cup boiling water in saucepan; cool.
Combine .... butter, 1 cup plus 2 tablespoons sugar and vanilla in large mixer bowl.
Beat .... with electric mixer at high speed until fluffy.
Add .... egg yolks 1 at a time, beating well after each addition.
Stir .... in melted chocolate gradually.
Combine .... flour, soda and salt.
Add .... to creamed mixture alternately with buttermilk, beating well after each addition.

Fold . . . . in stiffly beaten egg whites.
Pour . . . . into prepared baking pans.
Bake . . . . at 350 degrees until cakes test done.
Frost . . . . with Coconut-Pecan Frosting.

Coconut-Pecan Frosting

2/3 c. evaporated milk
2/3 c. sugar
1/4 c. butter
1 egg, slightly beaten
1 c. coconut
3/4 c. chopped pecans
1/2 tsp. vanilla extract

Combine . . . . first 4 ingredients in saucepan.
Bring . . . . to a boil over medium heat.
Boil . . . . for 2 minutes; cool.
Add . . . . coconut, pecans and vanilla.
Cool . . . . until of spreading consistency, stirring occasionally.

Linda Lou Thompson
Cleveland H. S., Cleveland, Oklahoma

BIG GERMAN SWEET CHOCOLATE CAKE

1 4-oz. package German's sweet chocolate
1 c. margarine, softened
2 c. sugar
4 eggs, separated
1 tsp. vanilla extract
2 1/4 c. sifted flour
1 tsp. soda
1/2 tsp. salt
1 c. buttermilk
1 recipe Coconut-Pecan Frosting

Melt . . . . chocolate in 1/2 cup boiling water in saucepan.
Cream . . . . . . margarine and sugar in bowl until fluffy.
Add . . . . egg yolks 1 at a time, beating well after each addition.
Blend . . . . . . in vanilla and chocolate.
Sift . . . . dry ingredients together.
Add . . . . to creamed mixture alternately with buttermilk, beating well after each addition.
Fold . . . . in stiffly beaten egg whites.
Pour . . . . into 3 waxed paper-lined 9-inch round cake pans.

Bake . . . . at 350 degrees for 30 to 35 minutes.
Frost . . . . with Coconut-Pecan Frosting.

Coconut-Pecan Frosting

1 c. evaporated milk
3 egg yolks, slightly beaten
1 tsp. vanilla extract
1 c. sugar
1/2 c. butter
1 1/3 c. coconut
1 c. chopped pecans

Combine . . . . first 5 ingredients in saucepan.
Cook . . . . over medium heat for 12 minutes or until thick.
Add . . . . coconut and pecans.
Cool . . . . until of spreading consistency, beating occasionally.

Patricia L. Kubat
Former State Officer, 1973-74
Okeene H. S., Okeene, Oklahoma
Kindra Doll
Ringwood H. S., Ringwood, Oklahoma

HEAVENLY HASH CAKE

1 c. sugar
3/4 c. self-rising flour
2 eggs
1 tsp. vanilla extract
2 c. chopped pecans
Melted margarine
4 tbsp. cocoa
Miniature marshmallows
3/4 box confectioners' sugar
3 to 4 tbsp. evaporated milk

Combine . . . . first 5 ingredients with 1/2 cup margarine and 2 tablespoons cocoa in bowl, mixing well.
Pour . . . . into prepared 9 x 13-inch baking pan.
Bake . . . . at 350 degrees for 1/2 hour.
Spread . . . . . marshmallows over hot cake.
Combine . . . . remaining ingredients with 2 tablespoons margarine and 2 tablespoons cocoa in bowl, mixing well.
Spread . . . . . over marshmallows.

Lori Kemp
Rattan H. S., Rattan, Oklahoma

GO-COLA CAKE

2 eggs
1 3/4 c. sugar
1/2 c. buttermilk
2 c. flour
1 tsp. soda
1 1/2 c. butter, softened
1 1/2 tsp. vanilla extract
6 tbsp. cocoa
1 1/3 c. Coca-Cola
1 1/2 c. miniature marshmallows
1 box confectioners' sugar
1 c. nuts, chopped

Blend . . . . . . first 5 ingredients with 1 cup butter, 1 teaspoon vanilla and 3 tablespoons cocoa in bowl.
Beat . . . . with electric mixer at medium speed for 1 minute.
Add . . . . 1 cup Coca-Cola, blending well.
Fold . . . . in marshmallows.
Pour . . . . into greased 8 x 12-inch baking pan.
Bake . . . . at 350 degrees for 45 minutes.
Combine . . . . confectioners' sugar, nuts and remaining 1/2 cup butter, 1/2 teaspoon vanilla, 3 tablespoons cocoa and 1/3 cup Coca-Cola in bowl, mixing well.
Spread . . . . . over top of cooled cake.

Irene Garman
Okeene Public Schools, Okeene, Oklahoma

MAYONNAISE CAKE

2 c. salad dressing
2 c. sugar
4 c. sifted flour
2 tsp. soda
2 tsp. baking powder
1/2 tsp. salt
6 tbsp. cocoa
2 tsp. vanilla extract

Blend . . . . . . salad dressing and sugar together in bowl until smooth.
Combine . . . . dry ingredients.
Add . . . . to sugar mixture alternately with 2 cups water and vanilla, beating well after each addition.
Pour . . . . into greased baking pan.

Bake . . . . at 350 degrees for 35 minutes or until cake tests done.
Frost . . . . with orange or German chocolate frosting.

Kristi Clester
Okeene H. S., Okeene, Oklahoma

MISSISSIPPI MUD

2 c. sugar
2 c. flour
1 1/2 c. butter
1/2 c. cocoa
1/2 c. sour milk
1 tsp. soda
2 eggs, slightly beaten
2 tsp. vanilla extract
6 tbsp. milk
1 box confectioners' sugar

Sift . . . . sugar and flour into bowl.
Combine . . . . 1 cup butter, 1 cup water and 1/4 cup cocoa in saucepan.
Bring . . . . to a boil, stirring constantly.
Pour . . . . over flour mixture.
Add . . . . sour milk, soda, eggs and 1 teaspoon vanilla, mixing well.
Pour . . . . into greased baking pan.
Bake . . . . at 400 degrees for 20 minutes.
Combine . . . . remaining 1/2 cup butter, 1/4 cup cocoa and milk in saucepan.
Bring . . . . to boiling point.
Blend . . . . . . in confectioners' sugar and remaining 1 teaspoon vanilla.
Pour . . . . over hot cake.

Edie Madison
Nowata H. S., Nowata, Oklahoma

CHOCOLATE-OATMEAL CAKE

1 c. oatmeal
3/4 stick margarine
1 bar German's chocolate
1 1/2 c. sifted flour
1/2 c. sugar
1/2 tsp. salt
1 tsp. soda
2 eggs
1 c. packed brown sugar
3 tbsp. milk
1 c. chopped nuts
1 c. coconut
1 tsp. vanilla extract

Pour . . . . 1 1/2 cups boiling water over oatmeal, margarine and half the chocolate in bowl, stirring until melted.

Stir . . . . in next 5 ingredients with 1/2 cup brown sugar, mixing well.

Pour . . . . into greased and floured pan.

Bake . . . . at 350 degrees for 30 minutes.

Combine . . . . milk, remaining brown sugar and chocolate in saucepan.

Cook . . . . over low heat until melted, blending well.

Stir . . . . in remaining ingredients.

Spread . . . . . over hot cake.

Bake . . . . until bubbly.

Jequetta Kaiser
Nowata H. S., Nowata, Oklahoma

TEXAS CAKE

2 sticks margarine
4 tbsp. cocoa
2 c. flour
2 c. sugar
1/2 c. sour cream
1 tsp. soda
1/2 tsp. salt
1 tsp. vanilla extract

Combine . . . . margarine and cocoa with 1 cup water in saucepan.

Bring . . . . to a boil.

Add . . . . remaining ingredients.

Pour . . . . into baking pan.

Bake . . . . at 350 degrees until cake tests done.

Lea Ann Casebolt
State Secretary
Cleveland H. S., Cleveland, Oklahoma

WACKY CAKE

3 c. flour
6 tbsp. cocoa
1 tsp. salt
2 tsp. soda
2 c. sugar
2 tbsp. vinegar
2 tsp. vanilla extract
3/4 c. oil

Sift . . . . first 5 ingredients together into 9 x 13-inch cake pan.

Make . . . . 3 wells in mixture.

Pour . . . . vinegar in first well, vanilla in second and oil in third.

Cover . . . . . . with 2 cups cold water, mixing with fork.

Bake . . . . at 350 degrees for 30 minutes.

Audine Cooper
Allen H. S., Allen, Oklahoma

WALDORF ASTORIA RED CAKE

1 c. milk
2 1/4 c. flour
1 c. shortening
2 1/2 c. sugar
2 eggs
Dash of salt
1 tbsp. cocoa
1 c. buttermilk
1 tbsp. vinegar
1 tsp. soda
3 tbsp. red food coloring
2 tsp. vanilla extract
1 stick margarine, softened

Cook . . . . milk and 1/4 cup flour together in saucepan until thick, stirring constantly.

Set . . . . aside to cool.

Cream . . . . . . 1/2 cup shortening, 1 1/2 cups sugar and eggs in large bowl.

Sift . . . . 2 cups flour, salt and cocoa together.

Add . . . . to creamed mixture alternately with buttermilk, beating well after each addition.

Mix . . . . vinegar and soda together in small bowl.

Add . . . . to batter, beating well.

Fold . . . . in food coloring and 1 teaspoon vanilla.

Pour . . . . into 3 greased and floured 8-inch round cake pans.

Bake . . . . at 350 degrees for 30 minutes.

Cream . . . . . . margarine, 1/2 cup shortening, 1 cup sugar and 1 teaspoon vanilla together in bowl.

Beat . . . . in cooled milk mixture until fluffy.

Frost . . . . between layers and over top of cooled cake.

Shannon Stephen
Cache H. S., Cache, Oklahoma

WALNUT-COCOA CAKE

1/2 c. shortening
3/4 c. sugar
2 eggs
1/2 c. honey
2 tsp. grated orange rind
2 c. sifted cake flour
1/3 c. cocoa
1 tsp. soda
1/2 tsp. salt
1/4 tsp. each cinnamon, nutmeg
2/3 c. buttermilk
3/4 c. finely chopped California walnuts
Cocoa Icing
1/2 c. chopped California walnuts

Cream . . . . . . shortening and sugar in bowl until light and fluffy.
Add . . . . eggs 1 at a time, beating well after each addition.
Beat . . . . in honey and orange rind.
Sift . . . . flour, cocoa, soda, salt and spices together.
Add . . . . to creamed mixture alternately with buttermilk, beating well after each addition.
Stir . . . . in finely chopped walnuts.
Pour . . . . into 2 greased and floured 9-inch layer cake pans.
Bake . . . . at 350 degrees for 25 to 30 minutes.
Let . . . . stand for 5 minutes.
Invert . . . . . . on wire racks to cool.
Spread . . . . . Cocoa Icing between layers and over sides and top of cakes.
Pat . . . . chopped walnuts around sides of cake.

Cocoa Icing

1/2 c. butter, melted
1/4 c. cocoa
1 lb. confectioners' sugar
1/4 c. light cream
1/2 tsp. vanilla extract
1/2 tsp. grated orange rind

Blend . . . . . . butter and cocoa in bowl.
Beat . . . . in confectioners' sugar and cream.
Add . . . . vanilla and orange rind, beating until smooth.

Beat . . . . in additional cream if necessary to make of spreading consistency.

Photograph for this recipe on page 114.

COCONUT DELIGHT

2 sticks margarine, softened
1/2 c. shortening
2 c. sugar
5 eggs, separated
2 c. flour
1 tsp. soda
1/8 tsp. salt
1 c. buttermilk
1 box confectioners' sugar
1 pkg. cream cheese, softened
1 tsp. vanilla extract
1 c. coconut

Cream . . . . . . 1 stick margarine, shortening and sugar in bowl.
Add . . . . egg yolks 1 at a time, beating well after each addition.
Combine . . . . flour, soda and salt.
Add . . . . to creamed mixture alternately with buttermilk, beating well after each addition.
Fold . . . . in stiffly beaten egg whites.
Pour . . . . into 3 prepared 9-inch cake pans.
Bake . . . . at 350 degrees until cakes test done.
Blend . . . . . . confectioners' sugar, cream cheese, 1 stick margarine and vanilla in bowl.
Spread . . . . . between layers and on top of cake, sprinkling coconut over frosting.

Stephanie Ann Wright
Union City H. S., Union City, Oklahoma

ENGLISH JIFFY CAKE

3/4 c. margarine, softened
3/4 c. castor sugar
2 eggs
2 c. flour
2 tsp. baking powder
1/2 c. milk

Combine . . . . all ingredients in large mixer bowl.

Beat . . . . with electric mixer at medium speed for 2 to 3 minutes.

Pour . . . . into greased and floured 9-inch round cake pan.

Bake . . . . at 350 degrees for 35 minutes.

Carrie Owens
Union City H. S., Union City, Oklahoma

GINGERBREAD

1 3/4 c. sifted flour
3/4 c. cornmeal
1 tsp. baking powder
3/4 tsp. salt
3/4 tsp. soda
1 tsp. cinnamon
1 tsp. ginger
1/4 tsp. mace
1/3 c. butter, softened
1/2 c. packed brown sugar
2 eggs
1/2 c. light molasses
3/4 c. buttermilk

Sift . . . . first 8 ingredients together; set aside.

Cream . . . . . . butter and sugar together in bowl.

Beat . . . . in eggs and molasses.

Stir . . . . in dry ingredients, mixing well.

Add . . . . buttermilk.

Beat . . . . with electric mixer at low speed.

Pour . . . . into greased 9-inch square baking pan.

Bake . . . . at 350 degrees for 35 to 40 minutes.

Serve . . . . warm or cold.

Photograph for this recipe on this page.

ITALIAN CREAM CAKE

1 1/2 sticks margarine, softened
1/2 c. shortening
2 c. sugar
5 eggs, separated
2 c. flour
1 tsp. soda
1 c. buttermilk
1 c. nuts, chopped

2 sm. cans flaked coconut
2 tsp. vanilla extract
1 8-oz. package cream cheese, softened
1 box confectioners' sugar

Cream . . . . . . 1 stick margarine, shortening and sugar together in bowl.

Add . . . . egg yolks, beating well.

Blend . . . . . . in flour, soda and buttermilk.

Stir . . . . in nuts, 1 can coconut and 1 teaspoon vanilla.

Fold . . . . in beaten egg whites.

Pour . . . . into 4 prepared 9-inch cake pans.

Bake . . . . at 350 degrees until cakes test done.

Combine . . . . cream cheese, 1/2 stick margarine, confectioners' sugar and 1 teaspoon vanilla in bowl, beating well.

Spread . . . . . between layers and on top of cake, sprinkling 1 can coconut over frosting.

Edna Crow
State Dept. of Vo-Tech Ed., Stillwater, Oklahoma

LEMON DAISY CAKE

1 c. butter
1 3/4 c. sugar
6 egg whites
3/4 c. milk
1 tsp. vanilla extract
3 c. sifted cake flour
3/4 tsp. salt
4 tsp. baking powder
Lemon Filling

Cream . . . . . . butter and sugar in bowl until light and fluffy.
Add . . . . egg whites 2 at a time, beating well after each addition.
Mix . . . . milk, vanilla and 1/2 cup water.
Sift . . . . dry ingredients together.
Add . . . . to creamed mixture alternately with milk mixture, beginning and ending with dry ingredients, beating well after each addition.
Pour . . . . into 2 greased and floured 9-inch round cake pans.
Bake . . . . at 350 degrees for 30 to 35 minutes or until cakes test done.
Spread . . . . . Lemon Filling between cooled cake layers.
Frost . . . . with favorite fluffy white frosting.
Garnish . . . . . with thin lemon rind strips.

Lemon Filling

8 egg yolks, beaten
1 1/2 c. sugar
Juice and grated rind of 2 lemons
1/4 c. butter

Combine . . . . all ingredients in saucepan.
Cook . . . . over very low heat until thick, stirring constantly.

Photograph for this recipe on this page.

LISA'S PINEAPPLE UPSIDE-DOWN CAKE

1 c. packed brown sugar
1/2 c. butter, melted
6 to 8 slices pineapple, drained
1/2 c. chopped pecans
6 to 8 maraschino cherry halves
3 eggs, separated
1 c. sugar
5 tbsp. pineapple juice
1 c. flour
1 tsp. baking powder

Add . . . . sugar to butter in heavy skillet, mixing well.
Arrange . . . . . pineapple and pecans in skillet, placing cherry in center of each pineapple slice.
Mix . . . . beaten egg yolks, sugar and pineapple juice in bowl.
Stir . . . . in sifted dry ingredients.
Fold . . . . in stiffly beaten egg whites.
Spoon . . . . . . over pineapple.
Bake . . . . at 350 degrees for 45 to 60 minutes.

Lisa Wright
Okeene Public Schools, Okeene, Oklahoma

PLUM CAKE

2 c. sugar
2 c. flour
1 c. oil
3 eggs
2 sm. jars baby food plums
1/2 tsp. soda
1/2 tsp. salt
1/2 tsp. cloves
1 tsp. cinnamon
1 1/2 tbsp. red food coloring

Combine . . . . all ingredients in bowl.
Beat . . . . with electric mixer for 4 minutes.
Pour . . . . into greased and floured bundt pan.

Bake .... at 350 degrees for 1 hour or until cake tests done.
Cool .... in pan for 10 minutes.

Twanda Page
Weatherford H. S., Weatherford, Oklahoma

POPPY SEED POUND CAKE

1/2 c. poppy seed
1/2 c. milk
Sugar
1 1/2 c. butter, softened
2 tbsp. grated lemon rind
1 tbsp. grated orange rind
8 eggs, separated
2 c. sifted cake flour
3/4 tsp. salt
1/2 c. lemon juice
1/4 c. orange juice

Soak .... poppy seed in milk in small bowl for 2 hours.
Rinse ...... under cold running water, draining well.
Beat .... 1 1/4 cups sugar gradually into creamed butter.
Add .... rinds and egg yolks 1 at a time, beating well after each addition, then beat for 5 minutes longer.
Add .... 1/4 cup sugar gradually to softly beaten egg whites, beating until stiff.
Sift .... flour and salt, 1/3 at a time, over yolk mixture, folding in after each addition.
Fold .... in egg whites, 1/4 at a time, and poppy seed.
Pour .... into greased 10-inch bundt pan.
Bake .... at 350 degrees for 1 hour or until cake tests done.
Cool .... on wire rack for 5 minutes before removing from pan.
Combine .... juices with 1/3 cup sugar, stirring until dissolved.
Spoon ...... slowly over cake until surface is well moistened but not soggy.
Serve .... cooled cake with whipped cream flavored with 1 teaspoon each lemon and orange rind.

Virginia Lamb
Home Ec. Dept. Head, Central State U.
Edmond, Oklahoma

SEVEN-UP POUND CAKE

4 sticks margarine
Sugar
5 eggs
3 c. sifted flour
1 bottle of 7-Up
1 tsp. vanilla extract
1 tsp. lemon extract

Cream ...... margarine with 3 cups plus 3 tablespoons sugar in bowl.
Add .... eggs 1 at a time, beating well after each addition.
Add .... flour and 7-Up alternately, beating well after each addition.
Stir .... in flavorings.
Pour .... into greased and floured bundt pan.
Bake .... at 350 degrees for 1 1/2 hours.
Cool .... for 15 minutes before removing from pan.

Tami Lundquist
Lindsay H. S., Lindsay, Oklahoma

ZUCCHINI CAKE

3 eggs, beaten
1 c. oil
2 c. sugar
2 tsp. vanilla extract
2 c. flour
3 tsp. cinnamon
2 tsp. soda
1 tsp. salt
1/2 tsp. baking powder
2 c. coarsely grated peeled zucchini
1 8-oz. can crushed pineapple
1/2 c. chopped nuts (opt.)

Combine .... first 4 ingredients in bowl, mixing well.
Blend ...... in dry ingredients.
Stir .... in zucchini, pineapple and nuts.
Pour .... into greased and floured 10-inch bundt pan.
Bake .... at 350 degrees for 55 to 60 minutes.
Cool .... in pan for 20 minutes.

Carrie Young
Chisholm H. S., Enid, Oklahoma

ITALIAN SOUR CREAM CAKE WITH AMARETTO

2 eggs, separated
1/2 c. packed brown sugar
1 c. coconut
Ground pecans
1 pkg. butter cake mix with pudding
1 c. sour cream
Amaretto
2 eggs
1 c. sifted confectioners' sugar
2 tbsp. cocoa
1 tbsp. margarine, softened
1 tbsp. corn syrup
6 maraschino cherries

Beat .... 2 egg whites in small bowl until foamy.
Add .... brown sugar gradually, beating for 3 minutes or until stiff.
Fold .... in coconut and 1/2 cup ground pecans.
Spread ..... on bottom and up side of generously greased 10-inch tube pan.
Beat .... cake mix, sour cream, 1/2 cup Amaretto, 1/2 cup water, 2 egg yolks and 2 eggs in bowl with electric mixer at low speed until moistened.
Beat .... on high for 2 minutes.
Spread ..... evenly in prepared pan.
Bake .... at 350 degrees for 55 to 65 minutes or until cake tests done.
Cool .... in pan for 10 minutes.
Invert ...... onto serving plate.
Blend ...... confectioners' sugar, cocoa, 2 tablespoons Amaretto, margarine, corn syrup and 2 to 4 teaspoons water in bowl until smooth.
Spoon ...... over cool cake.
Decorate .... with 2 teaspoons ground pecans and maraschino cherries.

Laurie Adam
Okeene H. S., Okeene, Oklahoma

PUMPKIN CAKE

3 1/4 c. sifted flour
Sugar
2 tsp. soda

1 1/2 tsp. salt
1/4 tsp. baking powder
1 tsp. cinnamon
1/2 tsp. ground cloves
3/4 tsp. nutmeg
3/4 c. shortening
Frozen Florida orange juice, thawed
1 15-oz. can applesauce
3 eggs
1 1/2 c. raisins
1 c. chopped nuts
2 egg whites
1/2 tsp. cream of tartar
1 tsp. vanilla extract
Food coloring
1/2 sm. banana

Sift .... flour, 2 1/2 cups sugar and next 6 ingredients into large mixing bowl.
Add .... shortening, 6 tablespoons each orange juice, water and applesauce.
Beat .... with electric mixer at medium speed for 2 minutes.
Add .... eggs.
Beat .... for 2 minutes longer.
Stir .... in raisins and nuts.
Pour .... into greased and floured 10-inch tube pan.
Bake .... at 350 degrees for 1 1/4 hours or until cake tests done.
Cool .... for 15 to 20 minutes before removing from pan.
Combine .... egg whites, 1 1/2 cups sugar, cream of tartar, 1/2 cup orange juice and vanilla in double boiler pan over boiling water.
Beat .... with electric mixer at high speed for 5 to 7 minutes or until peaks form.
Tint .... 1/2 cup frosting with green food coloring.
Add .... several drops of yellow and red food coloring to remaining frosting to tint orange.
Trim .... cake to resemble pumpkin.
Place .... on serving plate.
Stand ...... banana in center for stem.
Frost .... cake with orange frosting and stem with green frosting.

Photograph for this recipe on page 104.

CREAM CHEESE QUICKIE

1 box chocolate cake mix
3 eggs
1 tsp. vanilla extract
1 stick butter
1 box confectioners' sugar
1 8-oz. package cream cheese, softened

Combine .... cake mix, 1 egg, 1/2 teaspoon vanilla and butter in bowl, mixing well.
Pat .... into greased 9 x 13-inch baking pan.
Mix .... remaining ingredients in bowl.
Pour .... over first mixture.
Bake .... at 350 degrees for 30 minutes.

Debbie Orgain
Hammon School, Hammon, Oklahoma

COCONUT-PINEAPPLE REFRIGERATOR CAKE

1 box yellow cake mix
1 15-oz. can crushed pineapple
1 c. sugar
1 box vanilla instant pudding mix
1 c. coconut
1 carton Cool Whip
Nuts

Prepare ..... cake using package directions.
Punch ...... holes in baked cake with knife.
Simmer ..... pineapple and sugar in saucepan.
Pour .... over cake; chill.
Prepare ..... pudding mix using package directions and adding coconut.
Spread ..... over top of cake.
Top .... with Cool Whip.
Sprinkle .... with nuts.

Ramona Weidner
Hennessey H. S., Hennessey, Oklahoma

GOOEY BUTTER CAKE

1 stick margarine, softened
1 box yellow cake mix
4 eggs
1 8-oz. package cream cheese, softened
1 1-lb. box confectioners' sugar

Combine .... first 2 ingredients and 2 eggs in bowl, mixing well.
Pour .... into greased and floured 9 x 13-inch baking pan.

Combine .... remaining ingredients in bowl, beating well.
Pour .... over first mixture.
Bake .... at 350 degrees for 35 to 40 minutes.

Lana Taylor
Mustang H. S., Mustang, Oklahoma
Nancy Schultz
Okeene H. S., Okeene, Oklahoma

GLAZED RUM CAKE

1/2 c. chopped nuts
1 box yellow cake mix
3 eggs, beaten
3/4 c. oil
3/4 c. light rum
1 c. sugar
1 stick margarine, melted

Sprinkle .... oiled bundt pan with chopped nuts.
Mix .... next 3 ingredients with 1/2 cup rum and 1/2 cup warm water in bowl.
Pour .... into prepared pan.
Bake .... at 275 degrees for 1 hour.
Mix .... remaining ingredients together.
Pour .... over warm cake.

Michele Blakley
Wilson H. S., Wilson, Oklahoma

SOCK-IT-TO-ME CAKE

Sugar
3 tsp. cinnamon
1 butter cake mix
4 tsp. butter flavoring
4 eggs
3/4 c. oil
1 c. sour cream
1 c. nuts

Coat .... greased bundt pan with mixture of 3 tablespoons sugar and cinnamon.
Mix .... remaining ingredients with 1/2 cup sugar in bowl.
Pour .... into prepared pan.
Bake .... at 350 degrees for 40 to 60 minutes or until cake tests done.

Jerri Newville
Moore West Mid-H. S., Oklahoma City, Oklahoma

Candies and Cookies

BROWNIES

CHOCOLATE BARS

PEANUT BUTTER BARS

SUGAR COOKIES

MICROWAVE CANDY

PEANUT BUTTER COOKIES

CHOCOLATE COOKIES

CHOCOLATE CHIP COOKIES

CHOCOLATE CANDY

BUTTERMILK FUDGE

1 tsp. soda
1 c. buttermilk
2 c. sugar
1/4 c. light corn syrup
2 tbsp. butter
1 tsp. vanilla extract
1 c. nuts

Dissolve . . . . soda in buttermilk in saucepan.
Stir . . . . in sugar and syrup.
Cook . . . . to soft-ball stage or 240 degrees on candy thermometer.
Stir . . . . in remaining ingredients.
Beat . . . . . . until creamy.
Pour . . . . into buttered pan.
Cut . . . . in squares when cool.

Sharon Richardson
Moore West H. S., Oklahoma City, Oklahoma

CARAMELS

1 c. butter, melted
1 lb. brown sugar
Dash of salt
1 c. light corn syrup
1 can sweetened condensed milk
1 tsp. vanilla extract

Blend . . . . . . first 4 ingredients in saucepan.
Stir . . . . in condensed milk gradually.
Cook . . . . over medium heat to firm-ball stage or 245 degrees on candy thermometer, stirring constantly.
Stir . . . . in vanilla.
Pour . . . . into buttered 9 x 9-inch pan.
Cut . . . . into squares when cool.

Valerie Riggs
Ringwood H. S., Ringwood, Oklahoma

BONBONS

2 lb. confectioners' sugar
1/4 lb. butter, softened
1/4 tsp. almond extract
Dash of salt
1 can sweetened condensed milk
1 lg. package coconut
Chopped cherries
Chopped nuts
1 lg. package chocolate chips
1 box paraffin

Blend . . . . . . first 5 ingredients in large bowl.
Mix . . . . in coconut, cherries and nuts.
Shape . . . . . . into balls; chill.
Melt . . . . chocolate chips and paraffin in double boiler, blending well.
Dip . . . . Bonbons in chocolate.
Cool . . . . on waxed paper.

Melissa Blakely
Wilson H. S., Wilson, Oklahoma

CHOCOLATE-DIPPED MARSHMALLOWS

1 8-oz. milk chocolate bar
1 tsp. shortening
30 lg. marshmallows
Chopped peanuts
Graham cracker crumbs
Flaked coconut

Melt . . . . chocolate bar with shortening in double boiler over hot water.
Remove . . . . from heat to cool slightly.
Dip . . . . marshmallows with toothpicks into melted chocolate, covering completely.
Scrape . . . . . . off excess chocolate on side of pan.
Dip . . . . in peanuts, graham cracker crumbs or coconut.
Place . . . . on waxed paper-lined cookie sheet.
Remove . . . . toothpicks, swirling chocolate.
Chill . . . . for 15 minutes.
Yields . . . . . . 30 pieces.

Photograph for this recipe on page 1.

CHOCOLATE KISS DIVINITY

2 1/2 c. sugar
1/2 c. light corn syrup
2 egg whites, stiffly beaten
1 tsp. vanilla extract
1/2 tsp. mint flavoring
1/4 tsp. salt
Several drops of red or green food coloring
1/2 c. chopped nuts (opt.)
30 milk chocolate kisses

Combine . . . . sugar, corn syrup and 1/2 cup water in 2-quart saucepan.

Bring . . . . to a boil over medium heat, stirring constantly until sugar dissolves.

Cook . . . . to hard-ball stage or 260 degrees on candy thermometer; do not stir.

Pour . . . . slowly over egg whites, beating with electric mixer at high speed.

Add . . . . flavorings and salt.

Beat . . . . until candy holds shape.

Fold . . . . in food coloring and nuts.

Drop . . . . by teaspoonfuls onto waxed paper.

Press . . . . unwrapped chocolate kiss on top.

Store . . . . in airtight container.

Yields . . . . . . 30 pieces.

Photograph for this recipe on page 1.

EASY CREAMY COCOA FUDGE

3/4 c. cocoa
1/2 c. butter, melted
1   14-oz. can sweetened condensed milk
1 lb. confectioners' sugar, sifted
2 tsp. vanilla extract
1 c. chopped nuts (opt.)

Blend . . . . . . cocoa and butter in saucepan until smooth.

Stir . . . . in condensed milk.

Cook . . . . over low heat for 5 minutes or until thickened; remove from heat.

Beat . . . . in confectioners' sugar and vanilla until smooth.

Fold . . . . in nuts.

Pour . . . . into buttered 9-inch square pan.

Garnish . . . . . with walnut halves.

Yields . . . . . . 20 squares.

Photograph for this recipe on page 1.

NUT CLUSTER CUPS

1 c. semisweet chocolate chips
1 tsp. shortening
1 c. broken pecans

Melt . . . . chocolate chips with shortening in double boiler over hot water.

Stir . . . . in pecans.

Drop . . . . by heaping teaspoonfuls into 1-inch paper candy cups.

Chill . . . . until firm.

Yields . . . . . . 14-16 cups.

Photograph for this recipe on page 1.

ROCKY ROAD

2   8-oz. milk chocolate bars
3 c. miniature marshmallows
3/4 c. coarsely broken walnuts

Melt . . . . chocolate bars in double boiler over warm water.

Stir . . . . in marshmallows and walnuts.

Spread . . . . . in buttered 8-inch square pan.

Chill . . . . until firm.

Yields . . . . . . 16 squares.

Photograph for this recipe on page 1.

DATE LOAF CANDY

2 c. sugar
1 c. milk
2 tbsp. corn syrup
2 tbsp. butter
1 c. finely chopped dates
1 c. chopped nuts
1/2 tsp. vanilla extract

Combine . . . . first 4 ingredients in saucepan.

Cook . . . . to soft-ball stage or 235 degrees on candy thermometer.

Stir . . . . in remaining ingredients.

Cook . . . . for 5 minutes, stirring constantly.

Remove . . . . from heat.

Beat . . . . until stiff enough to shape into roll on moist tea towel sprinkled with confectioners' sugar.

Slice . . . . for serving.

Pat Kellner
Okeene Public Schools, Okeene, Oklahoma

PEANUT BRITTLE

2 c. sugar
1 c. light corn syrup
2 c. raw peanuts
2 tsp. soda
1 tsp. vanilla extract
1 tbsp. butter

Combine .... sugar and syrup in saucepan.
Cook .... to soft-crack stage or 285 degrees on candy thermometer, stirring frequently.
Stir .... in peanuts.
Cook .... until golden brown, stirring constantly.
Remove .... from heat.
Stir .... in remaining ingredients quickly.
Pour .... immediately onto buttered baking sheet, spreading thinly.
Break ...... into pieces when cool.

Paula Schultz
Okeene H. S., Okeene, Oklahoma

FESTIVE PEANUT BUTTER FUDGE

3/4 c. evaporated milk
1/4 c. margarine
2 1/4 c. sugar
1 7-oz. jar marshmallow creme
1 tsp. vanilla extract
1 12-oz. package peanut butter chips
1 c. broken pecans
1/4 c. red candied cherries

Combine .... first 4 ingredients in 3-quart saucepan, mixing well.
Boil .... for 5 minutes, stirring constantly.
Remove .... from heat.
Stir .... in remaining ingredients until chips are completely melted.
Pour .... into buttered 8 x 8-inch pan.
Garnish ..... with additional pecans and cherries.

Janine Dorsey
Ft. Cobb H. S., Ft. Cobb, Oklahoma

QUICK PEANUT FUDGE

2 c. sugar
3 tbsp. butter
1 c. evaporated milk
1 c. miniature marshmallows
1 12-oz. jar chunk-style peanut butter
1 tsp. vanilla extract

Combine .... first 3 ingredients in electric skillet.
Bring .... to a boil or 280 degrees.
Boil .... for 5 minutes, stirring constantly.
Turn .... off skillet.
Add .... marshmallows, peanut butter and vanilla, stirring until blended.
Pour .... into buttered 8-inch square pan.
Cut .... into squares when cool.
Yields ...... 2 pounds.

Photograph for this recipe on this page.

PEANUT SPONGE

3 c. sugar
2 c. corn syrup
3 c. salted peanuts
2 tsp. soda

Combine .... sugar, syrup and 1/2 cup water in heavy saucepan.
Bring .... to a boil over medium heat, stirring constantly.
Cook .... to 280 degrees on candy thermometer.
Add .... peanuts gradually.
Cook .... to 300 degrees on candy thermometer, stirring frequently.

Remove .... from heat.
Blend ...... in soda.
Pour .... onto 2 greased baking sheets.
Break ...... into pieces when cool.
Yields ...... 2 1/2 pounds.

Photograph for this recipe on this page.

STRAWBERRY DIVINITY

1 sm. package strawberry gelatin
2 egg whites, stiffly beaten
3 c. sugar
3/4 c. light corn syrup

Beat .... dry gelatin into stiffly beaten egg whites.
Combine .... sugar, syrup and 3/4 cup hot water in saucepan.
Boil .... until mixture threads from spoon.
Pour .... over egg whites mixture, beating constantly until stiff.
Drop .... by teaspoonfuls onto waxed paper.

Mary K. Leonhart
Terral School, Terral, Oklahoma

MICROWAVE CHOCOLATE PEANUT CANDY

12 oz. chocolate chips
12 oz. peanut butter chips
3 c. salted peanuts

Place .... chips in large glass dish.
Microwave .. on Medium until melted.
Stir .... in peanuts.
Drop .... by spoonfuls onto waxed paper.

Beverly Burton
Skiatook H. S., Skiatook, Oklahoma

MICROWAVE CARAMEL FUDGE

1/2 c. butter
1 c. packed brown sugar
1/4 c. milk
1/2 tsp. vanilla extract
3 1/4 c. confectioners' sugar
1/2 c. chopped nuts

Place .... butter in 1-quart glass bowl.
Microwave .. on High for 1 minute or until melted.

Blend ...... in brown sugar.
Microwave .. on High for 2 minutes.
Stir .... until slightly thickened.
Blend ...... in remaining ingredients in order given.
Spread ..... in buttered 8-inch cake pan.
Chill .... for 1 hour before cutting into pieces.

Kim Maynard
Pawhuska H. S., Pawhuska, Oklahoma

MICROWAVE PECAN BRITTLE

1 c. sugar
1/2 c. light corn syrup
1 c. frozen pecans
1 tsp. vanilla extract
1 tbsp. butter
1 tsp. soda

Blend ...... sugar and syrup in glass bowl.
Microwave .. on High for 4 minutes.
Stir .... in pecans.
Microwave .. on High for 3 minutes.
Stir .... in vanilla and butter.
Microwave .. on High for 2 minutes.
Stir .... in soda and pour into buttered pan.

Shelia Fisher
Okeene Public Schools, Okeene, Oklahoma

APRICOT BARS

1/2 c. margarine
1 1/2 c. graham cracker crumbs
1 6-oz. package dried apricots, chopped
1 can sweetened condensed milk
1 3 1/2-oz. can flaked coconut
1/2 c. coarsely chopped nuts

Melt . . . . margarine in 9 x 13-inch baking dish.
Spread . . . . . crumbs and apricots in dish.
Pour . . . . condensed milk evenly over all.
Top . . . . with coconut and nuts, pressing gently.
Bake . . . . at 350 degrees for 25 to 30 minutes or until lightly browned.

Norita Adam
Okeene, Oklahoma

BUTTERSCOTCH BARS

3/4 c. butter, melted
1 pkg. brown sugar
3 eggs
3 c. flour
3 tsp. baking powder
3/4 tsp. salt
1 tsp. vanilla extract
Nuts

Blend . . . . . . butter and brown sugar in bowl.
Add . . . . remaining ingredients, mixing well.
Spread . . . . . in greased baking dish.
Bake . . . . at 300 degrees until bars test done.
Cut . . . . into bars while warm.

Duane Billey
Reydon H. S., Reydon, Oklahoma

LEMON SQUARES

2 sticks margarine
1/2 c. confectioners' sugar
1/2 tsp. salt
Flour
4 eggs
1/2 tsp. vanilla extract
2 c. sugar
2 tbsp. lemon juice

Combine . . . . first 3 ingredients with 2 cups flour in bowl, mixing until crumbly.
Pat . . . . into buttered 8 x 8-inch baking dish.
Bake . . . . at 350 degrees for 25 minutes.
Combine . . . . remaining ingredients with 6 tablespoons flour in bowl.
Beat . . . . for 1 minute.
Pour . . . . over crust.
Bake . . . . for 30 minutes longer.
Cut . . . . into squares, sprinkling with additional confectioners' sugar.

Gina Bidack
Chandler H. S., Chandler, Oklahoma

BROWNIES FOR A CROWD

8 eggs, beaten
4 1/2 c. sugar
2 c. flour
1 tsp. vanilla extract
1/2 lb. chocolate, melted
1 lb. butter, melted
1 1/2 lb. chopped nuts

Combine . . . . eggs, sugar and flour, beating well.
Stir . . . . in remaining ingredients, mixing well.
Spread . . . . . 3/4 inch thick in 2 greased 10 x 15-inch pans.
Bake . . . . at 350 degrees for 40 minutes. Do not overbake.
Cut . . . . into 2 x 3-inch pieces and remove from pan immediately.
Yields . . . . . . enough to serve any teen-age crowd on Saturday night.

Lenorah Polk
Central State University, Edmond, Oklahoma

BROWNIES WITH CARAMEL ICING

2 sticks margarine, softened
1 c. sugar
2 eggs, separated
4 tbsp. cocoa
1/2 c. flour
1 c. chopped nuts
2 tsp. vanilla extract
1 lb. brown sugar
1 c. whipping cream

Cream ...... 1 stick margarine and sugar in bowl.
Beat .... in egg yolks and next 3 ingredients with 1 teaspoon vanilla.
Fold .... in stiffly beaten egg whites.
Spread ..... into greased 8 x 8-inch baking pan.
Bake .... at 350 degrees for 30 minutes.
Combine .... brown sugar, cream and 1 stick margarine in saucepan.
Cook .... to soft-ball stage or 240 degrees on candy thermometer.
Beat .... in 1 teaspoon vanilla until of spreading consistency.
Frost .... cooled brownies.

> Sherry Somner
> Reporter, McLoud FHA

CARAMEL BROWNIES

7 oz. caramels, melted
1/4 c. evaporated milk
1 pkg. Duncan Hines Brownie Mix

Blend ...... caramels and evaporated milk over hot water until smooth.
Prepare ..... brownie mix using package directions for chewy fudge.
Spread ..... half the batter in greased 8-inch square pan.
Layer ...... caramel mixture and remaining batter on top.
Bake .... at 350 degrees for 30 to 35 minutes.

> Jeanie L. Taylor
> Hinton H. S., Hinton, Oklahoma

CHOCOLATE BROWNIES

1 c. sugar
1/2 tsp. vanilla extract
2 eggs, beaten
1/2 c. butter, melted
1/2 c. sifted flour
1/3 c. cocoa
1/4 tsp. each baking powder, salt
1/2 c. chopped nuts (opt.)

Add .... sugar and vanilla to eggs gradually, beating constantly.
Blend ...... in butter.
Add .... combined dry ingredients gradually, mixing well.

Stir .... in nuts.
Pour .... into greased 8-inch square pan.
Bake .... at 350 degrees for 20 to 35 minutes or until brownies pull away from edge of pan.

> Tresa Dawn Rateliff
> Wilson H. S., Wilson, Oklahoma
> Denise Morgan
> Moore West H. S., Moore, Oklahoma

PRALINE-TOPPED BROWNIES

3/4 c. sifted flour
1/2 tsp. salt
3/4 c. butter, softened
1 c. sugar
2 eggs
1/2 tsp. vanilla extract
2 oz. unsweetened chocolate, melted
1 c. finely chopped pecans
1/2 c. packed brown sugar
2 tbsp. cream

Sift .... flour and salt together.
Cream ...... 1/2 cup butter and sugar in bowl until light and fluffy.
Add .... eggs 1 at a time, beating well after each addition.
Blend ...... in vanilla and chocolate.
Stir .... in flour mixture.
Fold .... in 1/2 cup pecans.
Pour .... into greased 8-inch square baking pan.
Bake .... at 450 degrees for 30 to 35 minutes.
Cream ...... brown sugar and remaining 1/4 cup butter in bowl until light and fluffy.
Blend ...... in cream.
Stir .... in remaining pecans.
Spread ..... over hot brownies.
Broil .... on low until topping is bubbly.
Cut .... into squares while warm.
Remove .... from pan to wire rack to cool.

Photograph for this recipe on page 128.

GERMAN CHOCOLATE-CARAMEL COOKIES

60 caramels
Evaporated milk
1 pkg. German chocolate cake mix
3/4 c. melted margarine
1 c. chopped nuts (opt.)
1 c. semisweet chocolate chips

Melt .... caramels with 1/2 cup evaporated milk in saucepan.
Combine .... cake mix, margarine, 1/3 cup evaporated milk and nuts, mixing until crumbly.
Press .... half the mixture into greased 9 x 13-inch baking pan.
Bake .... at 350 degrees for 8 to 10 minutes.
Sprinkle .... with chocolate chips.
Spread ..... caramel mixture over chips.
Top .... with remaining nut mixture.
Bake .... for 18 to 20 minutes longer.
Cut .... into bars.

Tonya Bullard
Duncan Senior H. S., Duncan, Oklahoma
Carol Franks
Hennessey H. S., Hennessey, Oklahoma

MAGIC COOKIE BARS

1 stick butter
1 1/2 c. graham cracker crumbs
1 c. coconut
1 c. chocolate chips
1 c. butterscotch chips
1 c. chopped pecans
1 can sweetened condensed milk

Melt .... butter in 9 x 13-inch baking dish.
Press .... crumbs into butter.
Layer ...... coconut, chips and pecans over crumbs.
Drizzle ..... condensed milk over top.
Bake .... at 350 degrees for 30 minutes.
Cut .... into bars when cooled.

Jennifer Hingle
Rush Springs H. S., Rush Springs, Oklahoma

NO-BAKE COOKIES

1 c. sugar
1 stick butter

1/2 c. cocoa
1/2 c. milk
1 tsp. vanilla extract
1/2 c. peanut butter
3 c. oatmeal

Combine .... first 5 ingredients in saucepan.
Boil .... for 3 minutes.
Stir .... in peanut butter and oatmeal.
Drop .... by teaspoonfuls onto waxed paper.

Donna Harris
Muskogee H. S., Muskogee, Oklahoma

NUT-CHOCOLATE BARS

1/3 c. shortening
1 c. packed brown sugar
1 egg
1 tsp. vanilla extract
1 c. flour
1/4 tsp. soda
1/4 tsp. salt
1/2 c. chocolate chips
1/2 c. chopped nuts

Cream ...... shortening and brown sugar in bowl.
Beat .... in egg and vanilla.
Mix .... in sifted dry ingredients.
Stir .... in chips and nuts.
Spread ..... in greased 7 x 11-inch baking dish.
Bake .... at 350 degrees for 20 to 25 minutes or until brown.
Cut .... into bars while warm.

B. Koehn
Delaware H. S., Delaware, Oklahoma

SPECIAL K BARS

1/2 c. sugar
1/2 c. light corn syrup
3/4 c. crunchy peanut butter
1 tsp. vanilla extract
4 c. Special K cereal
3 oz. chocolate chips, melted
1 c. butterscotch chips, melted

Combine .... sugar and corn syrup in large saucepan.
Bring .... to a boil; remove from heat.
Blend ...... in peanut butter and vanilla.
Stir .... in cereal.

Press .... into buttered 9 x 13-inch baking
dish.
Spread ..... chips over cereal mixture.
Cut .... cooled mixture into finger-sized
bars.

Relda I. Coley
Binger H. S., Binger, Oklahoma

PEANUT BUTTER SURPRISES

1 c. sugar
1 c. light corn syrup
1 1/2 c. chunky peanut butter
1 tsp. vanilla extract
4 1/2 c. Special K cereal

Combine .... sugar and syrup in saucepan.
Bring .... to a boil.
Remove .... from heat.
Stir .... in peanut butter and vanilla.
Pour .... over cereal in large bowl, mixing
well.
Press .... into buttered pan.
Cut .... into bars when cool.

Carol Teel
Rush Springs H. S., Rush Springs, Oklahoma

PEANUT BUTTER AND CHOCOLATE CHIP COOKIES

1 c. butter, softened
3/4 c. packed brown sugar
3/4 c. sugar
2 eggs
1/2 tsp. vanilla extract
2 1/4 c. flour
1 tsp. soda
1/2 tsp. salt
1 c. chocolate chips
1 1/2 c. peanut butter chips

Combine .... first 5 ingredients in bowl, mix-
ing until fluffy.
Add .... combined flour, soda and salt,
mixing well.
Stir .... in chips.
Spread ..... in greased 10 x 15-inch baking
pan.
Bake .... at 350 degrees for 25 to 30 min-
utes or until golden brown.
Cut .... into bars when cool.

Stacey Basham
Thomas H. S., Thomas, Oklahoma

SODA CRACKER COOKIES

40 saltine crackers
1 c. butter, melted
1 c. packed brown sugar
2 c. chocolate chips
Nuts

Line .... large cookie sheet with foil,
coating with oil.
Arrange ..... saltines in single layer on foil.
Combine .... butter and brown sugar in
saucepan.
Boil .... for 2 1/2 minutes.
Pour .... over crackers.
Bake .... at 300 degrees for 5 minutes or
until crackers float.
Sprinkle .... chocolate chips over crackers,
spreading to cover when melted.
Press .... nuts into chocolate.
Cut .... while warm.

Phillis Smith
Silo H. S., Durant, Oklahoma

APRICOT-CHIP COOKIES

1/4 c. butter
1/4 c. shortening
1/3 c. packed light brown sugar
1/3 c. sugar
1 egg
1/2 tsp. vanilla extract
1 c. flour
1/2 tsp. salt
1/2 tsp. soda
*2/3 c. finely chopped dried California
apricots*
1/2 c. semisweet chocolate chips

Cream ...... first 4 ingredients in bowl.
Beat .... in egg and vanilla.
Stir .... in dry ingredients gradually until
smooth.
Fold .... in apricots and chocolate chips.
Drop .... by heaping 1/2 teaspoonfuls
onto baking sheets.
Bake .... at 375 degrees for 8 to 10 min-
utes or until lightly browned.
Cool .... on wire racks.
Yields ...... 4 dozen.

Photograph for this recipe on page 74.

BONBON COOKIES

1 c. butter, softened
1 egg, well beaten
1 c. confectioners' sugar
2 1/2 c. flour
1 tsp. baking powder
Nuts

Combine .... all ingredients except nuts in bowl, mixing well.
Chill .... for 1 hour.
Shape ...... into balls, placing nut in center indentation.
Place .... on cookie sheet.
Bake .... at 375 degrees for 12 to 15 minutes.

Alexa Kay Callahan
Sentinel H. S., Sentinel, Oklahoma

BUFFALO CHIP COOKIES

1 c. vegetable shortening
1 c. butter
2 c. packed brown sugar
2 c. sugar
4 eggs
1 tbsp. vanilla extract
4 c. flour
2 tsp. soda
2 tsp. baking powder
1 tsp. salt
2 c. each oatmeal, crushed corn flakes
1 c. each chocolate chips, coconut, nuts

Combine .... first 6 ingredients in bowl, mixing well.
Mix .... in flour, soda, baking powder and salt.
Stir .... in remaining ingredients.
Chill .... for 1 hour.
Drop .... by spoonfuls onto baking sheet.
Bake .... at 350 degrees for 10 to 12 minutes.

Shelli Trusty
Rush Springs H. S., Rush Springs, Oklahoma

CHOCOLATE CHIP-NUT COOKIES

2/3 c. shortening
2/3 c. butter, softened
1 c. sugar
1 c. packed brown sugar
2 eggs

2 tsp. vanilla extract
3 c. flour
1 tsp. soda
1 tsp. salt
1 c. chopped nuts
1 12-oz. package chocolate chips

Combine .... first 6 ingredients in bowl, mixing well.
Mix .... in remaining ingredients.
Drop .... by teaspoonfuls onto baking sheet.
Bake .... at 375 degrees for 8 to 10 minutes.
Yields ...... 7 dozen.

Ginny Barefoot
Ryan Public School, Ryan, Oklahoma

KIM'S CHOCOLATE CHIP COOKIES

1 c. shortening
1 c. packed brown sugar
1/2 c. sugar
1 tsp. vanilla extract
2 eggs
2 c. flour
1 tsp. soda
1 tsp. salt
1 c. chopped nuts
2 c. chocolate chips

Cream ...... first 4 ingredients in bowl until fluffy.
Beat .... in eggs.
Add .... combined dry ingredients, mixing well.
Stir .... in nuts and chips.
Drop .... by teaspoonfuls onto cookie sheet.
Bake .... at 375 degrees for 8 to 10 minutes.
Yields ...... 7 dozen.

Kim Robison
Pawhuska H. S., Pawhuska, Oklahoma

CHOCOLATE DROPS

2 c. sugar
4 tbsp. cocoa
1/2 c. milk
1 stick margarine
Dash of salt

1/2 c. peanut butter
3 c. quick-cooking oats
2 tsp. vanilla extract

Combine . . . . first 4 ingredients in saucepan.
Boil . . . . for 1 minute.
Stir . . . . in remaining ingredients.
Drop . . . . by teaspoonfuls onto waxed paper.

Kendra George
Eisenhower H. S., Lawton, Oklahoma

CHOCOLATE KRINKLE COOKIES

1/2 c. oil
2 c. sugar
4 sq. chocolate, melted
4 eggs
2 tsp. vanilla extract
2 c. sifted flour
2 tsp. baking powder
1/2 tsp. salt
Confectioners' sugar

Blend . . . . . . first 3 ingredients in bowl.
Add . . . . eggs and vanilla 1 at a time, beating well after each addition.
Mix . . . . in flour, baking powder and salt.
Chill . . . . for 1 hour.
Shape . . . . . . into balls.
Roll . . . . in confectioners' sugar and place on greased baking sheet.
Bake . . . . at 350 degrees for 10 to 12 minutes.

Roxanne Outhier
Okeene H. S., Okeene, Oklahoma

DOUBLE CHOCOLATE NUGGETS

1 pkg. devil's food cake mix
1/2 c. oil
2 eggs
1 6-oz. package semisweet chocolate chips
Pecan halves (opt.)

Combine . . . . first 3 ingredients in bowl, mixing well.
Stir . . . . in chocolate chips.
Drop . . . . by teaspoonfuls onto cookie sheet.
Top . . . . with pecan half.
Bake . . . . at 350 degrees for 10 to 12 minutes or until cookies test done.

Cool . . . . for 1 minute before removing to rack.

Gina Boren
Mustang H. S., Mustang, Oklahoma

TIGER COOKIES

2 c. sifted flour
1 tsp. soda
1/2 tsp. salt
1 c. soft butter
1 c. sugar
2 eggs
1 tsp. vanilla extract
3 c. crushed sugared corn flakes
1 c. semisweet chocolate chips, melted

Sift . . . . first 3 ingredients together.
Cream . . . . . . butter and sugar in bowl until light and fluffy.
Beat . . . . in eggs and vanilla.
Add . . . . sifted ingredients, mixing well.
Fold . . . . in cereal.
Swirl . . . . chocolate into batter, leaving streaks of chocolate.
Drop . . . . by teaspoonfuls onto baking sheets.
Bake . . . . at 375 degrees for 12 minutes.
Yields . . . . . . 5 dozen.

Photograph for this recipe below.

WHOOPIE PIES

1/2 c. margarine, softened
1 c. packed brown sugar
2 tsp. vanilla extract
2 eggs, beaten
1 1/2 to 2 c. sifted flour
1/2 tsp. salt
1 tsp. soda
1/2 c. cocoa
Milk
3/4 c. shortening
2 c. confectioners' sugar
1 egg white

Cream ...... margarine and brown sugar together in bowl.
Beat .... in 1 teaspoon vanilla and eggs.
Add .... sifted dry ingredients alternately
with 1/2 cup milk, beating well
after each addition.
Drop .... by teaspoonfuls 2 to 3 inches
apart onto greased cookie sheet.
Bake .... at 375 degrees for 10 to 12
minutes.
Beat .... remaining ingredients with 2 tablespoons milk and 1 teaspoon
vanilla in bowl until fluffy.
Spread ..... between 2 cookies to make a
sandwich.

Mrs. Terry Kellner
Okeene, Oklahoma

GINGER CREAMS

1/3 c. shortening
1/2 c. sugar
1 egg
1/2 c. molasses
2 c. flour
1/4 tsp. salt
1/2 tsp. soda
1 tsp. ginger
1/2 tsp. each nutmeg, cloves, cinnamon

Combine .... first 4 ingredients with 1/2 cup
water, mixing well.
Stir .... in combined dry ingredients.
Drop .... by teaspoonfuls onto greased
baking sheet.
Bake .... at 400 degrees for 8 minutes or
until cookies test done.

Penny Battles
Wilson H. S., Wilson, Oklahoma

PEACH DROPS

Margarine, softened
1 3-oz. package cream cheese, softened
1/4 c. packed brown sugar
3/4 c. peach preserves
1 1/4 c. flour
1 1/2 tsp. baking powder
1 tsp. cinnamon
1/4 tsp. salt
1/2 c. walnuts
1 c. confectioners' sugar

Cream ...... 1/2 cup margarine, cream cheese
and brown sugar in bowl until
fluffy.
Beat .... in 1/2 cup preserves.
Combine .... next 4 ingredients, mixing well.
Add .... to creamed mixture, mixing
well.
Stir .... in walnuts.
Drop .... by spoonfuls on greased baking
sheet.
Bake .... at 350 degrees for 12 minutes.
Blend ...... confectioners' sugar, 1 table-
spoon margarine and 1/4 cup
preserves in bowl.
Frost .... cooled cookies.

Nelda Love
Anadarko H. S., Anadarko, Oklahoma

ORANGE-PECAN DIABETIC COOKIES

1 /4 c. shortening
1 egg
2 tsp. Sucaryl or Sweet 10
6 tbsp. frozen unsweetened orange juice,
thawed
1 c. sifted flour
1/4 tsp. baking powder
1/4 tsp. salt
1 tsp. vanilla extract
1/4 c. chopped pecans

Combine .... first 4 ingredients with 2 tablespoons water in bowl, mixing
well.
Blend ...... in combined dry ingredients.
Stir .... in vanilla and pecans.
Drop .... by teaspoonfuls onto greased
baking sheet.

Bake .... at 375 degrees for 12 to 15 minutes or until lightly browned.

Kim Heinze
State V. P., West District, 1982
Okeene H. S., Okeene, Oklahoma

PAM'S POTATO CHIP COOKIES

1 c. margarine, softened
1 c. packed brown sugar
1 c. sugar
2 eggs
1 tsp. vanilla extract
2 c. crushed potato chips
1 6-oz. package butterscotch chips
2 1/2 c. flour
1 tsp. baking powder

Cream ...... margarine and sugars together in bowl.
Beat .... in eggs and vanilla.
Stir .... in chips and sifted dry ingredients, mixing well.
Drop .... by teaspoonfuls onto greased baking sheet.
Bake .... for 10 to 12 minutes.

Pam Dunn
Hennessey, Oklahoma

SNICKERDOODLES

1 /2 c. butter, softened
1/2 c. shortening
2 eggs
Sugar
2 3/4 c. flour
1 tsp. salt
2 tsp. cream of tartar
Cinnamon

Combine .... butter, shortening, eggs and 1 1/2 cups sugar in bowl, mixing well.
Add .... combined flour, salt and cream of tartar, mixing well.
Shape ...... into balls.
Roll .... in mixture of sugar and cinnamon, placing on baking sheet.
Flatten ..... with fork.
Bake .... at 400 degrees for 8 to 10 minutes.

Patricia Evans
Ringwood H. S., Ringwood, Oklahoma

EVELYN'S SUGAR COOKIES

1 c. butter, softened
1 c. shortening
1 c. confectioners' sugar
Sugar
2 eggs
4 c. flour
1 tsp. cream of tartar
1 tsp. soda
1 1/2 tsp. vanilla extract

Cream ...... first 3 ingredients with 1 cup sugar in bowl.
Add .... eggs, beating well.
Sift .... dry ingredients together.
Add .... to creamed mixture with vanilla, mixing well.
Roll .... into small balls.
Sprinkle .... with sugar.
Place .... on greased baking sheet.
Flatten ..... with glass dipped in sugar.
Bake .... at 350 degrees for 8 to 10 minutes or until golden brown.

Evelyn Minton
Oakwood, Oklahoma

SOUR CREAM-SUGAR COOKIES

1 3/4 c. sugar
1 c. shortening
1 tsp. lemon extract
1 tsp. salt
2 eggs
1 tsp. soda
3/4 c. sour cream
5 c. (or more) flour

Combine .... first 4 ingredients in bowl, beating until creamy.
Beat .... in eggs.
Blend ...... soda with sour cream.
Add .... to batter, mixing well.
Add .... 4 cups flour, 1 cup at a time, mixing well after each addition.
Knead ...... on floured surface, adding enough flour to make stiff dough.
Roll .... and cut as desired, sprinkling with sugar.
Place .... on baking sheet.
Bake .... at 350 degrees until brown.

Mrs. Ed. Luetkemeyer
Okeene, Oklahoma

Fun-Raiser Ideas

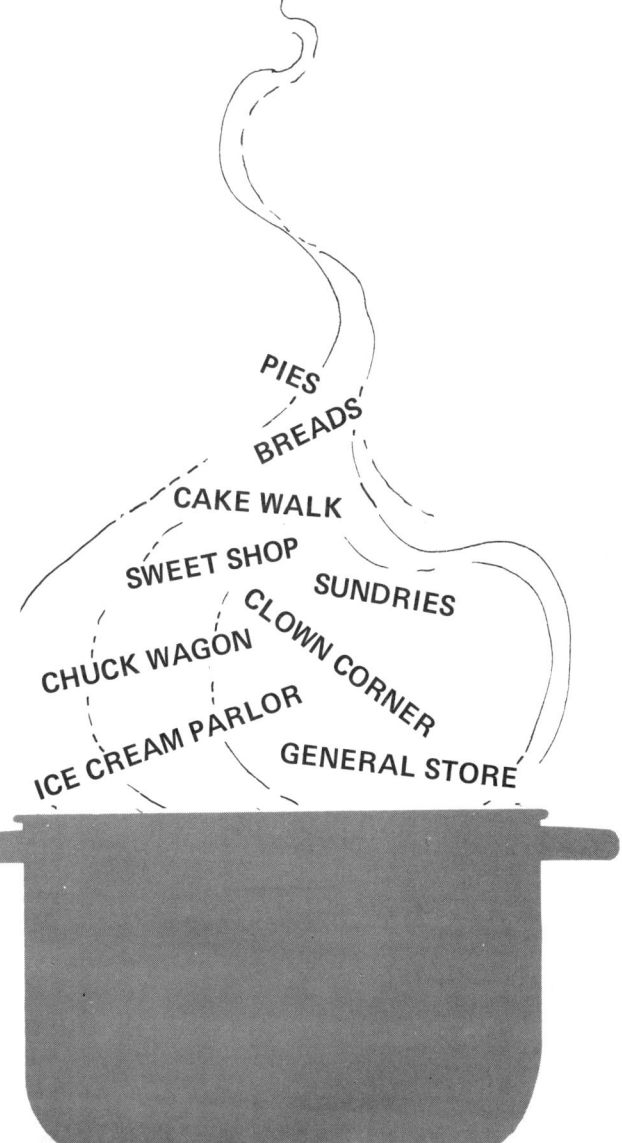

PIES

BREADS

CAKE WALK

SWEET SHOP   SUNDRIES

CLOWN CORNER

CHUCK WAGON

ICE CREAM PARLOR   GENERAL STORE

GENERAL STORE

SOUTHERN SWEET CHOCOLATE PIE
CHERRY PIE
ORANGE-PECAN PIE
DOG-TICK PIE

SPICED NUTS
EASY COCOA MIX
BASIC SEASONING SALT
SWEET RELISH
BANANA BUTTER

SPUDNUTS
CINNAMON ROLLS
OATMEAL BREAD

BASIC SEASONING SALT

1   26-oz. box table salt
1 tbsp. each onion salt, garlic salt
2 tbsp. each celery salt, paprika
4 tbsp. each black and white pepper
1 tbsp. dillweed
2 tbsp. monsodium glutamate
4 tbsp. sugar

Combine . . . . all ingredients in large container, mixing well.
Let . . . . stand in darkness for 24 hours.
Package . . . . . in salt shakers or spice jars.

Deanna Hardesty
Tuttle Public Schools, Tuttle, Oklahoma

CABANA BANANA BUTTER

4 lg. bananas
2 tbsp. lemon juice
1 1/2 c. sugar
1/2 tsp. cinnamon
1/8 tsp. cloves

Cut . . . . bananas into chunks.
Sprinkle . . . . with lemon juice.
Process . . . . . in blender container to mash.
Add . . . . to remaining ingredients in saucepan.

Simmer . . . . . for 15 minutes, stirring constantly.
May . . . . store, covered, in refrigerator for several weeks.
Yields . . . . . . 2 1/2 cups.

Photograph for this recipe on opposite page.

MICROWAVE SPICED WALNUTS

1/2 c. packed brown sugar
1/2 tsp. salt
1/2 tsp. cinnamon
1/4 tsp. allspice
1/8 tsp. each nutmeg, cloves
1 1/2 c. walnut halves

Combine . . . . all ingredients except walnuts with 1 1/2 tablespoons water in 2-quart glass bowl.
Microwave . . on High for 3 minutes, stirring occasionally.
Stir . . . . in walnuts 1/2 cup at a time until well coated.
Microwave . . on High for 5 minutes or until syrup hardens slightly.
Spoon . . . . . . onto waxed paper.

Cindy Allen
Ringling H. S., Ringling, Oklahoma

SWEET RELISH

9 tbsp. salt
4 qt. ground cucumbers
2 qt. ground onions
6 c. sugar
2 tsp. turmeric
3/4 tsp. ground cloves
6 c. vinegar
1 1/2 tsp. celery seed
2 tsp. mustard seed

Combine . . . . 4 tablespoons salt with cucumbers and 1 tablespoon salt with onions.
Let . . . . stand for 2 hours; drain well.
Combine . . . . remaining ingredients in large kettle.
Bring . . . . to a boil.
Stir . . . . in cucumbers and onions.

Cook . . . . for 10 minutes, stirring constantly. Do not boil.

Spoon . . . . . . into hot sterilized jars leaving 1/2-inch headspace; seal.

Mildred Mitchell
Medford School, Medford, Oklahoma

SPUDNUTS

2 pkg. dry yeast
2 eggs
2/3 c. melted shortening
2/3 c. sugar
1 c. mashed potatoes
1 tsp. vanilla extract
1 tsp. baking powder
1 1/2 tsp. salt
6 to 7 c. flour
Oil for deep frying

Dissolve . . . . yeast in 1 1/2 cups warm water.

Beat . . . . next 5 ingredients in large bowl.

Add . . . . yeast mixture, beating well.

Combine . . . . dry ingredients.

Add . . . . to potato mixture, mixing well.

Knead . . . . . . on floured surface until smooth and elastic.

Place . . . . in greased bowl, turning to grease surface.

Let . . . . rise until doubled in bulk.

Punch . . . . . . dough down.

Store . . . . covered, in refrigerator for up to 2 weeks until needed.

Roll . . . . out; cut with doughnut cutter.

Let . . . . rise until doubled in bulk.

Fry . . . . in hot deep fat until golden brown.

Roberta Henderson
Fort Gibson H. S., Fort Gibson, Oklahoma

DONNA'S CINNAMON ROLLS

1 pkg. yeast
Sugar
Butter, softened
1 egg
1 tsp. salt
3 1/2 c. flour
Cinnamon
1 c. packed brown sugar

2 tbsp. corn syrup
2/3 c. nuts

Combine . . . . yeast, 1/4 cup sugar and 1 cup warm water in large bowl.

Stir . . . . in 1 tablespoon butter, egg, salt and flour.

Chill . . . . overnight.

Roll . . . . dough into 1/4-inch thick rectangle.

Sprinkle . . . . with sugar and cinnamon to taste.

Roll . . . . as for jelly roll.

Slice . . . . into 12 rolls.

Mix . . . . remaining ingredients with 2/3 cup butter in bowl.

Spread . . . . . in baking pan.

Arrange . . . . . rolls over mixture.

Let . . . . rise for 30 minutes.

Bake . . . . at 375 degrees for 30 minutes.

Invert . . . . . . immediately on serving platter.

Donna Moad
Washita Heights School, Corn, Oklahoma

EASY COCOA MIX

4 c. nonfat dry milk
1 1/2 c. presweetened cocoa powder
3/4 c. nondairy creamer

Combine . . . . all ingredients in bowl, mixing well.
Store . . . . in covered container.
Mix . . . . 1/3 cup mix with 2/3 cup boiling water to serve.

Angie Sanders
Tomlinson Wolves, Lawton, Oklahoma

OATMEAL BREAD

1 c. quick oats
1/2 c. whole wheat flour
1/2 c. packed brown sugar
1 tbsp. salt
2 tbsp. margarine
1 pkg. dry yeast
5 c. all-purpose flour

Combine . . . . first 5 ingredients in large bowl.
Stir . . . . in 2 cups boiling water; cool to lukewarm.
Dissolve . . . . yeast in 1/2 cup warm water.
Add . . . . dissolved yeast and all-purpose flour to oats mixture, mixing well.
Knead . . . . . . on floured surface for 5 to 10 minutes.
Place . . . . in greased bowl, turning to grease surface.
Let . . . . rise, covered, until doubled in bulk.
Punch . . . . . . down and let rise again.
Shape . . . . . . into 2 loaves.
Place . . . . in greased 5 x 9-inch loaf pans.
Let . . . . rise until doubled in bulk.
Bake . . . . at 350 degrees for 30 to 40 minutes.
Cool . . . . on rack, brushing lightly with additional margarine.

Barbara Idell, Advisor
Madill H. S., Madill, Oklahoma

SUPER CHERRY PIE

1 1/4 c. sugar
3 tbsp. cornstarch
1/4 tsp. salt
1/4 c. cherry juice
1/2 tsp. red food coloring
1/8 tsp. almond extract
2 cans water-pack cherries, drained
1 tbsp. butter
Pie Crust

Blend . . . . . . first 6 ingredients in saucepan.
Cook . . . . until thick and clear, stirring constantly.
Add . . . . cherries.
Bring . . . . to a boil; remove from heat.
Stir . . . . in butter; cool.
Pour . . . . into pastry-lined 9-inch pie plate.
Weave . . . . . . lattice strips over top, pressing ends moistened with water to bottom crust; flute.
Bake . . . . at 400 degrees for 40 minutes or until golden brown.

Pie Crust

2 c. flour
1 tsp. salt
2/3 c. shortening
4 to 6 tbsp. milk

Sift . . . . flour and salt into bowl.
Cut . . . . in shortening until crumbly.
Sprinkle . . . . milk evenly over mixture, tossing with fork to mix.
Press . . . . together on waxed paper; divide in half.
Roll . . . . each portion 1/8 inch thick.
Line . . . . pie plate with 1 portion.
Cut . . . . remaining pastry into 1/2-inch wide strips for lattice top.

Beatrice, Rhonda and Kristi Paul
Chisholm H. S., Enid, Oklahoma

SOUTHERN SWEET CHOCOLATE PIE

4 oz. German's sweet chocolate
1/4 c. butter
1 14 1/2-oz. can evaporated milk
1 1/2 c. sugar
3 tbsp. cornstarch
1/8 tsp. salt
2 eggs, beaten
Vanilla extract to taste
1 unbaked 9-in. pie shell
1 1/3 c. flaked coconut
1/2 c. chopped pecans

Melt .... chocolate with butter in saucepan.
Remove .... from heat.
Blend ...... in milk.
Combine .... sugar, cornstarch and salt in bowl.
Beat .... in eggs and vanilla.
Add .... chocolate mixture gradually, mixing well.
Pour .... into pie shell.
Sprinkle .... coconut and pecans over top.
Bake .... at 375 degrees for 40 minutes.
Cover ...... loosely with foil.
Bake .... for 20 minutes longer or until top is puffed and cracked.
Cool .... for 3 hours or longer.

Sherie Martin
Bray-Doyle H. S., Bray, Oklahoma

ORANGE-PECAN PIE

1 c. light corn syrup
1/4 c. butter
1/4 c. sugar
1 c. chopped pecans
1 tbsp. orange juice
1 tbsp. grated orange rind
3 eggs, well beaten
1/2 tsp. salt
1 unbaked 9-in. pie shell

Combine .... first 8 ingredients in medium bowl, mixing well.
Pour .... into pie shell.
Bake .... at 350 degrees for 45 minutes.

Gladys Brown
Jenks H. S., Jenks, Oklahoma

DOG-TICK PIE

1 1/2 c. sugar
4 tbsp. flour
1 egg, well beaten
3 tbsp. lemon juice
2 tsp. grated lemon rind
1/8 tsp. salt
1 c. raisins
1 recipe 2-crust pie pastry

Blend ...... first 3 ingredients in double boiler.

Add .... next 4 ingredients with 2 cups water, mixing well.
Cook .... for 15 minutes or until thick, stirring occasionally.
Cool .... for 5 to 10 minutes.
Pour .... into pastry-lined 9-inch pie plate.
Top .... with lattice-woven pastry strips.
Bake .... at 450 degrees for 10 minutes.
Reduce ..... temperature to 350 degrees.
Bake .... for 20 minutes longer or until lightly browned.

Phyllis A. Stratton
Muskogee H. S., Muskogee, Oklahoma

SWEET SHOP

PECAN ROLLS
REESE CUP CANDIES
SALTWATER TAFFY
HEATH BARS

HEAVENLY BROWNIES
SOUTHERN PECAN BARS

SESAME SEED COOKIES
CHERRY WINKS

RHONDA'S HEATH BARS

1 c. butter, melted
1 1/3 c. sugar
1 tbsp. corn syrup
1 c. toasted almonds
9 Hershey bars

Combine .... first 3 ingredients with 3 tablespoons water in saucepan.
Cook .... to hard-crack stage or 300 degrees on candy thermometer.
Stir .... in almonds.
Spread ..... in well-greased baking sheet.
Arrange ..... chocolate bars over hot toffee, spreading to cover.
Break ...... into pieces when cool.

Rhonda Deann Sanner
Wilson H. S., Wilson, Oklahoma

CHERRY WINKS

1 c. shortening
1 3-oz. package cream cheese, softened
1 c. sugar
1 egg
1 tsp. almond extract
2 1/2 c. flour
1/4 tsp. soda
1/2 tsp. salt
1 1/4 c. finely chopped pecans
36 maraschino cherries, halved

Cream . . . . . . shortening and cream cheese in bowl.
Add . . . . sugar gradually, beating until light and fluffy.
Beat . . . . in egg and flavoring.
Add . . . . combined dry ingredients, beating well.
Chill . . . . for 1 hour.
Shape . . . . . . into 1-inch balls.
Roll . . . . in pecans.
Place . . . . on cookie sheet, pressing cherry into center of each.
Bake . . . . at 350 degrees for 12 to 15 minutes.
Yields . . . . . . 6 dozen cookies.

Daresa Dell
Medford H. S., Medford, Oklahoma

HEAVENLY BROWNIES

2/3 c. shortening
5 oz. chocolate
1 c. sugar
2 eggs, beaten
1 1/2 tsp. vanilla extract
1 1/4 c. flour
1/2 tsp. baking powder
1 tsp. salt
1 c. chopped walnuts
1 c. miniature marshmallows
2 tbsp. butter
3 tbsp. coffee
2 c. sifted confectioners' sugar

Melt . . . . shortening and 3 ounces chocolate in saucepan.
Combine . . . . sugar and eggs in bowl, beating well.
Stir . . . . in 1 teaspoon vanilla and chocolate mixture.

Sift . . . . flour, baking powder and 1/2 teaspoon salt together.
Add . . . . to chocolate mixture with walnuts, mixing well.
Pour . . . . into greased 9-inch round baking pan.
Bake . . . . at 325 degrees for 25 to 30 minutes.
Top . . . . hot brownies with marshmallows, spreading evenly when melted.
Melt . . . . butter with 2 ounces chocolate in saucepan.
Add . . . . 1/2 teaspoon vanilla, 1/2 teaspoon salt and remaining ingredients, beating until glossy.
Spread . . . . . over brownies.

Dede Speed
FHA/HERO Oklahoma State President
Duncan H. S., Duncan, Oklahoma

SESAME SEED COOKIES

1/3 c. sesame seed
1 c. butter
1 c. sugar
1 egg
2 c. flour
1 tsp. baking powder
1/4 tsp. salt
3 c. sifted confectioners' sugar
3 tbsp. milk
1 tsp. vanilla extract

Saute . . . . . . sesame seed in 1/2 cup butter in skillet until golden brown.
Blend . . . . . . 1/2 cup butter with sugar and egg in bowl.
Stir . . . . in 2 tablespoons sauteed sesame seed and 2 tablespoons water.
Add . . . . combined flour, baking powder and salt, mixing well.
Drop . . . . by teaspoonfuls onto cookie sheet.
Flatten . . . . . with greased glass dipped in sugar.
Bake . . . . at 350 degrees for 10 minutes or until lightly browned.
Mix . . . . remaining ingredients and sesame seed together in bowl.
Frost . . . . cooled cookies.

Kim Westfahl Jech
Okeene H. S., Okeene, Oklahoma

SOUTHERN PECAN BARS

1/3 c. butter, softened
3/4 c. packed brown sugar
1/2 tsp. baking powder
Flour
1/4 c. finely chopped pecans
2 eggs, well beaten
3/4 c. dark corn syrup
1/2 tsp. salt
1 tsp. vanilla extract
3/4 c. chopped pecans

Cream . . . . . . butter and 1/2 cup brown sugar in bowl.
Mix . . . . in baking powder and 1 1/3 cups flour until crumbly.
Stir . . . . in finely chopped pecans.
Press . . . . into 8 x 12-inch baking dish.
Bake . . . . at 350 degrees for 10 minutes.
Combine . . . . remaining ingredients except pecans with 3 tablespoons flour and 1/4 cup brown sugar, mixing well.
Pour . . . . over crust.
Sprinkle . . . . pecans over top.
Bake . . . . for 25 to 30 minutes longer.
Cut . . . . into bars when cooled.
Note . . . . topping may be doubled for extra goodness.

Mary Ann Luther
Feature Writer, Enid Morning News and Daily Eagle
Enid, Oklahoma

HEAVENLY FUDGE

4 1/2 c. sugar
1/2 stick butter
1 can evaporated milk
1 16-oz. milk chocolate bar, crushed
1 16-oz. package chocolate chips
1 16-oz. jar marshmallow whip
2 c. chopped nuts

Combine . . . . first 3 ingredients in saucepan.
Boil . . . . for 7 minutes, stirring constantly.
Combine . . . . remaining ingredients in large bowl.
Cover . . . . . . with boiling syrup.
Beat . . . . until smooth and thick.
Drop . . . . by teaspoonfuls onto waxed paper.

Christine Bidwell
Okeene H. S., Okeene, Oklahoma

PECAN ROLL

1 12-oz. package penuche fudge mix
1/2 lb. caramels
1/4 c. milk
1 1/2 c. chopped pecans

Prepare . . . . . fudge mix using package directions.
Shape . . . . . . into 4 rolls 1 inch in diameter.
Melt . . . . caramels with milk in saucepan over low heat, stirring constantly.
Spread . . . . . over rolls.
Roll . . . . in pecans; chill.
Cut . . . . into 1/2-inch slices.
Yields . . . . . . 32 pieces.

Annette Campbell
Ringwood H. S., Ringwood, Oklahoma

SALT WATER TAFFY

2 c. sugar
1 c. light corn syrup
1 1/2 tsp. salt
2 tbsp. butter
1/4 tsp. oil of peppermint
7 drops of green food coloring

Combine . . . . first 3 ingredients with 1 cup water in 2-quart saucepan.
Cook . . . . until sugar dissolves, stirring constantly.
Cook . . . . to hard-ball stage or 265 degrees on candy thermometer. Do not stir.
Remove . . . . from heat.
Stir . . . . in remaining ingredients.
Pour . . . . into buttered 12 x 15-inch pan.
Let . . . . stand until cool enough to handle.
Pull . . . . with buttered hands until light colored and difficult to pull.
Cut . . . . into 4 portions.
Pull . . . . each into 1/2-inch thick strand.
Cut . . . . into bite-sized pieces with buttered scissors.
Yields . . . . . . 1 1/4 pounds.

Juli Royalty
Hydro H. S., Hydro, Oklahoma

REESE CUPS

1/4 lb. each margarine and butter,
* softened*
1 1/2 lb. confectioners' sugar
1 1/2 tsp. vanilla extract
2 c. peanut butter
1 6-oz. package semisweet chocolate
* chips, melted*
1 oz. paraffin, melted (opt.)

Cream . . . . . . first 3 ingredients with 1 cup
                    peanut butter in bowl.
Blend . . . . . . in remaining peanut butter.
Shape . . . . . . into balls.
Blend . . . . . . chocolate and paraffin in double
                    boiler.
Dip . . . . peanut butter balls in chocolate
                    mixture using toothpicks.
Cool . . . . on waxed paper.
Yields . . . . . . 65 pieces.

Lana Guinn
Hennessey H. S., Hennessey, Oklahoma

CHUCK WAGON

CAMPFIRE SPAGHETTI
CHUCK WAGON STEW
LINDA'S REAL TEXAS CHILI
GREEN CHILI ENCHILADAS
FRENCH-FRIED ONION RINGS
HOT BEAN SALAD
NINE-DAY SLAW
RANCH YEAST BISCUITS

CAMPFIRE SPAGHETTI

1 lb. ground beef
2 tbsp. butter
2 med. onions, chopped
1 clove of garlic, minced
1 4-oz. can mushrooms
1 1-lb. can tomatoes
1 6-oz. can tomato paste
1/2 c. dry red wine (opt.)
2 tsp. salt
1 bay leaf
1/8 tsp. thyme
1/2 tsp. Tabasco sauce
1 tsp. Worcestershire sauce
8 oz. spaghetti, cooked

Saute . . . . . . ground beef in butter in heavy
                    skillet for several minutes.
Add . . . . onions and garlic.
Saute . . . . . . until ground beef is browned.
Stir . . . . in undrained mushrooms and re-
                    maining ingredients.
Simmer . . . . . for 1/2 hour or until thickened.
Serve . . . . over spaghetti.
Yields . . . . . . 6 servings.

Photograph for this recipe on opposite page.

CHUCK WAGON STEW

1 lb. ground beef
1 med. onion, chopped
1 tsp. chili powder
1/2 tsp. garlic powder
Salt and pepper to taste
1 16-oz. can tomatoes
1 16-oz. can corn, drained
1 16-oz. can red kidney beans, drained
1 green pepper, chopped

Brown . . . . . . ground beef in skillet, stirring
                    until crumbly; drain.
Add . . . . onion and seasonings.
Cook . . . . until onion is tender, stirring
                    occasionally.
Stir . . . . in tomatoes, corn and beans.
Cook . . . . covered, for 30 minutes.
Stir . . . . in green pepper.
Cook . . . . for 5 minutes longer.
Serve . . . . with corn bread and grated
                    cheese.

Sonja Tyree
Tomlinson Jr. H. S., Lawton, Oklahoma

LINDA'S REAL TEXAS CHILI

3 lb. stew beef
2 tbsp. oil
2 or 3 cloves of garlic, minced
4 to 6 tbsp. chili powder
2 tsp. cuminseed
3 tbsp. flour
1 tbsp. oregano
2 cans beef broth
1 tsp. salt
1/4 tsp. pepper
1 can pinto beans

Saute . . . . . . beef in oil in heavy 4-quart
                    stock pot over medium heat.

Reduce . . . . . temperature, stirring in garlic.
Combine . . . . next 3 ingredients; sprinkle evenly over beef.
Sprinkle . . . . oregano over beef.
Stir . . . . in 1 1/2 cans broth, mixing well.
Season . . . . . with salt and pepper.
Simmer . . . . . for 1 1/2 hours, stirring occasionally.
Add . . . . remaining broth.
Cook . . . . for 30 minutes longer.
Stir . . . . in beans.
Chill . . . . . . to improve flavor; reheat.

Linda Clinton
Eufaula H. S., Eufaula, Oklahoma

GREEN CHILI ENCHILADAS

1 lb. hamburger
Garlic, salt and pepper to taste
1 can chopped green chiles
1 sm. package corn tortillas
1 carton French onion dip
1 sm. can evaporated milk
Monterey Jack cheese
Picante sauce

Saute . . . . . . hamburger with seasonings in skillet until brown and crumbly.
Stir . . . . in green chiles.
Fill . . . . each tortilla with spoonful chili mixture; roll and place in casserole.
Combine . . . . next 3 ingredients in saucepan.
Cook . . . . over low heat until blended, stirring constantly.
Pour . . . . over enchiladas.
Top . . . . with picante sauce.
Bake . . . . at 350 degrees for 20 minutes.

Gayle, Kristen and Jill Ritchie
Chisholm H. S., Enid, Oklahoma

FRENCH-FRIED ONION RINGS

3 lg. Spanish onions, sliced 1/4 in. thick
1/2 c. milk
1 egg, beaten
3/4 c. flour
1/2 tsp. salt
Oil for deep frying

Separate . . . . onion slices into rings.
Combine . . . . next 4 ingredients in bowl, beating until smooth.

Dip . . . . onion rings in batter, draining excess batter from rings.
Fry . . . . in 1-inch deep oil heated to 375 degrees in skillet for 2 minutes or until brown.

Lyn Cooper
Rattan H. S., Rattan, Oklahoma

HOT BEAN SALAD

3/4 lb. bacon, diced
1 med. onion, diced
2 c. packed brown sugar
1 can cut green beans, drained
1 can kidney beans, drained
1 can lima beans, drained
1 can pork and beans
1 tsp. seasoned salt

Saute . . . . . . bacon and onion in skillet until lightly browned.
Add . . . . remaining ingredients, mixing well.
Pour . . . . into 9 x 13-inch baking dish.
Bake . . . . at 350 degrees for 1 hour.
Yields . . . . . . 10-12 servings.

Sue Reynolds
Bartlesville H. S., Bartlesville, Oklahoma

NINE-DAY SLAW

3 lb. cabbage
1 green pepper
1 bunch onions
1 sm. jar pimentos
2 c. sugar
1 c. oil
1 c. vinegar
2 tsp. celery seed
2 tsp. salt

Mix .... first 4 ingredients together in bowl.
Place .... remaining ingredients in saucepan.
Bring .... to a boil.
Pour .... over cabbage mixture.
Store .... in refrigerator for 9 days before serving.

Jamae Hobbs
Dover School, Dover, Oklahoma

RANCH YEAST BISCUITS

1 pkg. yeast
1/4 c. melted shortening
1/4 c. sugar
2 c. buttermilk
4 1/2 c. flour
4 tsp. baking powder
1/3 tsp. soda
1 tsp. salt

Dissolve .... yeast in 1/2 cup warm water in large bowl.
Add .... remaining ingredients in order given, mixing well.
Roll .... on floured surface.
Cut .... with biscuit cutter.
Bake .... at 400 degrees for 15 to 20 minutes or until brown.

Charlene Heronema
Reydon H. S., Reydon, Oklahoma

CAKE WALK

TUNNEL OF FUDGE
BLUE RIBBON BANANA CAKE
FRESH APPLE CAKE
ORANGE SLICE CAKE

LEVONN'S FRESH APPLE CAKE

1 box spice cake mix
1 box instant vanilla pudding mix
1/2 c. oil
3 eggs
1 tsp. soda
4 c. apples, peeled, cored, diced
1 3-oz. package cream cheese, softened
1/4 c. margarine, softened
Confectioners' sugar
Chopped nuts
1 tsp. vanilla extract

Mix .... first 4 ingredients with 1 cup water in large bowl.
Sprinkle .... soda over apples in bowl, stirring well.
Fold .... apples into batter.
Pour .... into greased and floured bundt pan.
Bake .... at 350 degrees for 50 to 60 minutes.
Beat .... cream cheese and margarine together in bowl.
Add .... enough confectioners' sugar to make spreading consistency.
Stir .... in nuts and vanilla.
Spread ..... on warm cake.
Note .... may use yellow cake mix.

Levonn Bohnstedt
Yale H. S., Yale, Oklahoma

TUNNEL OF FUDGE CAKE

1 1/2 c. butter, softened
6 eggs
1 1/2 c. sugar
2 c. flour
1 pkg. double Dutch dry frosting mix
2 c. chopped walnuts

Cream ...... butter with electric mixer at high speed until fluffy.
Add .... eggs 1 at a time, beating well after each addition.
Beat .... in sugar gradually until fluffy.
Blend ...... in flour, frosting mix and walnuts.
Pour .... into greased tube pan.
Bake .... at 350 degrees for 55 to 60 minutes.

Paula Dawdy
Cyril H. S., Cyril, Oklahoma

BLUE RIBBON BANANA CAKE

3/4 c. shortening
1 1/2 c. sugar
2 eggs
1 c. mashed bananas
2 c. sifted cake flour
1/2 tsp. salt
1 tsp. soda
1 tsp. baking powder
1/2 c. buttermilk
1 tsp. vanilla extract
1/2 c. chopped pecans (opt.)
1 c. coconut (opt.)
Creamy Nut Filling
White Snow Frosting

Cream . . . . . . shortening and sugar together in bowl until fluffy.
Beat . . . . in eggs with electric mixer on medium speed for 2 minutes.
Stir . . . . in bananas.
Sift . . . . dry ingredients together.
Add . . . . to creamed mixture alternately with buttermilk and vanilla, beating well after each addition.
Beat . . . . for 2 minutes longer.
Stir . . . . in pecans.
Pour . . . . into 2 greased and floured 9-inch cake pans.
Sprinkle . . . . 1/2 cup coconut on each layer.
Bake . . . . at 375 degrees for 25 to 30 minutes.
Cool . . . . in pans for 10 minutes.
Spread . . . . . cooled Creamy Nut Filling between layers.
Frost . . . . with White Snow Frosting.

Creamy Nut Filling

1/2 c. sugar
2 tbsp. flour
1/2 c. cream
2 tbsp. butter
1/2 c. chopped pecans
1 tsp. vanilla extract

Combine . . . . first 4 ingredients in saucepan, cooking until thick.
Stir . . . . in pecans and vanilla.

White Snow Frosting

1/4 c. shortening
1/4 c. butter

1 egg white
1/2 tsp. coconut extract
1/2 tsp. vanilla extract
2 c. sifted confectioners' sugar

Cream . . . . . . first 5 ingredients together in bowl until fluffy.
Add . . . . confectioners' sugar gradually, beating until light and fluffy.

Goldie Purvine
Okeene H. S., Okeene, Oklahoma

ORANGE SLICE CAKE

2 c. chopped dates
1 lb. candy orange slices, chopped
2 c. chopped nuts
2 c. coconut
3 1/2 c. flour
1 c. butter, softened
3 1/2 c. sugar
4 eggs
1 tsp. soda
1/2 c. buttermilk
1 1/4 tsp. vanilla extract
1 tsp. lemon juice
2/3 c. orange juice

Combine . . . . first 4 ingredients with 1/2 cup flour in bowl, mixing well.
Cream . . . . . . butter and 2 cups sugar in bowl.
Add . . . . eggs, beating well.
Combine . . . . 3 cups flour with soda.
Add . . . . to creamed mixture alternately with buttermilk, beating well after each addition.
Beat . . . . in vanilla and lemon juice.
Stir . . . . in fruit mixture.
Pour . . . . into greased and floured tube pan.
Bake . . . . at 250 degrees for 2 hours or until cake tests done.
Combine . . . . orange juice and 1 1/2 cups sugar in saucepan.
Bring . . . . . . to a rolling boil; cool.
Beat . . . . for a few minutes.
Pour . . . . over cake.
Let . . . . stand for 12 hours before cutting.

Karla Eischen
Okarche School, Okarche, Oklahoma

ICE CREAM PARLOR

RICH CHOCOLATE ICE CREAM
BUTTERFINGER ICE CREAM
TUTTI-FRUTTI ICE CREAM
STRAWBERRY-BANANA ICE CREAM
FRESH APRICOT ICE CREAM
MENDIE'S PUDDING POPS
TEA PUNCH
ORANGE JULIUS

FRESH APRICOT ICE CREAM

2 lb. fresh apricots
1 1/4 c. sugar
2 c. light cream
2 c. heavy cream
1 c. milk
1/8 tsp. salt
1 tsp. vanilla extract

Dip . . . . apricots in boiling water for 1/2 minute.
Plunge . . . . . . into cold water; peel.
Cut . . . . into halves, removing pits.
Puree . . . . . . in blender container.
Combine . . . . with remaining ingredients in 1-gallon ice cream freezer container.
Freeze . . . . . . using freezer directions.

Photograph for this recipe above.

LEA ANN'S BUTTERFINGER ICE CREAM

1 3/4 c. sugar
5 eggs, beaten
1 tsp. vanilla extract
1 can sweetened condensed milk
7 lg. Butterfingers, crushed
Dash of salt
1/2 gal. milk

Combine . . . . first 3 ingredients in bowl, mixing well.
Stir . . . . in condensed milk.
Mix . . . . in remaining ingredients.
Pour . . . . into 1-gallon ice cream freezer container.
Freeze . . . . . . using freezer directions.

Lea Ann Cummins
Ringling H. S., Ringling, Oklahoma

RICH CHOCOLATE ICE CREAM

2 c. sugar
2/3 c. cocoa
1/4 c. flour
1/4 tsp. salt
2 c. milk
2 eggs, slightly beaten
1 tbsp. vanilla extract
4 c. light cream
1 c. heavy cream

Combine . . . . sugar, cocoa, flour and salt in saucepan.
Stir . . . . in milk.
Bring . . . . to a boil over medium heat, stirring constantly.
Boil . . . . for 1 minute, stirring constantly; remove from heat.
Stir . . . . a small amount of hot mixture into eggs.
Stir . . . . eggs into hot mixture.
Blend . . . . . . in remaining ingredients.
Chill . . . . in refrigerator.
Fill . . . . ice cream freezer container 2/3 full.
Freeze . . . . . . using freezer directions.
Yields . . . . . . 8 servings.

Tamra Dee Rateliff
Wilson H. S., Wilson, Oklahoma

STRAWBERRY-BANANA ICE CREAM

1 sm. package strawberry gelatin
2 pkg. frozen strawberries
3 ripe bananas, mashed
2 cans sweetened condensed milk
1 qt. half and half
3 tbsp. vanilla extract
Milk

Dissolve .... gelatin in 1 cup boiling water in large bowl; cool.
Add .... remaining ingredients except milk, mixing well.
Pour .... into ice cream freezer container.
Add .... milk to fill line.
Freeze ...... using manufacturer's instructions.

Teresa Carpenter
Merritt School, Elk City, Oklahoma

MENDIE'S PUDDING POPS

1 pkg. instant chocolate pudding mix
2 c. cold milk

Combine .... pudding mix and milk in bowl.
Beat .... with rotary beater for 2 minutes.
Pour .... into 6 Tupperware Popsicle molds.
Freeze ...... until firm.

Mendie Adam
Okeene Public Schools, Okeene, Oklahoma

DRUMMOND ORANGE JULIUS

1 6-oz. can frozen orange juice
1/2 c. milk
1 tsp. vanilla extract
1/4 c. sugar

Combine .... all ingredients in blender container with 1/2 cup water and enough ice cubes to fill container.
Process ..... until liquified.
Yields ...... 1 quart.

Chris George
Drummond H. S., Drummond, Oklahoma

TEA PUNCH

5 oz. lemon juice
2 c. sugar
2 tbsp. almond extract
1 tbsp. vanilla extract
1   1-qt. tea bag
2 qt. ginger ale, chilled

Combine .... first 4 ingredients with 1 quart water in large container.
Steep ...... tea bag in 1 cup boiling water; cool and remove tea bag.
Add .... tea and ginger ale to sugar mixture.
Serve .... over ice.
Yields ...... 20-25 servings.

Myrtle Chapman
El Reno H. S., El Reno, Oklahoma

CLOWN CORNER

FUN FACE COLORING
CHILDREN'S COOKED PLAY DOUGH
CARAMEL CORN

REALLY GOOD POPCORN BALLS
TUTTI-FRUTTI COOKIES
CARAMEL APPLES

FUN FACE COLORING

2 tsp. white shortening
5 tsp. cornstarch
1 tsp. flour
2 or 3 drops of glycerin
Food coloring

Blend ...... first 3 ingredients in bowl until smooth.
Add .... glycerin, blending until creamy.
Blend ...... in food coloring 1 drop at a time until desired shade is reached.
Stroke ...... over face with fingers in 1 direction only.
Remove .... with shortening, cold cream or baby oil.
Note .... for brown coloring, add 2 1/2 teaspoons cocoa.

Erwana Ferrell, Advisor
McLoud H. S., McLoud, Oklahoma

CHILDREN'S COOKED PLAY DOUGH

1 c. flour
1/4 c. salt
1 tbsp. cream of tartar
1 tbsp. oil
Several drops of food coloring
Several drops of oil of cloves,
*   wintergreen or peppermint (opt.)*

Combine . . . . all ingredients and 1 cup water in saucepan.
Cook . . . . for 3 minutes or until mixture forms ball, stirring constantly.
Set . . . . aside to cool.
Store . . . . in airtight container.

Debbie Watson
Dale H. S., Dale, Oklahoma

CARAMEL APPLES

1 can sweetened condensed milk
1 c. sugar
1/2 c. light corn syrup
1/8 tsp. salt
1 tsp. vanilla extract
6 med. apples
6 wooden skewers

Combine . . . . first 4 ingredients in heavy 2-quart saucepan.
Heat . . . . to boiling point and until sugar dissolves, stirring constantly.
Cook . . . . over low heat to 230 degrees on candy thermometer, stirring constantly.
Remove . . . . from heat.
Stir . . . . in vanilla.
Cool . . . . for 5 minutes.
Insert . . . . . . skewers in apples.
Dip . . . . apples in candy to coat.
Cool . . . . on greased baking sheet.

Photograph for this recipe on page 142.

TUTTI-FRUTTI BARS

1/2 lb. marshmallows
1/4 c. butter
1/2 tsp. vanilla extract
1/2 c. chopped candied cherries
1/2 c. coarsely chopped pecans
1   15 1/2-oz. package crisp rice cereal

Melt . . . . marshmallows and butter in double boiler.
Beat . . . . in vanilla.
Stir . . . . in cherries and pecans.
Pour . . . . over cereal in large bowl, mixing well.
Press . . . . into 9 x 12-inch pan.
Garnish . . . . . with additional cherries and pecans.
Let . . . . stand for 1 hour or until firm.
Cut . . . . into bars.

Junetta Stoy
Barnsdall H. S., Barnsdall, Oklahoma

CARAMEL CORN

2 sticks margarine
2 c. packed brown sugar
1/2 c. corn syrup
1 tsp. salt
1 tsp. vanilla extract
1/2 tsp. soda
6 qt. popped popcorn

Combine . . . . first 4 ingredients in saucepan.
Boil . . . . for 5 minutes, stirring constantly.
Remove . . . . from heat.
Stir . . . . in vanilla and soda.
Pour . . . . over popcorn in baking dish, mixing well.
Bake . . . . at 250 degrees for 45 minutes, stirring every 15 minutes.

Kristie Kay
Drummond H. S., Drummond, Oklahoma

REALLY-GOOD POPCORN BALLS

1 box brown sugar
1 can sweetened condensed milk
1 c. light corn syrup
1 stick margarine
1 tsp. vanilla extract
3 gal. popped popcorn

Combine . . . . first 5 ingredients in saucepan.
Cook . . . . to soft-ball stage or 250 degrees on candy thermometer.
Pour . . . . over popcorn.
Shape . . . . . . into balls with buttered hands.
Yields . . . . . . 20-25 popcorn balls.

Rachel Lyles
Ringling H. S., Ringling, Oklahoma

CALORIE CHART

Almonds, shelled, 1/4 cup 213
Apples: 1 med. 70
   chopped, 1/2 cup 30
Apple juice, 1 cup .117
Applesauce: sweetened 1/2 cup 115
   unsweetened, 1/2 cup 50
Apricots: fresh, 3 55
   canned, 1/2 cup .110
   dried, 10 halves .100
Apricot nectar, 1 cup 140
Asparagus: fresh, 6 spears 19
   canned, 1/2 cup 18
Avocado, 1 med. 265
Bacon, 2 sl. crisp-cooked, drained 90
Banana, 1 med. 100
Beans: baked, 1/2 cup 160
   dry, 1/2 cup 350
   green, 1/2 cup 20
   lima, 1/2 cup 95
   soy, 1/2 cup 95
Bean sprouts, 1/2 cup 18
Beef, cooked, 3 oz. serving:
   roast, rib 375
   roast, heel of round 165
   steak, sirloin 330
Beer, 12 oz. 150
Beets, cooked, 1/2 cup 40
Biscuit, from mix, 1 90
Bologna, all meat, 3 oz. 235
Bread: roll, 1 85
   white, 1 slice 65
   whole wheat, 1 slice 65
Bread crumbs, dry, 1 cup 390
Broccoli, cooked, 1/2 cup 20
Butter: 1/2 cup 800
   1 tbsp. 100
Buttermilk, 1 cup 90
Cabbage: cooked, 1/2 cup 15
   fresh, shredded, 1/2 cup 10
Cake: angel food, 1/12 pkg. prepared 140
   devil's food, 1/12 pkg. prepared 195
   yellow, 1/12 pkg. prepared 200
Candy: caramel, 1 oz. 115
   chocolate, sweet, 1 oz. 145
   hard candy, 1 oz. 110
Marshmallows, 1 oz. 90
Cantaloupe, 1/2 med. 60
Carrots, cooked, 1/2 cup 23
   fresh, 1 med. 20
Catsup, 1 tbsp. 18
Cauliflower: cooked, 1/2 cup 13

   fresh, 1/2 lb. 60
Celery, chopped, 1/2 cup 8
Cereals: bran flakes, 1/2 cup 53
   corn flakes, 1/2 cup 50
   oatmeal, cooked, 1/2 cup 65
Cheese: American, 1 oz. 105
   Cheddar: 1 oz. 113
      shredded, 1 cup 452
   Cottage: creamed, 1/2 cup 130
      uncreamed, 1/2 cup 85
   Cream, 1 oz. 107
   Mozzarella, 1 oz. 80
      shredded, 1 cup 320
   Parmesan, 1 oz. .110
   Velveeta, 1 oz. 84
Cherries: canned, sour in water, 1/2 cup 53
   fresh, sweet, 1/2 cup 40
Chicken, meat only, 4 oz. serving:
   boned, chopped 1/2 cup 170
   broiled 155
   canned, boned .230
   roast, dark meat 210
   roast, light meat 207
Chili peppers: green, fresh, 1/2 lb. 62
   red, fresh, 1/2 lb. 108
Chili powder with seasonings, 1 tbsp. 51
Chocolate, baking, 1 oz. 143
Cocoa mix, 1-oz. package 115
Cocoa powder, baking, 1/3 cup 120
Coconut, dried, shredded, 1/4 cup 166
Coffee 0
Corn: canned, cream-style, 1/2 cup 100
   canned, whole kernel, 1/2 cup 85
Corn bread, mix, prepared, 1 x 4-in. piece. 125
Corn chips, 1 oz. .130
Cornmeal, 1/2 cup 264
Cornstarch, 1 tbsp. 29
Crab, fresh, meat only, 3 oz. 80
   canned, 3 oz. 85
Crackers: graham, 2 1/2-in. square 28
   Ritz, each 17
   saltine, 2-in. square 13
Cracker crumbs, 1/2 cup 281
Cranberries: fresh, 1/2 lb. 100
   juice, cocktail, 1 cup 163
   sauce, 1/2 cup .190
Cream: half-and-half, 1 tbsp. 20
   heavy, 1 tbsp. 55
   light, 1 tbsp. 30
Creamer, imitation powdered, 1 tsp. 10
Cucumber, 1 med. 30

Dates, dried, chopped, 1/2 cup 244
Eggs: 1 whole, large 80
   1 white 17
   1 yolk 59
Eggplant, cooked, 1/2 cup 19
Fish sticks, 5 200
Flour: rye, 1 cup 286
   white: 1 cup 420
   1 tbsp. 28
   whole wheat, 1 cup 400
Fruit cocktail, canned, 1/2 cup 98
Garlic, 1 clove 2
Gelatin, unflavored, 1 env. 25
Grapes: fresh, 1/2 cup 35-50
   juice, 1 cup 170
Grapefruit: fresh, 1/2 med. 60
   juice, unsweetened, 1 cup 100
Ground beef, patty, lean 185
   regular 245
Haddock, fried, 3 oz. 140
Ham, 3 oz. servings:
   boiled 200
   fresh, roast 320
   country-style 335
   cured, lean 160
Honey, 1 tbsp. 65
Ice cream, 1/2 cup 135
Ice milk, 1/2 cup 96
Jams and preserves, 1 tbsp. 54
Jellies, 1 tbsp. 55
Jell-O, 1/2 cup 80
Lamb, 3 oz. serving, leg roast 185
   1 1/2 oz., rib chop 175
Lemon juice, 1 tbsp. 4
Lemonade, sweetened, 1 cup 110
Lentils, cooked, 1/2 cup 168
Lettuce, 1 head 40
Liver, 2 oz. serving: beef, fried 130
   chicken, simmered 88
Lobster, 2 oz. 55
Macaroni, cooked, 1/2 cup 90
Mango, 1 fresh 134
Margarine: 1/2 cup 800
   1 tbsp. 100
Mayonnaise: 1 tbsp. 100
Milk: whole, 1 cup 160
   skim, 1 cup 89
   condensed, 1 cup 982
   evaporated, 1 cup 345
   dry nonfat, 1 cup 251
Muffin, plain 120
Mushrooms: canned, 1/2 cup 20
   fresh, 1 lb. 123
Mustard: prepared, brown, 1 tbsp. 13
   prepared, yellow, 1 tbsp. 10
Nectarine, 1 fresh 30
Noodles: egg, cooked, 1/2 cup 100

fried, chow mein, 2 oz. 275
Oil, cooking, salad, 1 tbsp. 120
Okra, cooked, 8 pods 25
Olives: green, 3 lg. 15
   ripe, 2 lg. 15
Onion: chopped, 1/2 cup 32
   dehydrated flakes, 1 tbsp. 17
   green, 6 20
   whole, 1 40
Orange: 1 whole 65
   juice, 1 cup 115
Oysters, meat only, 1/2 cup 80
Pancakes, 4-in. diameter, 1 60
Peaches: fresh, 1 med. 35
   canned, 1/2 cup 100
   dried, 1/2 cup 210
Peanuts, shelled, roasted, 1 cup 420
Peanut butter, 1 tbsp. 100
Pears: fresh, 1 med. 100
   canned, 1/2 cup 97
   dried, 1/2 cup 214
Peas: black-eyed, 1/2 cup 70
   green, canned, 1/2 cup 83
   green, frozen, 1/2 cup 69
Pecans, chopped, 1/2 cup 400
Peppers: sweet green, 1 med. 14
   sweet red, 1 med. 19
Perch, white, 4 oz. 50
Pickles: dill, 1 lg. 15
   sweet, 1 average 30
Pie crust, mix, 1 crust 626
Pie, 8-in. frozen, 1/6 serving
   apple 234
   cherry 300
   peach 280
Pimento, canned, 1 avg. 10
Pineapple: fresh, diced, 1/2 cup 36
   canned, 1/2 cup 90
   juice, 1 cup 135
Plums: fresh, 1 med. 30
   canned, 3 101
Popcorn, plain, popped, 1 cup 54
Pork, cooked, lean:
   Boston butt, roasted, 4 oz. 280
   chop, broiled, 3.5 oz. 260
   loin, roasted, 4 oz. 290
Potato chips, 1 oz. 322
Potatoes, white:
   baked, 1 sm. with skin 93
   boiled, 1 sm. 70
   French-fried, 10 pieces 155
   hashed brown, 1/2 cup 225
   mashed, with milk and butter, 1/2 cup 90
Potatoes, sweet:
   baked, 1 avg. .155
   candied, 1 avg. 295
   canned, 1/2 cup 110

Prune: 1 lg. 19
    dried, cooked, 1/2 cup 137
    juice, 1 cup 197
Puddings and pie fillings, prepared:
    banana, 1/2 cup .165
    butterscotch, 1/2 cup 190
    chocolate, 1/2 cup 190
    lemon, 1/2 cup .125
Puddings, instant, prepared:
    banana, 1/2 cup .175
    butterscotch, 1/2 cup 175
    chocolate, 1/2 cup 200
    lemon, 1/2 cup .180
Pumpkin, canned, 1/2 cup 38
Raisins, dried, 1/2 cup 231
Rice: cooked, white, 1/2 cup 90
    cooked, brown, 1/2 cup 100
    precooked, 1/2 cup 105
Salad dressings, commercial:
    blue cheese, 1 tbsp. 75
    Fresh, 1 tbsp. 70
    Italian, 1 tbsp. 83
    mayonnaise, 1 tbsp. 100
    mayonnaise-type, 1 tbsp. 65
    Russian, 1 tbsp. 75
    Thousand Island, 1 tbsp. 80
Salami, cooked, 2 oz. 180
Salmon: canned, 4 oz. 180
    steak, 4 oz. 220
Sardines, canned, 3 oz. 175
Sauces: barbecue, 1 tbsp. 17
    hot pepper, 1 tbsp. 3
    soy, 1 tbsp. 9
    white, med. 1/2 cup 215
    Worcestershire, 1 tbsp. 15
Sauerkraut, 1/2 cup 21
Sausage, cooked, 2 oz. 260
Sherbet, 1/2 cup .130
Shrimp: cooked, 3 oz. 50
    canned, 4 oz. 130
Soft drinks, 1 cup 100
Soup, 1 can, condensed:
    chicken with rice 116
    cream of celery 215
    cream of chicken 235
    cream of mushroom 331
    tomato 220
    vegetable-beef .198

Sour cream, 1/2 cup 240
Spaghetti, cooked, 1/2 cup 80
Spinach: fresh, 1/2 lb. 60
    cooked, 1/2 cup 20
Squash: summer, cooked, 1/2 cup 15
    winter, cooked, 1/2 cup 65
Strawberries, fresh, 1/2 cup 23
Sugar: brown, packed, 1/2 cup 410
    confectioners', sifted, 1/2 cup 240
    granulated: 1/2 cup 385
    1 tbsp. 48
Syrups: chocolate, 1 tbsp. 50
    corn, 1 tbsp. 58
    maple, 1 tbsp. 50
Taco shell, 1 shell 50
Tea, 1 cup 0
Tomatoes: fresh, 1 med. 40
    canned, 1/2 cup 25
    juice, 1 cup 45
    paste, 6-oz. can 150
    sauce, 8-oz. can 34
Toppings: caramel, 1 tbsp. 70
    chocolate fudge, 1 tbsp. 65
    Cool Whip, 1 tbsp. 14
    Dream Whip, prepared, 1 tbsp. 8
    Strawberry, 1 tbsp. 60
Tortilla, corn, 1 65
Tuna: canned in oil, drained, 4 oz. 230
    canned in water, 4 oz. 144
Turkey: dark meat, roasted, 4 oz. 230
    light meat, roasted, 4 oz. 200
Veal: cutlet, broiled, 3 oz. 185
    roast, 3 oz. 230
Vegetable juice cocktail, 1 cup 43
Vinegar, 1 tbsp. 2
Waffles, 1 130
Walnuts, chopped, 1/2 cup 410
Water chestnuts, sliced, 1/2 cup 25
Watermelon, fresh, cubed, 1/2 cup 26
Wheat germ, 1 tbsp. 29
Wine: dessert, 1/2 cup 140
    table, 1/2 cup 85
Yeast: compressed, 1 oz. 24
    dry, 1 oz. 80
Yogurt: plain, w/whole milk, 1 cup 153
    plain, w/skim milk, 1 cup 123
    with fruit, 1 cup 260

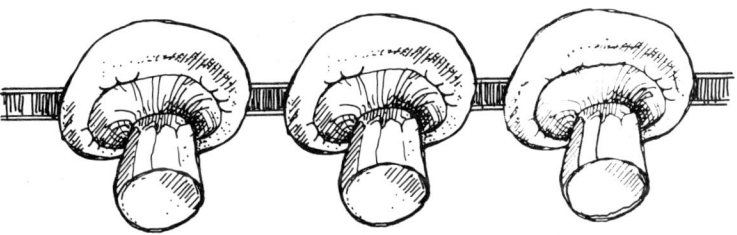

CANDY TESTING CHART

PRODUCT	TEST IN COLD WATER*	DEGREES F. ON CANDY THERMOMETER			
		SEA LEVEL	2000 FEET	5000 FEET	7500 FEET
FUDGE, PANOCHA, FONDANT	SOFT BALL (can be picked up but flattens)	234° - 240° F.	230° - 236° F.	224° - 230° F.	219° - 225° F.
CARAMELS	FIRM BALL (holds shape unless pressed)	242° - 248° F.	238° - 244° F.	232° - 238° F.	227° - 233° F.
DIVINITY, TAFFY AND CARAMEL CORN	HARD BALL (holds shape though pliable)	250° - 268° F.	246° - 264° F.	240° - 258° F.	235° - 253° F.
BUTTERSCOTCH, ENGLISH TOFFEE	SOFT CRACK (separates into hard threads but not brittle)	270° - 290° F.	266° - 286° F.	260° - 280° F.	255° - 275° F.
BRITTLES	HARD CRACK (separates into hard and brittle threads)	300° - 310° F.	296° - 306° F.	290° - 300° F.	285° - 295° F.

* Drop about 1/2 teaspoon of boiling syrup into one cup water, and test firmness of mass with fingers.

METRIC CONVERSION CHART

VOLUME

1 tsp.	=	4.9 cc
1 tbsp.	=	14.7 cc
1/3 c.	=	28.9 cc
1/8 c.	=	29.5 cc
1/4 c.	=	59.1 cc
1/2 c.	=	118.3 cc
3/4 c.	=	177.5 cc
1 c.	=	236.7 cc
2 c.	=	473.4 cc
1 fl. oz.	=	29.5 cc
4 oz.	=	118.3 cc
8 oz.	=	236.7 cc

1 pt.	=	473.4 cc
1 qt.	=	.946 liters
1 gal.	=	3.7 liters

CONVERSION FACTORS

Liters	X	1.056	=	Liquid quarts
Quarts	X	0.946	=	Liters
Liters	X	0.264	=	Gallons
Gallons	X	3.785	=	Liters
Fluid ounces	X	29.563	=	Cubic centimeters
Cubic centimeters	X	0.034	=	Fluid ounces
Cups	X	236.575	=	Cubic centimeters
Tablespoons	X	14.797	=	Cubic centimeters
Teaspoons	X	4.932	=	Cubic centimeters
Bushels	X	0.352	=	Hectoliters
Hectoliters	X	2.837	=	Bushels

WEIGHT

1 dry oz.	=	28.3 Grams
1 lb.	=	.454 Kilograms

CONVERSION FACTORS:

Ounces (Avoir.)	X	28.349	=	Grams
Grams	X	0.035	=	Ounces
Pounds	X	0.454	=	Kilograms
Kilograms	X	2.205	=	Pounds

EQUIVALENT CHART

	WHEN RECIPE CALLS FOR:	YOU NEED:
BREAD & CEREAL	1 c. soft bread crumbs	2 slices
	1 c. fine dry bread crumbs	4-5 slices
	1 c. small bread cubes	2 slices
	1 c. fine cracker crumbs	24 saltines
	1 c. fine graham cracker crumbs	14 crackers
	1 c. vanilla wafer crumbs	22 wafers
	1 c. crushed corn flakes	3 c. uncrushed
	4 c. cooked macaroni	1 8-oz. package
	3 1/2 c. cooked rice	1 c. uncooked
DAIRY	1 c. freshly grated cheese	1/4 lb.
	1 c. cottage cheese or sour cream	1 8-oz. carton
	2/3 c. evaporated milk	1 sm. can
	1 2/3 c. evaporated milk	1 tall can
	1 c. whipped cream	1/2 c. heavy cream
SWEET	1 c. semisweet chocolate pieces	1 6-oz. package
	2 c. granulated sugar	1 lb.
	4 c. sifted confectioners' sugar	1 lb.
	2 1/4 c. packed brown sugar	1 lb.
MEAT	3 c. diced cooked meat	1 lb., cooked
	2 c. ground cooked meat	1 lb., cooked
	4 c. diced cooked chicken	1 5-lb. chicken
NUTS	1 c. chopped nuts	4 oz. shelled
		1 lb. unshelled
VEGETABLES	4 c. sliced or diced raw potatoes	4 medium
	2 c. cooked green beans	1/2 lb. fresh or 1 16-oz. can
	1 c. chopped onion	1 large
	4 c. shredded cabbage	1 lb.
	2 c. canned tomatoes	1 16-oz. can
	1 c. grated carrot	1 large
	2 1/2 c. lima beans or red beans	1 c. dried, cooked
	1 4-oz. can mushrooms	1/2 lb. fresh
FRUIT	4 c. sliced or chopped apples	4 medium
	2 c. pitted cherries	4 c. unpitted
	3 to 4 tbsp. lemon juice plus 1 tsp. grated peel	1 lemon
	1/3 c. orange juice plus 2 tsp. grated peel	1 orange
	1 c. mashed banana	3 medium
	4 c. cranberries	1 lb.
	3 c. shredded coconut	1/2 lb.
	4 c. sliced peaches	8 medium
	1 c. pitted dates or candied fruit	1 8-oz. package
	2 c. pitted prunes	1 12-oz. package
	3 c. raisins	1 15-oz. package

COMMON EQUIVALENTS

1 tbsp. = 3 tsp.	6 1/2 to 8-oz. can = 1 c.
2 tbsp. = 1 oz.	10 1/2 to 12-oz. can = 1 1/4 c.
4 tbsp. = 1/4 oz.	14 to 16-oz. can (No. 300) = 1 3/4 c.
5 tbsp. + 1 tsp. = 1/3 c.	16 to 17-oz. can (No. 303) = 2 c.
8 tbsp. = 1/2 c.	1-lb. 4-oz. can or 1-pt. 2-oz. can (No. 2) = 2 1/2 c.
12 tbsp. = 3/4 c.	1-lb. 13-oz. can (No. 2 1/2) = 3 1/2 c.
16 tbsp. = 1 c.	3-lb. 3-oz. can or 46-oz. can or 1-qt. 14-oz. can =
1 c. = 8 oz. or 1/2 pt.	5 3/4 c.
4 c. = 1 qt.	6 1/2-lb. or 7-lb. 5-oz. can (No. 10) = 12 to 13 c.
4 qt. = 1 gal.	

SUBSTITUTIONS CHART

	INSTEAD OF:	USE:
BAKING	1 tsp. baking powder	1/4 tsp. soda plus 1/2 tsp. cream of tartar
	1 c. sifted all-purpose flour	1 c. plus 2 tbsp. sifted cake flour
	1 c. sifted cake flour	1 c. minus 2 tbsp. sifted all-purpose flour
	1 tsp. cornstarch (for thickening)	2 tbsp. flour or 1 tbsp. tapioca
SWEET	1 1-oz. square chocolate	3 to 4 tbsp. cocoa plus 1 tsp. shortening
	1 2/3 oz. semisweet chocolate	1 oz. unsweetened chocolate plus 4 tsp. sugar
	1 c. granulated sugar	1 c. packed brown sugar or 1 c. corn syrup, molasses, honey minus 1/4 c. liquid
	1 c. honey	1 to 1 1/4 c. sugar plus 1/4 c. liquid or 1 c. molasses or corn syrup
DAIRY	1 c. sweet milk	1 c. sour milk or buttermilk plus 1/2 tsp. soda
	1 c. sour milk	1 c. sweet milk plus 1 tbsp. vinegar or lemon juice of 1 c. buttermilk
	1 c. buttermilk	1 c. sour milk or 1 c. yogurt
	1 c. light cream	7/8 c. skim milk plus 3 tbsp. butter
	1 c. heavy cream	3/4 c. skim milk plus 1/3 c. butter
	1 c. sour cream	7/8 c. sour milk plus 3 tbsp. butter
	1 c. bread crumbs	3/4 c. cracker crumbs
SEASONINGS	1 c. catsup	1 c. tomato sauce plus 1/2 c. sugar plus 2 tbsp. vinegar
	1 tbsp. prepared mustard	1 tsp. dry mustard
	1 tsp. Italian spice	1/4 tsp. each oregano, basil, thyme, rosemary plus dash of cayenne
	1 tsp. allspice	1/2 tsp. cinnamon plus 1/8 tsp. cloves
	1 medium onion	1 tbsp. dried minced onion or 1 tsp. onion powder
	1 clove of garlic	1/8 tsp. garlic powder or 1/8 tsp. instant minced garlic or 3/4 tsp. garlic salt or 5 drops of liquid garlic
	1 tsp. lemon juice	1/2 tsp. vinegar

INDEX

APPETIZERS
ants on a log 10
artichoke balls 10
cheese
   and ham pinwheels 10
   balls
      Erwana's 13
      fried 10
      pecan, deviled 12
   drops, spicy 12
   football 12
   rolls
      Dedria's 12
      party 13
chili nachos 10
dips
   beef, microwave 14
   cheese
      and crunch 13
      chili, hot 14
      dazzle 13
      macho nacho 14
   guacamole 13
   Mexican, easy 14
   olive 14
   skinny dip 14
   taco pizza 15
   two-meat 15
   vegetable, fresh, tangy 15
ham
   and cheese pinwheels 10
   rolls with pickle-fruit kabobs 11
party snack 12
pepperoni balls 11
pepper snacks, poco 11
pickle-fruit kabobs with ham rolls 11
pizza, bite-sized 10
vegetable confetti 15
Banana Butter, cabana 144
BEEF
barbecued, in buns 28
chili
   baked 28
   Texas, Linda's 150
corned beef 32
goulash on noodles 29
ground beef, see Ground Beef
Mexican fricassee 29
roasts
   drip beef 30
   pot roast 30
   super 31
skillet meal 28
spaghetti, southern-style 29
steaks
   round steak 31
      Swiss 32
   Spanish 31
stew, deviled 28
stroganoff, Aunt Catherine's 29

sukiyaki 30
BEVERAGES
apple cider nog, hot 112
cocoa mix, easy .146
eggnog, New Year's 113
milk, hot and spicy 113
orange Julius, Drummond 155
punch
   apricot-pineapple 112
   banana 112
   bob-for-orange 113
   cranberry, hot 113
   tea 155
BREADS
apple
   Donna's 87
   fresh apple 86
apricot, fruit and nutty 87
banana
   bran 88
   nut 88
   pecan, Tamie's 87
biscuits
   cheese twist 76
   ranch 152
bowknots, cinnamon-sugar 76
breakfast bars 76
breakfast puffs, raisin 82
carrot 88
cheese
   Cheddar-nut 89
   herbed 90
   savory 91
   supper bread 90
coffee cakes
   apricot, crunchy 76
   bubble bread 77
   cranberry-nut 77
   cream cheese 78
   favorite 77
   maple-walnut rings, stacked 79
   monkey bread 78
   peach kuchen 78
   Plucket bread 78
corn bread
   hush puppies
      Gloria's 84
   jalapeno 83
   ring 82
   Tennessee mountain 83
doughnuts
   applesauce 79
   cake 79
   overnight 80
   raised 80
   spudnuts 145
fry bread
   Becky's 80
   taco, Navajo 80
graham crackers 83

muffins
  beer 84
  blueberry
    cream cheese 84
    oatmeal 85
  bran
    batter, make-ahead 85
    nut 86
  breakfast, French 85
  oatmeal 86
  peanut-bacon 86
  poppy seed 86
oatmeal 146
pancakes
  apple, diet 81
  lefse, Norwegian 81
  peanut, southern 81
  Roberta's 81
pumpkin, spicy 89
rolls
  cinnamon
    cake mix 93
    Donna's 145
  dinner, double-quick 91
  honey, golden 92
  Michelle's 92
  wonder dough 93
  yeast, quick 93
squash
  summer 90
  zucchini-nut 90
strawberry 89
toast, fried 82
CAKES
apple
  favorite 116
  frosted 116
  Levonn's 152
  Rosemary's 116
  with buttermilk sauce 116
banana
  blue ribbon 153
  nut 117
butter, gooey 127
chocolate
  applesauce 117
  cream cheese quickie 127
  devil's food, delicious 118
  fudge 118
  German chocolate
    big 119
    Linda's 118
  go-cola 120
  heavenly hash .119
  mayonnaise 120
  Mississippi mud 120
  oatmeal 120
  red, Waldorf Astoria 121
  square 117
  Texas 121
  tunnel of fudge 152
  wacky 121
  walnut-cocoa 122

coconut
  delight 122
  pineapple refrigerator cake 127
cream, Italian 123
gingerbread 123
jiffy, English 122
lemon daisy cake 124
orange slice 153
pineapple upside-down, Lisa's 124
plum 124
pound cake 125
rum, glazed 127
sock-it-to-me 127
sour cream with Amaretto, Italian 126
zucchini 125
CANDIES
caramel apples 156
caramels 130
chocolate
  bonbons 130
  fudge, see fudge
  Heath bars, Rhonda's 147
  nut cluster cups 131
  pecan, microwave 133
  Reese cups 150
  rocky road 131
date loaf 131
divinity
  chocolate kiss .130
  strawberry 133
fudge
  buttermilk 130
  caramel, microwave 133
  chocolate
    creamy, easy 131
    heavenly 149
  peanut butter, festive 132
  peanut, quick 132
marshmallows, chocolate-dipped 130
microwave candy 133
peanut brittle 132
  microwave 133
  sponge 132
pecan roll 149
taffy, salt water .149
CHEESE
chili relleno casserole 57
Mexican
  chili casserole 57
  meal-in-one casserole 57
quiche Lorraine 56
Cheesecakes
cherry 101
Milnot 102
Washington 102
CHICKEN
and rice
  easy 52
  Tammy's 52
  with sausage 51
barbecued 46
breasts
  cordon bleu, microwave 48

divan for eight 49
Eden 49
Kiev, microwave 49
nuggets
    baked 45
    pancake 46
chili casserole 49
continental 51
crunchy casserole 52
divan
    microwave 48
    noodle 50
enchiladas, sour cream 53
honied 47
King Ranch 52
lemon, luscious 147
marinada 47
Mexican
    Michelle's 53
    Sherry's 52
not-the-same-old-chicken 48
Rita's casserole 50
salad, hot 50
stew, Brunswick 47
taco pie 53
tetrazzini 50
three-cheese 51
Waikiki 48

COOKIES
apricot
    bars 134
    chip 137
bonbon 138
brownies
    caramel 135
    chocolate 135
    for a crowd 134
    heavenly 148
    praline-topped 135
    with caramel icing 134
butterscotch bars 134
cherry winks 148
chocolate
    buffalo chip 138
    chocolate chip 138
    drops 138
    German chocolate-caramel 136
    krinkle 139
    no-bake 136
    nuggets, double chocolate 139
    nut bars 136
    soda cracker 137
    Special K 136
    tiger cookies 139
ginger creams 140
lemon squares 134
magic bars 136
orange-pecan diabetic cookies 140
peach drops 140
peanut butter
    and chocolate chips 137
    surprises 137
pecan bars, southern 149

potato chip, Pam's 141
sesame seed 148
snickerdoodles 141
sugar 141
tutti-frutti bars 156
whoopie pies 140

DESSERTS
angel food cake dessert 96
apple
    caramel 156
    crisp 96
    pizza pie 96
    pudding 96
baked Alaska
    orange 105
    strawberry 102
banana
    banana split cake 96
    pudding
        creamy 97
        no-bake 97
bread pudding, fruit-topped 97
cherry
    pineapple 97
    stuff 98
chocolate
    and vanilla pudding 98
    delight 98
    fudge, baked 98
    Mississippi mud, Janelle's 98
coconut torte 99
French pudding, Tiffin 107
fruit
    frozen 105
    pizza 99
lemon squares 99
peach kuchen, Dutch 100
rice Chantilly 100
sherbet, orange 105
spumoni 106
strawberry
    Bavarian crown 100
    dream 101
    fluff 106
    pizza 101
sweetened condensed milk
        homemade 102

EGGS
and cheese dish, baked 56
omelet, health nut 56
quiche Lorraine 56
salad casserole 55

Enchiladas
green chili 151

Face Coloring, fun 155

Grits Casserole, cheese 71

GROUND BEEF
bologna 33
enchiladas
    cheese 39
    green chili 151
lasagna, Sherrie's 41

loaves
  all-star 33
  glazed 33
meatballs
  casserole 34
  porcupines, oven 40
patties
  bachelor steak 34
  rice-a-burgers 37
  unusual 37
pies
  corn bread 37
  Gina's 38
  tamale 38
  zesty 39
  zucchini 38
pizzas
  casserole 41
  in-a-burger 41
  popover 42
  potato bake 41
  taco 42
rice sabrosia 38
Saturday night special 39
shooting stars 39
spaghetti
  campfire 150
  Italian 42
  Texas 42
stew, chuck wagon .150
tacos
  casserole 40
  Navajo 40
  salad, crowd-sized 40
Ham see Pork
Hominy Casserole 72
ICE CREAM
  apricot, fresh 154
  banana 107
  bars, peanut crunch 106
  Butterfinger
    Lea Ann's 154
    Teresa's 107
  caramel delight 105
  chocolate, rich 154
  peach 107
  see Pies
  strawberry-banana 155
  vanilla
    country 108
    Marilyn's 108
    old-fashioned .108
NOODLES
  casserole, Case 72
  egg
    glob 72
    homemade 72
  manicotti, microwave, Ginger's 56
Pie Pastry
  fried 112
  Margaret's 112
PIES
  apple-marmalade .108

butterscotch 109
cherry, super 146
chocolate
  Black Forest 109
  brownie 109
  chess 109
  pudding, microwave 110
  sweet chocolate, southern 146
dog-tick 147
ice cream, butter brickle 105
lemonade, peanutty .110
millionaire, frozen 110
orange-pecan 147
peach, fresh 110
pear, with hot cinnamon sauce 110
pecan 111
strawberry, fresh 111
Play Dough, cooked, children's 156
Popcorn
  balls, really good .156
  caramel 156
Popsicles
  pudding pops, Mendie's 155
PORK
  ham
    and fresh vegetable medley 44
    mini loaves and glazed Louisiana
      yams 44
    roll-ups, Swiss, microwave 44
  Mexican skillet dinner 44
  sausage
    casseroles
      noodle 45
      Vickie's 45
    lasagna, Sherrie's 41
  see Appetizers
  spareribs, Shirley's 45
Relish
  hot sauce, Horton's 17
  sweet 144
RICE
  casseroles
    Mexi-chili 57
    mushroom 73
    vegetable 73
  fried, Chinese 72
  honey, Katrina's 72
  San Francisco treat 73
  Spanish, quick and easy 73
SALADS
  chicken, hot 50
  darn good 19
  fruit
    a la mode 20
    apricot 17
    avocado kabobs, sweet and spicy 21
    Champagne 21
    cherry
      and sour cream 18
      fluff 18
    cranberry, Karen's 18
    Debi's 19
    delicious 19

lemon 18
melon cups, iced 20
orange 18
pineapple
  cherries and sour cream 18
  strawberry-sour cream 21
macaroni
  Acini DePePe 19
  seashell, Treasure Island 25
pretzel salad torte 21
taco, crowd-sized 40
tuna 18
vegetable
  banner 22
  bean 22
    hot 151
  broccoli 22
  cabbage
    coleslaw
      confetti 24
      Herman's 24
      Judy's 24
      nine-day 152
    pom-pom 23
  carrot 22
  Florentine 24
  frozen 23
  mushroom, fresh 23
  potato-peanut butter 24
  sauerkraut 23
  seven-layer 25
  Swedish 25
  sweet-sour 25
Sandwiches
  corned beef bun camper 32
  super hero 33
  tuna special 55
SAUCES
  barbecue
    Gladys' 17
    never-fail 17
    Sue's 17
  hot, Loretta's 16
SEAFOOD
  salmon croquettes 54
  scallops amandine 54
  tuna
    ring with cheese sauce 54
    sauce with spaghetti 54
    special 55
Seasoning Salt, basic 144

SOUPS
  cabbage patch 15
  chowder, clam 16
  gumbo
    chicken 16
    shrimp and okra 16
Spaghetti, campfire 150
Chuck Wagon Stew 150
Toppings
  peanut butter Chantilly 71
  walnut crumbs for vegetables, savory 71
Turkey
  quiche, Swiss 53
VEGETABLES
  asparagus 60
  beans
    baked
      Boston 60
      stove top 60
      Tonna's 61
    casseroles
      green beans 61
  broccoli
    and rice
      casseroles
        family favorite 62
        Mrs. Bernard's 63
      holiday 62
    casseroles 62
    with mild cheese sauce 62
  carrots
    elegant 63
    scalloped 63
  cauliflower
    tangy mustard, microwave 64
  corn 64
    pudding 64
  eggplant casserole, microwave 64
  onion rings, French-fried 151
  potatoes 66
  spinach pie casserole 66
  squash
    casserole, Stacy's 67
    patties 66
    pie 67
    spaghetti squash 67
    zucchini 71
  sweet potatoes 68
  tomatoes, baked stuffed, Dothan 67
Walnuts, spiced, microwave 144

PHOTOGRAPHY CREDITS: Cover — Micheal Jones; Hershey Foods Corporation; American Dairy Association; Thomas J. Lipton Company; Florida Citrus Commission; United Fresh Fruit and Vegetable Association; Sunkist Growers, Inc.; Blue Bonnet Margarine; Pickle Packers International; Ruth Lundgren, Ltd.; Frozen Potato Products Institute; General Foods; National Dairy Council; Louisiana Yam Council; National Macaroni Institute; National Broiler Council; R. T. French Company; DIAMOND Walnut Kitchen; Frozen Southern Vegetable Council; Southeastern Peanut Growers; California Apricot Advisory Board; California Raisin Advisory Board; Planters Cocktail Peanuts; The Pillsbury Company; Best Foods: Division of Corn Products; The J. M. Smucker Company; Armour and Company; The Quaker Oats Company; Evaporated Milk Association; Kellogg Company; Standard Fruit and Steamship Company; Dudley-Anderson-Yutzy.

cooking up a STORM

AN ALL-PURPOSE COOKBOOK

**FAVORITE RECIPES® OF OKLAHOMA
FUTURE HOMEMAKERS OF AMERICA**

FOR ORDERING INFORMATION

WRITE TO

FAVORITE RECIPES PRESS
P. O. Box 77
Nashville, Tenneseee 37202

OR CALL

TOLL FREE Cookbook Hotline
1-800-251-1520